KU-547-357

Cultures, Communities, Identities

Also by Marjorie Mayo

COMMUNITIES AND CARING: The Mixed Economy of Welfare

COMMUNITY EMPOWERMENT: A Reader in Participation and Development (*co-editor*)

IMAGINING TOMORROW: Adult Education for Transformation

Cultures, Communities, Identities

Cultural Strategies for Participation and Empowerment

Marjorie Mayo
Reader in Community Development
Goldsmiths College
University of London

Consultant Editor: Jo Campling

First published 2000 by
PALGRAVE
Houndmills, Basingstoke, Hampshire RG21 6XS and
175 Fifth Avenue, New York, N.Y. 10010
Companies and representatives throughout the world

PALGRAVE is the new global academic imprint of
St. Martin's Press LLC Scholarly and Reference Division and
Palgrave Publishers Ltd (formerly Macmillan Press Ltd).

ISBN 0–333–71662–0

This book is printed on paper suitable for recycling and
made from fully managed and sustained forest sources.

A catalogue record for this book is available
from the British Library.

Library of Congress Cataloging-in-Publication Data
Mayo, Marjorie.
    Cultures, communities, identities : cultural strategies for participation
    and empowerment / Marjorie Mayo.
        p. cm.
    Includes bibliographical references and index.
    ISBN 0–333–71662–0
    1. Community power—Developing countries. 2. Community
    organization—Developing countries. 3. Community development—
    –Developing countries. 4. Political participation—Developing countries.
    5. Community action—Developing countries. I. Title.
    HM776 .M39 2000
    307.1'4'091724—dc21
                                                            00–033295

10   9   8   7   6   5   4   3   2   1
09 08 07 06 05 04 03 02 01 00

Printed and bound in Great Britain by
Antony Rowe Ltd, Chippenham, Wiltshire

To my sisters and brothers

Contents

Acknowledgements   viii

Introduction   1

1   Culture and Cultural Strategies in the Context of 'Global'
    Restructuring   13

2   Communities, Identities and Social Movements   36

3   'Race', Racism, Anti-Racism and Identities   62

4   Community, Culture and Cultural Strategies: Alternative
    Approaches in Community Development   87

5   Cultural Strategies and Community Economic
    Development   111

6   Nationality, Ethnicity, Identity and Displacement:
    Cultural Strategies to Find Ways of Feeling 'at Home'   133

7   Cultural Strategies for Health and Well-being   155

8   Wider Strategies: 'Globalisation from Below'?   178

References   194

Index   210

Acknowledgements

I owe particular thanks to all of those who have provided me with materials and given generously of their time, welcomed me to visit their projects, suggested additional sources and commented upon various chapters in draft. Their assistance has been invaluable. Although there was insufficient space to refer to them all in detail, these materials have all contributed to shaping the arguments and perspectives in the chapters which follow. Warmest thanks and appreciation to Jean Anastacio, Les Back, Malcolm Barry, Jean Besson, Augusto Boal and his colleagues at the Centre of the Theatre of the Oppressed – Rio, Brazil, Su Braden, Audrey Bronstein and a number of her colleagues at Oxfam, Pauline Conroy, CAFE (Creative Activity for Everyone) in Dublin, Community Arts Project (Cape Town, South Africa) Stanley Forman, Mayerlene Frow, John Gaventa, James Gibbs, Ben Gidley, Gill Gordon, Jenny Harris, Marianne Hille and her colleagues at ActionAid, Ute Kowarzik, Robert Mayo, Mandy McIlwaine, Juliet Merrifield, Brian Morris, Ines Newman, Nici Nelson, NPPHCN Media and Training Centre (Cape Town, South Africa), Barbara Orten, Peter Shanahan, Jessica Shaw, Kalbir Shukra, Anne-Marie Singh, Small World, Marilyn Taylor, Viviene Taylor, Video News, John Wilkinson, Elizabeth Wilson, Ken Worpole, Undercurrents and Sue Eden. Any remaining errors are, of course, my own.

Jo Campling, my consultant editor, encouraged me to pursue this project. My grateful thanks to her for her advice, her patience and support.

Finally, special thanks and continuing appreciation to my son Clyde Harris and to my daughter Scarlet Harris. They provided comments and critical insights, ranging from reflections on football, music and anti-racist strategies to alternative perspectives on Bourdieu. As always, they also provided support, including technical support, when technophobia threatened to become overwhelming.

MARJORIE MAYO

Introduction

Cultures, communities and identities; each of these concepts has emerged to the fore in contemporary academic debates, just as each has become the focus of current debates on policy and practice. Each has fundamentally contested meanings, and these, in turn, relate to alternative and competing perspectives within these debates. So why have these contested concepts come to the fore in contemporary academic debates, and why might it matter, in relation to debates on policy and practice for participation and empowerment?

Cultural Studies emerged as a significant influence on academic debates in the humanities and social sciences in the last two decades of the twentieth century. Questions of culture and ideology came to the fore, in contrast with the preoccupation with political economy, more characteristic of debates in the previous decade. The influence of postmodernist thinking has been a key factor too. Advocates and critics of postmodernism have both, in their different ways, been centrally concerned with questions of cultures and identities. The influence of discourses of the postmodern, across a range of academic disciplines has been profound. From whichever perspective you approach the issues, then, these are concerns that need to be addressed.

Cultures, communities and identities have also featured within debates on politics, both in theory and in practice. There has been increasing focus upon communities in the context of 'communitarianism'. Debates on the significance of 'community' have emerged – alongside debates on the family and family values – in the context of anxieties about increasing fragmentation, social dislocation and excessive individualism. There is a need to reassert the values of community, it has been argued, to redress the balance following decades of economic and social policies based upon the view that there is no such thing as society, but only individuals and their families (Kymlicka, 1990, Etzioni, 1993, Atkinson, 1994, Atkinson, 1995).

From the communitarian perspective, it has been suggested, 'two scenarios beckon us. The one suggests a grasping, individualistic, rapidly changing future in which the gap between those who have "made it" and those who "fall by the wayside" widens in divisive ways. The other scenario is less clearly defined, but indicates the need to find more responsible ways of caring for children and finding ways in which all can contribute to a more caring society' (Atkinson, 1995, p. 3). What the communitarian approach implies in practice has been the subject of further debate. Individuals, communitarians emphasise, have social responsibilities as well as rights in society – an emphasis which has implications for agendas of social control as well as for agendas of social care. This raises further issues in turn, questions about the communitarian perspective and questions about the 'Third Way' with which this has been associated.

More fundamentally, the definition of the concept of community itself continues to be contested along with the definitions of culture and identity. The notion of community in terms of shared locality or neighbourhood is problematic already, and increasingly so in urban industrialised societies, characterised by high rates of mobility and complex social networks (Crow and Allan, 1994). The notion of community in terms of 'common identity' is scarcely less problematic. 'Race', ethnicity, and sexual orientation have each been considered, for example, as markers of 'communities of identity'. The gay community's experiences of organising in San Francisco, for instance, have been analysed in these terms (Castells, 1983). But the notion of communities of identity raises further questions in its turn. What, if anything, do such 'identities' actually mean, and how might these meanings differ, from one cultural context to another? Is it really meaningful, for instance, to refer to 'black identity' as a fixed given, without taking account of the dynamics of change in differing contexts (Gilroy, 1987, Gilroy, 1993)? How are these identities acquired, in any case, by nature and/ or by nurture? (Weeks, 1987, Caplan, 1987). How do individuals and groups become conscious or fail to become conscious of themselves, in relation to these identities? By what processes do they define themselves, and how do they address the issues of overlapping and potentially competing identities – as black women, for example, or older people who have disabilities or young people who are gay or lesbian?

However problematic, the notion of 'communities of identity' has been central to the discussion of New Social Movements such as those campaigning for Black Liberation, Women's Liberation, and Gay and Lesbian Liberation, together with movements of older people and movements of people with disabilities.[1] These movements have been concerned with contesting the negative identities which have been associated with the prejudices of racist, sexist, homophobic, ageist and ableist societies – aiming to promote positive identities, alternative communities based upon shared cultures and values. The celebration of diversity and difference has been a central theme in debates about community politics, and indeed in debates about alternative approaches to politics more generally (Harvey, 1990, Harvey, 1993).

Increasingly critical of orthodox left politics in the 1960s – rooted in previous assumptions about the leading role of the working class, led by centralised left political parties, and focusing upon the sphere of political economy – critics such as Gortz and Touraine had already been exploring alternative approaches. From the 1970s, these critics were according greater prominence to the roles of the New Social Movements, based upon the politics of identity and difference, with greater emphasis upon the sphere of culture and ideology (Gortz, 1982; Touraine, 1974).

From the 1980s, postmodernist critics had already been challenging the notion that history could be meaningfully interpreted in terms of emancipatory class politics – or indeed in terms of any 'grand narrative' at all. The meta-theories of the past, the very notion of historical progress and the underlying assumptions of the 'Enlightenment' were to be subjected to fundamental reappraisal. In place of these previous approaches, in contrast, there was an increasing emphasis upon diversity and difference, and the significance of space and place, rather than the significance of time and the notion of development (Keith and Pile, 1993).

The collapse of 'actually existing socialist' states in the former Soviet Union and Eastern and Central Europe, at the end of the 1980s, seemed to provide confirmation of such criticisms. This was the period when the 'End of History' (that is, history as grand emancipatory narratives) was a significant topic for debate (Fukuyama, 1992). Capitalism was established globally, it was argued, in a postmodern

---

1 New Social Movements have not only been concerned with issues of identity of course. Environmental movements have also been key, along with urban social movements.

era, a postindustrial information-based society. Questions of culture, diversity and difference were centrally important, that is, subjectivity and desires rather than the uniformity and the over-emphasis upon rationality and materialism which had been associated with the era of modern mass production.

From alternative perspectives on the left, meanwhile, the celebration of diversity and difference was also being explored as part of attempts to reappraise the assumptions of the past – but without throwing out the baby with the bathwater. How could the agendas of the New Social Movements be understood in relation to the agendas of traditional class politics, and what might be the scope for developing alliances between them? How could the celebration of diverse identities and cultural differences be related to agendas for challenging the underlying causes of oppression and exploitation, rooted in the relations of production? And how could one develop an enhanced understanding of cultural, community and identity politics without abandoning a structural analysis which was rooted in political economy (Harvey, 1990).

But was this possible? Some critics of the political economy approach concluded that this was fundamentally incompatible with the politics of cultures and identities (Smart, 1992). Aronowitz and Giroux, for example, argued that the Marxist tradition was centrally concerned with the primacy of the economic sphere; this had resulted in the devaluing of 'politics, ideology and culture'. What needed to be stressed, they continued, was that any approach to developing a critical theory of emancipation demanded that 'the Marxist theory of class and history be discarded and that the theoretical terrains of culture and ideology be given primary importance as a constitutive force in the shaping of consciousness and historical agency' (Aronowitz and Giroux, 1986, p. 117).

Or alternatively, did questions of culture need to be reformulated in relation to analyses rooted in political economy – a matter not so much of whether these were to be addressed but how? And similarly with identity politics, was the issue to be reformulated – to focus upon *how* rather than *whether* these debates needed to be related to community politics and the mainstream of class politics? This was the starting point for this book.

My initial rationale for addressing these questions about cultures, communities, identities and cultural strategies tended to be somewhat defensive. It was clearly important to engage with these preoccupying debates. But I suspected that I might ultimately conclude that the significance of cultural issues was being somewhat overestimated. Might this emphasis upon cultural questions prove to be something of a diversion from the material issues affecting communities in an increasingly polarised scenario of growing poverty and deprivation? Could this represent some contemporary version of 'Bread and Circuses', I suspected (even if the bread seemed to be in somewhat short supply, too, in the context of contemporary welfare spending restrictions)?

As I began to reflect further, I became increasingly convinced that such defensiveness was quite unnecessary. Far from being peripheral, these questions were leading into some of the most central theoretical debates for community development, and for community practice more generally. Questions of culture and identity (however each of these is defined) relate to some of the most fundamental issues for communities, how they see themselves, how they analyse their situations and whether and how they come to envisage the possibilities for change. 'Culture' in the anthropological usage, as Worsley has demonstrated, tells us not only who we are, and what is what, but what is to be done. 'It supplies a project, a design for living' (Worsley, 1984, p. 43). Community development agendas have actually been and continue to be focused upon precisely these types of questions – with varying answers depending upon participants' underlying theoretical perspectives as to who was who, what was what, and what was to be done .

At one end of the theoretical spectrum, as Chapter 4 explains, the community development programmes which were developed in the Third World, in the post-Second World War period have been criticised for their underlying assumptions – that the task was essentially to diffuse 'modernising', that is, Western attitudes and values, to get communities of 'backward people in the right frame of mind' for development as defined by other interests on their behalf (Manghezi, 1976). There are a number of subsequent examples of community development programmes which have started from such questionable assumptions – that the poor need to be rescued from their 'culture of poverty' (ideas which lurked behind community programmes in both Britain and the USA in the 1960s and early 1970s, for example (Loney, 1983). There are some uncomfortable echoes, too, in more recent reflections on the supposedly problematic values and attitudes of the 'underclass' in deprived communities (Morris, 1994).

Alternatively, though, towards the other end of the theoretical spectrum, critics of such approaches to community development have also been concerned with questions of culture and identity, albeit from fundamentally different assumptions. While recognising that peoples' cultures and identities can be expected to have roots in their material circumstances, in summary, such critics have argued that the world of ideas cannot simply be reduced to such material roots in economistic ways. Drawing upon the work of writers such as Gramsci, they have emphasised the key importance of ideology and culture as continuing sites of struggle in their own right. The dominant culture is constantly being reproduced, it is argued, and alternative cultures and identities are continually faced with the problem of how to present effective challenges (Popple, 1995). In such a scenario, existing – and unequal – social relationships appear normal, legitimate even, or at least as way beyond current agendas for social change. This is the logic of the view that at the end of the day 'there is no alternative' to market-led economies, societies in which the requirements of private profitability represent the ultimate bottom line. And this is precisely the type of view which is to be challenged, if alternative agendas are to be developed for community empowerment and social transformation.

There are parallels here, with the challenges posed by the New Social Movements. The Women's Liberation Movement, for example, set out to question a set of assumptions about gender roles in society, and the supposed natures of women and men, which effectively reinforced existing gender relations, male dominance and female subordination. Deeply ingrained cultural assumptions about women's roles as wives, mothers and daughters were challenged as women both collectively and individually explored alternative definitions of their identities. Similar points could be made about other social movements empowering oppressed groups to imagine alternatives, as Chapter 2 considers in more detail.

Community development workers, youth workers and community education workers concerned with participation, empowerment and social transformation have seen their role in terms of social and political education, in this broad sense. Drawing upon the work of Freire, in particular, professionals informed by such approaches have set out to empower the communities they work with to question dominant assumptions – in Freire's terms to get the oppressor out of their own heads. Social and political education of this type aims to empower people to analyse the sources of their problems for themselves, to explore their own needs and develop their own strategies. 'Cultural action for freedom' as Freire has expressed this type of approach, has been central to debates on social transformation, both in Britain and beyond, informing a range of practice from adult education and social education with young people to participatory action research in both the First and Third Worlds. More specifically, too, these debates have informed a range of community programmes and projects involving the arts and media, including programmes and projects which are discussed in more detail subsequently in this book.

For professionals working with communities, whether communities based upon locality or communities of identity, or both, these are central issues. Whatever perspective the worker finds most relevant, in fact, one of the most basic issues which they need to address (and which is typically addressed in their professional training) is the issue of their own identity as a worker – having a critical awareness of self, in order to work effectively and professionally with others, whether this is on a one-to-one basis with individuals, or whether this is with groups and communities. Without such an awareness of self, workers risk distorting their professional interventions with their own cultural assumptions. In societies which are culturally laden with racism, sexism, homophobia, ageism and ableism, not to mention class prejudice, such awareness is central to empowering practice.

Practice has, in any case, been moving ahead, whether or not this was being mirrored at the theoretical level, or reflected in education and training for professionals in the community. There are numerous examples of creative practice both in relation to issues of culture and identity in general, and more specifically, in relation to community arts and media projects, both in the First and Third Worlds. As I began to read on and to visit more community arts and media projects, I became increasingly aware of the extent to which this has actually been the case for some very considerable time.

Community arts such as drama, mime, song and dance have been used in a variety of contexts as part of community development programmes – to put across development messages. Educational plays of this type include didactic points – about health education, the benefits of particular hygiene measures or the value of participating in literacy programmes, for example. It has been argued that, at least until relatively recently, community media have been predominantly used as vehicles for top-down persuasion or as channels to convey information from 'experts'/authorities to 'the people' (Melkote, 1991).

But there are also a range of examples to illustrate alternative approaches, based upon more active participation and dialogue. Such examples illustrate more fully empowering ways of working for social transformation. Freire's work on the development of critical consciousness through active participation and dialogue influenced the thinking of Boal, for example, as he developed the Theatre of the Oppressed from the 1960s in Latin America (Boal, 1979). Ngugi's work in Kenya provides another example of the use of drama for community educa-tion and for the development of critical consciousness and social change (Epskamp, 1989). This book focuses particularly on examples of this type of approach to the uses of arts and media to promote commu-nity empowerment for social change, building towards the ultimate transformation of exploitative and oppressive social relations.

Meanwhile, the arts and cultural activity have also become an increasingly important part of urban regeneration in Britain. Cultural industries have been increasingly identified as a dynamic, growing sector, both in Britain and beyond. While some of the claims may have been somewhat exaggerated (with some apparently inflated claims about the numbers employed in the industries) by the 1990s there was increasing recognition of the potential contribution which cultural policies could make to urban regeneration, and growing inter-est amongst local authorities concerned to promote local economic development (Landry *et al.*, 1996).

Once again, the issues were not so much whether but how cultural policies were to be developed. Policies which put the interests of upmarket tourism before the needs of local communities were poten-tially diminishing the quality of life for local people. At their crudest, such policies could be used to justify programmes to remove beggars and 'squeegy merchants' from the streets of city centres, in case they offend the sensibilities of the tourists they seek to proposition for alms. But alternative, participatory approaches to the cultural indus-tries can be and have been developed too, as part of programmes to promote urban regeneration. There are a range of examples of such alternative approaches, both in Britain and beyond.

Subsequent British policy reports, such as the Social Exclusion Unit's Policy Action Team Report 10, have reaffirmed this growing recognition of the potential significance of the contribution of the arts, sport, cultural and recreational activity, as part of wider strate-gies, including strategies to promote regeneration and to combat social exclusion in Britain:

> Art and sport, cultural and recreational activity, can contribute to neighbourhood renewal and make a real difference to health, crime, employment and education in deprived communities ... The principles of the community development approach in this report should underpin and build on the ways in which local

authority culture/leisure strategies and services are developed
provided (Department for Culture, Media and Sport, 1999, pp   ,
11).

Arts activities and cultural initiatives were also being identified by
local authorities and their organisations as contributing to regeneration in a number of important ways. 'The arts can not only improve
the quality of life for a few, but transform the social contexts, self-
confidence and imaginative capacity of whole urban districts'
(Chelliah, 1999, p. 11).

As subsequent chapters illustrate, there has been a wealth of examples which have pointed to such outcomes over a long period, both in
relation to cultural issues in general, and in relation to community
arts and media, more specifically. As the Local Government
Information Unit report *Arts and Regeneration* pointed out, '(T)he use
of arts activity to achieve social objectives is not new' (Chelliah, 1999,
p. 5). On the contrary, in fact, the creative arts have been linked to
social purposes, in the past, both by official agencies and by local
people themselves. The history of working-class adult learning, for
example, demonstrates the significance of reading, including the
reading of works of fiction, as a way into further study and further
activism. Kean's study of working-class reading, for instance, demonstrated the ways in which socialists and feminists saw reading,
including the reading of fiction and poetry, as mechanisms for the
development of the self, and self-identity, in a community of like-
minded individuals. As Kean argued 'The emphasis on the study of
literature and poetry was not an aberration from economic texts but a
continuation of ... mental growth and increased awareness ...' (Kean,
1995, pp. 59–60). More recent adult learning programmes have led to
similar conclusions. As a participant on a programme for the unemployed at Ruskin College, Oxford, reflected, however useful it was to
address practical issues, the cultural aspects of the programme were
crucial too, because:

for our own self-respect and self-help we need drama and discussion, poetry and literature to learn about ourselves, about what we
can offer society and about the best way forward (quoted in
Hughes, 1995, p. 106).

There are numerous contemporary examples too, illustrating ways
in which the arts, leisure and sport are being used, creatively, to reach

and engage with those who are not being reached in other ways. Such examples include the involvement of young people in challenging racism, through football initiatives against racism. And they include the use of music as well as the involvement of popular entertainers, highlighting issues that affect young people, both in their communities and in the workplace. Some of these examples are discussed in subsequent chapters. As these case studies illustrate, presenting the facts, however logically argued, is not the only, or necessarily the most effective way to engage people's interest. Cultural strategies can promote communication in other ways too, relating to people's enthusiasms. And non-verbal forms, such as dance, can enable people to communicate, when, for whatever reason, verbal communication becomes problematic (as refugees' experiences illustrate, in Chapter 6). Cultural strategies can complement other approaches, potentially reaching the parts that other strategies fail to reach.

This book starts, then, from the position that issues of culture and identity do matter to communities and to those who work with them. The point is not whether but how these issues are addressed, how to analyse the varying perspectives which underpin these developments and how to explore their differing implications for policies and for cultural strategies in practice.

The book's plan

The plan of the rest of the book is as follows. Chapter 1 takes up the questions which have already been raised about the different meanings of culture, as a way of life, and in the more specific sense of the arts and media, whether defined as 'high' or elite culture, or whether defined in terms which include 'popular' or mass culture. Why have these 'cultural' questions gained increasing prominence over the past twenty years or so? What types of explanations have been offered and from which competing perspectives? How have perspectives and experiences varied, in different contexts? How have they been affected by increasing globalisation? And what might be the differing implications for cultural strategies and for community and identity politics?

Chapter 2 moves on to focus upon questions of identity, and identity politics, in the context of debates on the New Social Movements and community politics, more generally. How have 'communities of interest' including communities based upon 'identities' such as gender and sexual orientation been understood, how have these debates related to debates on communities based upon locality, and from which perspectives? These debates on differing approaches to 'community', 'identity', 'social movements' and cultural strategies are taken up more specifically, in relation to 'race' and ethnicity in Chapter 3. This chapter draws upon examples of different approaches to culture and identity, including debates on young people, sport, music and hybrid forms of musical expression on both sides of the Atlantic.

On the basis of these discussions of differing definitions and competing theoretical perspectives, Chapter 4 moves on to consider key implications for policies and practice. Having set out alternative scenarios, this chapter explores some of the varying approaches to the role of culture, both in the broader sense of culture as a way of life, and more specifically to the role of community arts and media, within strategies for community development, adult, community and social education, both in the First and Third Worlds. What are the implications for developing strategies based upon active participation, critical engagement, and collective empowerment? Together these chapters set out the framework for the discussion of strategies, policies and practice, in the remaining chapters.

Chapter 5 moves on to explore examples of cultural strategies in relation to local community economic development. These examples include cultural programmes and projects which form part of strategies for the cultural industries. And they include examples of local community economic development initiatives, including co-operatives in the cultural industries. The chapter concludes by raising questions about the links between local economic initiatives and the wider context, globally (Think Global; Act Local).

Chapter 6 focuses upon cultural strategies which relate to the exploration of political identities and consciousness. In particular, the chapter explores strategies for combating political marginalisation and social exclusion and building solidarity, looking at examples of projects which focus upon questions of culture (such as community festivals, carnivals and dance) amongst marginalised and minority groups, including refugees and asylum seekers.

In Chapter 7, the emphasis shifts to social issues, with a focus upon health and well-being in both the First and Third Worlds, exploring strategies based upon active participation and dialogue, rather than simply transmitting health education messages. There are examples of the use of drama, including interactive drama to explore issues of health and well-being, including HIV/AIDS and sexual health more generally, as part of community health programmes. The focus is upon projects which set out to empower people individually and collectively to challenge oppression and to combat negative identities in relation to gender, sexual orientation and other forms of oppression.

Finally, Chapter 8 reflects upon the implications of these examples, relating these back to the framework of alternative theoretical perspectives outlined in the opening chapters. How far can participatory approaches to the use of community media contribute to the development of critical consciousness and solidarity between communities in different localities and communities with differing interests and identities? And how far can such approaches contribute to the promotion of sustainable development and to longer-term strategies for transformation, both at the local level and beyond?

1
Culture and Cultural Strategies in the Context of 'Global' Restructuring

Culture, it has been suggested, 'is probably the broadest concept of all those used in the historical social sciences. It embraces a very large range of connotations, and thereby it is the cause perhaps of the most difficulty' (Wallerstein, 1990, p. 31). Raymond Williams commented that 'Culture is one of the two or three most complicated words in the English language' (Williams, 1976). *The Blackwell Dictionary of Sociology* defines culture as 'the accumulated store of symbols, ideas, and material products associated with a social system, whether it be an entire social system or a family' (Johnson, 1995, p. 68). Culture, in the sociological sense, is 'learned behaviour', nurture rather than nature, humankind's social inheritance, 'the skills, knowledge and accepted ways of behaving of the society', '"the ways of life" of society's members', a design for living which is both learned and shared (Haralambos and Holborn, 1991, pp. 2–3). Without culture in this sense, there can be no human society.

The concept of culture, according to Giddens, 'consists of the values the members of a given group hold, the norms they follow, and the material goods they create' (Giddens, 1989, p. 310), emphasising the point that the concept of culture includes material as well as ideological aspects, a society's pattern of work as well as its customs, family life, religious ceremonies and leisure pursuits. In this, the sociological definition parallels the anthropological definition of culture as a whole way of life.

The more restricted usage defines culture as the arts and media in society – whether these are considered in terms of 'high' or elite notions of culture, such as classical music, or Shakespeare, in the British context, or alternatively in terms of 'popular' culture, such as 'pop' music and television 'soap operas' – or both. The anthropological and sociological definitions include such definitions but are absolutely not confined to these. On the contrary, in fact, from a social science perspective, culture in the sense of art, literature and film, for instance, both 'draws from and participates in the construction of culture as a way of life, a system of values and beliefs which, in turn, affects culture as a creative, representational practice' (King, 1991, p. 2). The wider context sets the framework for the arts and media, in society, and these, in their turn, reinforce or challenge accepted norms and values, including norms and values about what is produced, and how, on the basis of which social relations.

Said set out his own position on these interconnections, between culture as a way of life and culture as the arts, when he argued that culture is a 'sort of theatre where various political and ideological causes engage with one another'. Far from being 'antiseptically quarantined from its wordly affiliations', he argued, the work of art/literature is more fully understood and enjoyed, by taking into account its social context – including the prevalent norms and values. Said developed this argument by exploring the impact of the context of empire and the associated assumptions, including assumptions about 'race' which profoundly affected the works of late nineteenth- and early twentieth-century writers such as Conrad, Kipling, Gide and Loti, for example (Said, 1994, pp. xv–xviii) – issues which re-emerge in Chapter 3 and subsequent chapters, in the context of debates about culture and 'race'. Both the production and the consumption of the arts and media, according to such a view, relate to the wider 'culture' – culture defined in terms of a whole way of life, both ideological and material.

Wolff made a similar point when she argued for the importance of exploring the relationships between the different definitions and approaches, between for example, culture as 'values and beliefs, and culture as arts and media'. This would involve, for instance, analysing the ways in which cultural texts participate in the construction of wider cultural values and ideologies, such as values and norms about gender relations. And such an approach would include exploring the social relations, the economic and material factors as well as the ideologies which underpin the production of creative works (Wolff, 1991, p. 172).

These types of approaches challenge what their authors would see as false polarities, culture as a way of life/design for living versus culture as the arts and media (whether of the 'high' or 'low', 'elite' or 'popular' varieties) – or culture as ideologies, norms and values versus the economic and material bases of social relations. Rather than seeing these in terms of opposites – either/or – one or the other – in these types of analyses the questions become rephrased – how should one explore the dynamics of the interrelationships between them? Such explorations are key, it will be argued, for developing a critical understanding of the range of implications for policies and practice, in the fields of culture, community and identity politics? These debates set the framework for the discussion of cultural strategies for social change, in subsequent chapters, from Chapters 4 to 8.

This chapter sets out to summarise the development of these debates, based upon varying perspectives, over past decades. Why have cultural questions – however defined – taken on greater prominence, in this period? What types of explanation have been offered and from which competing perspectives? How far have these perspectives varied in different contexts, and how far have they affected and/or been affected by global factors? Inevitably, given the wide-ranging nature of these debates, this will be no more than an introductory summary. The aim is to sketch the framework for exploring the differing implications for cultural strategies and identity and community politics, policies and practice, in succeeding chapters – not to even attempt a more comprehensive account, within the space of one chapter.

Before addressing these questions, though, the following point of clarification needs to be added. This is a word of explanation about the particular focus of this chapter – the focus on cultural strategies as these have been developed from varying perspectives. Debates on cultural strategies are specifically highlighted, to set the context for the discussion of cultural strategies in practice, in the chapters which follow. But, this is not at all to imply that cultural strategies are *all* that matters – let alone to suggest that a work of art should be evaluated simply or even predominantly in terms of its contribution to any particular agenda for social change. The limitations of such a perspective on culture and the media-culture as propaganda/agitprop – should emerge subsequently in this chapter. Cultural strategies are the focus, here. But this is in no way to argue that the discussion of culture – in the sense of the creative arts – *could*, let alone *should*, be reduced to these considerations.

Debates on cultural strategies, adult education and progressive movements in the past

The Introduction started from the contemporary prominence of questions of culture, and cultural strategies along with questions of
identity and community, within both academic and policy debates,
not only in Britain, but internationally. Culture, according to
Wallerstein, has been characterised the 'Ideological Battleground of
the Modern World-System' in the late twentieth century (Wallerstein,
1991). But this contemporary focus upon culture and cultural politics
did not spring from nowhere, without identifiable roots or parallels.

On the contrary, in fact, in a chapter on 'Cultural Struggle or
Identity Politics' in relation to adult education, Steele has argued that:

> the seed of a cultural struggle in Britain after World War Two found
> fertile soil among the ranks of the new generation of adult educa-
> tors. Many of them saw it as a key element in the creation of a New
> Left which would be liberated from both Stalinised Marxism and
> from Fabian philistinism and believed that the members of the
> adult education movement could be prime actors in the new poli-
> tics.

What came to be installed in universities as a new academic discipline
of Cultural Studies, Steele suggested, 'owes its development to the
work of this generation of adult educators, who saw it as a programme
of popular education' (Steele, 1995, p. 47).

Cultural politics were seen as key to the construction of a new political common sense. In the wider sense of the term 'cultural' politics
(with 'cultural' defined in terms of a way of life) this involved challenging ruling-class norms and values. Democratic adult education
would empower working-class people to challenge prevailing bourgeois ideology and to promote a new popular critical consciousness.
In the more restricted sense of culture and cultural politics (defined in
terms of the arts), the study of cultural subjects would also provide a
vehicle for the cultivation of the active citizen, it was argued.

This latter argument had its own history in debates on adult education and social change from the nineteenth century onwards. As
Steele also pointed out, in the 1930s there had been furious debates
about the content of progressive working-class education.
Traditionalists argued for a focus upon the 'hard' disciplines – such as
economics and politics. For the traditionalists, literature and the arts

were 'women's' subjects, peripheral to the immediate concerns of trade union and labour movement struggles. The modernisers, in contrast, argued for a wider approach to adult education, an approach which positively valued the teaching of 'cultural' subjects, including literature and the arts.

This latter perspective, as Steele argued, was linked to the development of a New Left politics in the post-war period. As Raymond Williams (one of the key figures) and other adult educators perceived it, Cultural Studies could provide a mechanism for teaching politics by other means in the Cold War period which followed the Second World War, providing political education through adult and community education. Cultural Studies was seen as contributing to the new politics which was required, a politics which, as it has already been suggested, would be 'both critical of a Fabian-inspired Labourism but not content with the dogmas of Soviet-constructed Marxism' (Steele, 1995, p. 51) rooted in the values of democracy, and working-class traditions of community.

Steele quoted E.P. Thompson, for example, to illustrate this new interest in culture as a means of winning people for socialism of a less 'top-down' variety, changing people through cultural education, and engaging them in active participation, emphasising local self-determination and democratic vitality. Cultural Studies, from this New Left perspective was not, Steele argued:

> intended as the formation of a new academic discipline but an active politics conducted on the margins of the academy – rough, moralistic, unrefined but responsive to popular movements (Steele, 1995, pp. 53–4).

In the event, Steele went on to suggest, Cultural Studies blossomed, moving successfully into the academic mainstream. Some of the reasons for this will be explored in more detail, subsequently. But the post-war project of developing a popular critical education as part of a New Left politics was left, Steele argued, stranded in a time-warp – or at least awaiting further development in both theory and practice.

The subsequent history of Cultural Studies, as an area of academic study, is beyond the focus of this book, however. The key points to emphasise here are simply these. Recent debates on culture in general and more specifically in relation to community and identity politics, have a longer history. And this has been a history of contestation between differing approaches based upon competing perspectives about culture and cultural strategies and struggles in relation to politics and social movements. The post-war starting point for these debates, the question of how to develop a more participatory democratic Left politics, without separating the cultural sphere from political economy (including the political economy of culture itself) remains as relevant, if not more relevant than ever, it will be argued, in the rapidly changing 'global village' of the Millennium.

Differing perspectives

So what were these differing perspectives on culture and cultural strategies and struggles, and how have debates developed subsequently? The history of competing approaches to culture can be traced back through philosophical debates on culture and ideology, as well as through anthropological and sociological debates in the classical texts of those disciplines. Jenks started his discussion of debates on culture from the era of industrialisation, tracing the origins of debates on contemporary themes to this period, including debates on culture, ideology and social action versus materialism, on universalism and homogenisation/(globalisation) versus continuing cultural diversity and difference, and on elitism versus cultural egalitarianism (Jenks, 1993).

Jenks showed, for example, how the philosophical ideas of Kant were drawn upon by sociologists such as Weber in his work on the key importance of culture and ideology in explaining social change.[1] Weber's approach challenged Marxist perspectives, which, in contrast, emphasised the importance of material factors, such as the development of industrialisation, in explaining social and cultural change (although this dichotomy has actually been over-simplified, as it will be suggested subsequently in the discussion of contemporary approaches to tackling these questions of materialism, culture and cultural politics).

Debates within the anthropological classics from the nineteenth century onwards have similar contemporary implications. For the focus of this book, the debate between the evolutionists and the structuralists has particular relevance. Drawing upon the ideas of Darwin, the evolutionists approached the study of anthropology with the

---

1   Weber argued that the emergence of the Protestant Ethic was a key factor in the development of a culture which was favourable to capitalist industrialisation.

assumption that societies were to be located on a developmental scale, progressing from lower civilisations through to higher, more advanced civilisations (such as Western capitalist cultures). Structuralists such as Boas, Malinowski and Radcliffe-Brown, on the other hand, approached the study of each particular culture as having its own structure, with logic and validity in its own terms (Cheater, 1989). There are comparisons as well as contrasts here, with contemporary debates on globalisation and culture, just as there are comparisons and contrasts with contemporary debates on universalism, and 'grand theories' of modernisation, versus postmoderist critiques of these, and their emphasis upon diversity and difference – themes which re-emerge in Chaper 3 and subsequent chapters.

Similarly, there are parallels with past debates on culture as an elite activity, the pursuit of total perfection, reserved for the few, versus cultural egalitarianism. This latter approach has itself been the subject of further debate in the post-Second World War period. Should cultural egalitarianism take the form of bringing the 'high culture' to the many, a concern of many of those engaged in adult education? Or should this take the form of valuing working-class culture (in the tradition of Raymond Williams's insistence that culture is ordinary)? Or should this mean both (which would incidentally be the logic of taking an anthropological definition of culture as a way of life, in the first place, since 'ways of life' could hardly exclude working-class ways of life and popular culture, as well as the lifestyles of the cultural elite)? There are comparisons as well as contrasts here with more recent debates on cultural diversity and difference, including debates with postmodernist rejections of any hierarchies of cultures or tastes.

For the reader with an interest in exploring this history, Jenks's book provides a guide through these earlier debates, as well as to contemporary debates on culture, as these have developed across different disciplines. For the purposes of this book, however, the focus needs to shift forward to the post-Second World War era. It was from this period, as it has already been suggested, that debates on culture and cultural strategies and struggles developed on the New Left, attempting to combat what was seen as the economism of the past; the effective freezing of many debates on the Left, in the era of Stalin's predominance in the USSR and beyond. Anderson, for example, fiercely critical of Stalin's impact, characterised the Soviet Union, under his rule, as a cultural backwater 'formidable only by the weight of its censorship and the crudity of its propaganda' (Anderson, 1979, p. 20).

Ironically perhaps, this revival of interest in ideological debate on the Left was beginning to occur just as some sociologists were celebrating *The End of Ideology* (the title of an influential book of essays by the American sociologist, Daniel Bell subtitled: 'On the Exhaustion of Political Ideas in the Fifties' (Bell, 1965). Bell introduced these essays by describing his own perspective as anti-ideological. In the past decade (that is, the 1950s), he argued, it had become clear that nineteenth-century ideologies in general and Marxism in particular had been exhausted. The reasons for this were complex, including events such as the Moscow trials and the Soviet suppression of the Hungarian uprising in 1956, events which were seen as fatally discrediting Marxism – although Bell did also recognise that communism continued to have political weight in some European countries. Overall, however, Bell argued that in the Western world, by the beginning of the 1960s, there was 'a rough consensus amongst intellectuals on political issues: the acceptance of a Welfare State; the desirability of decentralized power; a system of mixed economy and of political pluralism' which signalled the end of the ideological age (Bell, 1961, p. 403). There are parallels as well as differences here with the subsequent publication of Francis Fukuyama's book *The End of History*, celebrating the global victory of liberal democratic capitalism (Fukuyama, 1992). As Mark Twain commented of his own (premature) obituary, such rumours of the death of ideology proved to be greatly exaggerated, however.

On the Left, in the 1950s and 1960s, the issue to be addressed was not the death of ideology but the need for reappraisal. Until Stalin's death in 1953, and indeed for some time after, Marxist approaches had been heavily influenced by Stalinist orthodoxies. Alternative approaches had, of course, been voiced both in Britain and elsewhere. In Germany the Frankfurt School developed a critical perspective which challenged Stalinist orthodoxies, with a particular focus upon the importance of ideology and culture as spheres of struggle. The ideas of the Frankfurt School were developed and had significant influence on debates within the New Left, in the 1960s and 1970s. But Left critics such as the Hungarian Marxist thinker and political activist, Lukacs, who were living and working in contexts which were more directly subject to Soviet influence, had had to contend with powerful pressures to conform. Official attacks on Lukacs's cultural and political activity in the post-war period, have, in fact, been described as signalling 'the complete Stalinization of culture and politics in Hungary' (Meszaros, 1991, p. 326).

Before moving on to consider New Left perspectives on culture, ideology and cultural strategies and struggles in more detail, it may be useful to summarise the approaches which they set out to challenge. These may be characterised as follows.

Marxism is a materialist perspective and hence it is material reality which shapes peoples' consciousness. The way of life, the culture of any particular society, is determined by economic forces. 'The social being of people, that is to say, the mode of production, determines their social consciousness, in other words everything that constitutes the spiritual life of society' as a Soviet political education text explained (Novosti Press Agency, 1983, p. 6). 'Bourgeois ideology reflects the position of the capitalist class and its interests' (Novosti Press Agency, 1983, p. 6). Without effective challenges to this pervasive bourgeois ideology, the working class 'would be doomed to wander in the dark' (Novosti Press Agency, 1983, p. 51) the text concluded, but the role of the Party was to provide an understanding of the theory of scientific communism, and to develop effective strategies for the class struggle.[2]

The point to emphasise about these approaches to ideology, culture and class struggle is not, of course, that they have no basis in Marx's own writings. They do. In a well-known and much quoted passage, Marx argued, for example, that 'ruling ideas are nothing more than the ideal expression of the dominant material relationships' (Marx, 1970, p. 64). But Marx's approach to questions of ideology and culture was more complex than this statement implies. Taken out of context, on its own, this statement offers no more than a partial account of Marx's analysis. The point that is being argued here, then, is that Marx's views were being interpreted and applied too rigidly and too dogmatically.

The New Left was critical of the tendency to oversimplify and to interpret ideological questions mechanistically, focusing upon injecting the working class with political consciousness as defined and approved by Stalin. In Stalin's USSR, the critics argued, the role of culture, in general, and the arts in particular, was seen as being primarily didactic. Socialist realist art and films such as Eisenstein's 'The Battleship Potemkin' and 'October' could demonstrate the evils of capitalism and celebrate the achievements of socialism (Taylor, 1979). Alternative and less one-dimensional approaches to culture

---

2 This text did also recognise the danger of reducing history to economic factors alone, however.

and the arts, such as the writings of Lukacs, were seen as potentially suspect if not actually counter-revolutionary.

If this is a caricature of Stalin's approach to questions of ideology, culture and the arts it was even more of a caricature of Marx's own approach. When the New Left set out to move beyond such Stalinist orthodoxies, they had only to turn to Marx's own works for a less deterministic set of analyses. Marx certainly emphasised the key importance of material factors; life itself, he argued, is 'not determined by consciousness, but consciousness by life' (Marx, 1970, p. 47) just as he argued that the ideas of the ruling class, the class which is the ruling material force, in every epoch are the ruling ideas. But he also argued that ideologies and cultures were phenomena in their own right and had to be taken seriously as such. Bourgeois ideology and culture (in the wider sense of norms and values as well as in the more specific sense of the arts) could not simply be dismissed as propaganda; on the contrary, they had to be critically explored and understood, if they were to be combated effectively.

Marx was concerned both with the role of culture and ideas, and with human actors and the ways in which they construct meaning, and strategies for action. As Marx himself put this, in another much-quoted passage, men (and women) do make their own history. Although he went on to qualify this statement by pointing to the structural constraints on making history, arguing 'they do not make it just as they please: they do not make it under circumstances chosen by themselves, but under circumstances directly encountered, given and transmitted from the past' (Marx, 'The Eighteenth Brumaire of Louis Bonaparte', in Marx and Engels, *Selected Works*, 1968, p. 98).

It was this less deterministic, less crudely mechanistic Marx which the New Left set out to rediscover. And in addition to rediscovering Marx's early philosophical and ideological works, the New Left also rediscovered the Italian Marxist, Gramsci. In an introductory essay to Simon's book *Gramsci's Political Thought* Stuart Hall reflected that 'Gramsci's influence on people like me, who first read him, in translation, in the early 1960s, has been profound' (Hall, 1991, p. 7).

> If I were to try to summarise, in a sentence, what Gramsci did for people of my generation, I would have to say something like this; simply, he made it possible for us to read Marx again, in a new way: that is, to go on 'thinking' the second half of the 20th century, face-to-face with the realities of the modern world, from a position somewhere within the legacy of Marx's thought, that is, not a

quasi-religious body of dogma but as a living, developing, constantly renewable stream of ideas (Hall, 1991, pp. 7–8).

Since the revival of interest in his writings in the sixties, Gramsci's ideas have been the subject of continuing debate and varying interpretation.

Gramsci himself was both a theorist and a trade union and working-class educator, until he was arrested in 1926; he spent almost a quarter of his short life in prison, under Mussolini's fascist rule. Gramsci's writings on ideology and culture were seen as especially relevant for the New Left, particularly his contribution to the development of the concept of 'hegemony'. Gramsci was concerned here with the issue which Marx had already identified – how bourgeois societies exercise power through legitimising their rule, in the eyes of the dominated classes. Ideology and culture assume crucial importance in relation to this question. Bourgeois culture (in the wider sense of culture, that is, including norms and values) is so predominant and pervasive that the relatively powerless consent to their situation within the status quo – they see this as legitimate, even reasonable, 'commonsense'. Bourgeois hegemonic power is thus perpetuated through cultural values, norms and beliefs, through persuasion as well as coercion. Mass education and mass communications in a modern, capitalist society reinforce this bourgeois hegemony, reaffirming that the status quo is legitimate. The rules of the game are capitalist, and there is no alternative game in town.

But Gramsci was absolutely not suggesting that there was nothing to be done to challenge bourgeois hegemony. On the contrary, in fact, hegemony was never static but constantly needed to be reproduced and renegotiated. This allowed scope for human agency; bourgeois hegemony *could* be contested. Gramsci demonstrated this through his own work for the counter-hegemonic project, the battle of ideas – developing socialist consciousness through his writings and his contributions to workers' study circles, as well as contributing to politics directly, first in the socialist party and then in the newly formed communist party.

Gramsci's thinking has been central to the development of transformative strategies for adult education and community development (Ledwith, 1997, Mayo, 1999). Subsequent chapters refer to Gramsci's contributions again, together with the contributions of Freire and others who have acknowledged their intellectual debts to Gramsci. There is not the space to go into further detail in this chapter. The key point, for the argument here, is the significance of Gramsci's concept of hegemony for moving beyond Stalinist orthodoxies on questions of ideology and culture (using the term here, both in the wider sense, including norms and values as well as the more specific sense). The implications of Gramsci's writings were that ideology and culture were very definitely to be taken seriously, representing key sites of class struggle.

Gramsci's work has been seen as particularly relevant by a range of academics and professionals engaged in the cultural sphere. His influence on the work of Stuart Hall (who succeeded Richard Hoggart) and his colleagues at the Centre for Contemporary Cultural Studies in Birmingham has already been illustrated. As it has also been suggested, Gramsci's ideas have been seen to be relevant to the development of progressive practice in a number of fields which are of central concern to this book, including community education and development in general and community arts work more specifically (Popple, 1995; Mayo, 1997). Gramsci's ideas have also been seen as particularly relevant for those concerned with the New Social Movements as Chapter 2 explores in more detail.

But did the New Left's developments of Gramsci's ideas go far enough to overcome the limitations of former cultural orthodoxies in the changing context of the latter part of the twentieth century? Or alternatively, was Marxism being distorted by the advocates of 'socialism with a human face', as Althusser amongst others argued, becoming idealist rather than materialist, petty-bourgeois rather than proletarian (Althusser, 1984)? Before exploring and evaluating some of the more recent debates on culture and cultural struggles, however, one specific criticism of Gramsci's approach needs to be addressed, because of its particular relevance to subsequent discussions, in later chapters of this book. This is the criticism that Gramsci 's concept of hegemony leads to an inadequate formulation of the notion of 'false consciousness'.

A brief digression on the notion of 'false consciousness'

In brief, it has been argued by critics such as Scott, that the implications of the concept of hegemony (as formulated by Gramsci) would be that the dominated classes – 'in the thrall of hegemonic social thought' – would be unable to draw the revolutionary implications from their concrete struggles (such as wage struggles or struggles over social welfare provision). 'It is this dominated consciousness that,

Gramsci claims, has prevented the working class from drawing the radical consequences inherent in much of its action' according to Scott (Scott, 1990, p. 90). Scott went on to reject this formulation and so to reject Gramsci's concepts of hegemony and false consciousness altogether.

In summary, he argued that the empirical evidence did seem to suggest that dominated groups in society make typically limited demands – demands for fairer wages for example – rather than making more far-reaching demands for social change. But this could absolutely not be taken to prove that these limited demands represented the sum total of their limited 'false' consciousness. On the contrary, in fact, in anything other than a revolutionary situation, it would be less than realistic or prudent for the dominated to express their demands in any terminology except that which has legitimacy with the powerful.

Peasant demands, before the French Revolution, for example, focused upon grievances within the existing order; to demand more would have risked serious retribution (Foucault's account of the torture and death meted out for regicide in pre-revolutionary France providing a gruesome illustration of the potential penalties for more fundamental challenges to the status quo in that era (Foucault, 1979).) So historically, the fact that the less powerful have tended to pose their demands in ways which could be seen as so legitimate and reasonable provides no concrete evidence about the actual state of their consciousness – false or otherwise. Indeed, these very limited and specific concessions (for example, an 8-hour day, a minimum wage, cooking and toilet facilities) were precisely the type of demands which the workers were putting forward in Russia in 1917, on the threshold of the Bolshevik revolution, Scott argued.

These arguments are particularly important to address, because they raise such fundamental issues, not only for those concerned with theory, but also for those concerned with practice, in such fields as community and youth work, community and social education and community media. If the concept of hegemony does actually imply that the less powerful are simply duped, victims of false consciousness, then how, if at all, does such a concept relate to progressive approaches to professional practice? If this is what the concept of hegemony really implies, then this would be incompatible with the adult educational work of Paulo Freire, for example, which has been so influential in community education and community work more generally on a global scale. Because, as the Introduction set out in summary, Freire started from the contrary assumption, that the oppressed are by no means empty vessels, waiting to be filled with knowledge. Education for social transformation, according to Freire, was not about providing 'true' rather than 'false' consciousness, but about engaging in processes of dialogue so that the oppressed themselves collectively engage in challenging the root causes of their oppression, including the oppressors' views which they have internalised in their own heads (Freire, 1972).

Is such an approach incompatible with Gramsci's concept of hegemony? Freire himself paid tribute to Gramsci's ideas and their influence on his work (Freire, 1995). Whilst Gramsci emphasised the importance of rigorous theoretical work and valued the contribution which intellectuals could make, he was absolutely not arguing that the dominated were simply steeped in false consciousness, passively waiting for the revolutionary party and/or the intelligentsia to put them right. On the contrary, as it has already been suggested, Gramsci specifically emphasised that the battle of ideas was a continuing struggle, of key importance in its own right. Intellectuals could contribute to this battle of ideas, according to Gramsci, but they needed to be organically linked to the political and social movements of the dominated.

Top-down strategies to promote political enlightenment, based upon the premise that the dominated were simply passive victims steeped in 'false consciousness', were precisely part of the problem which the New Left set out to challenge. The reality is far more complex. As subsequent chapters will argue, communities, and individuals within communities, *are* experts on their own situations – although this expertise can be enhanced, and peoples' critical awareness of alternative options can be sharpened in crucial ways, through a range of interactive projects and programmes, including community media initiatives. These criticisms of some of the ways in which 'hegemony' and the notion of 'false consciousness' have been (mis)applied have been particularly important to address, then. The point that has been argued here, however, is that this absolutely does not necessitate a rejection of Gramsci's concept per se.

The debates continue

As it has already been suggested, Gramsci's writings, including his writings on the concept of hegemony, have been particularly influential in the development of Cultural Studies. In Britain, research at the

Centre for Contemporary Cultural Studies took these ideas forward, focusing upon different aspects of the processes by which ideological and cultural struggles were being waged. Researchers explored the implications of Gramsci's premise that bourgeois hegemony was never finally achieved, being the subject of continuing contestation. There were studies of the legitimation processes by which bourgeois hegemony was being renewed (as each generation was socialised) together with the counter-hegemonic challenges which were repeatedly having to be met (Clarke *et al.*, 1979). Willis's study of the processes by which working-class boys acquired the norms and values of adult workers in working-class jobs, *Learning to Labour*, provides a classic example of this type of study of the processes involved in these continuing ideological and cultural struggles (Willis, 1977).

Meanwhile, alternative approaches to the problem of how to move beyond previous orthodoxies were also being developed. To critics such as Althusser, elements of the New Left were correct in criticising Stalin's errors ('some of which – and rather a lot – turned out to be crimes' (Althusser, 1984, p. 111)) in Althusser's view. The problem, he argued, was that a number of these criticisms of Stalin's legacy were being made in non-Marxist ways. In a reply to an article which had appeared in *Marxism Today*, the theoretical journal of the British Communist Party, in 1972, criticising his writings, Althusser argued that these theoretical criticisms were based upon humanist rather than Marxist premises. The baby of historical materialism was being thrown out with the Stalinist bath water. And so were the politics of the Workers' Movement. Althusser's reply to the article in *Marxism Today* started by commenting that this article had made no mention of the political context, despite the fact that in the period in question the movement had lived through many important events, including the Vietnam War, the Cultural Revolution in China, the occupation of Czechoslovakia and the student movement events of May 1968 in France.

Althusser's own approach focused upon the later, rather than the early Marx, attempting to rediscover a more scientific set of solutions to the problems posed by Stalin, rooted in Marx's analysis of the mode of production. Ideology was to be understood in this context. Althusser was deeply critical of those who, in his view, were *'exploiting the works of Marx's youth in order to draw out of them an ideology of Man, Liberty, Alienation, Transcendence, etc. – without asking whether the system of these notions (with) (sic) idealist or materialist, whether this ideology was petty-bourgeois or proletarian'* (Althusser,

1984, p. 121). But he, too, drew upon Gramsci's writings, to develop his own alternative approach to questions of ideology.

Ideology, in Althusser's view, represented 'the imaginary relationship of individuals to their real relations of existence' (Althusser, 1984, p. 36). As such, ideology represented a real force in human history. In capitalist society, the State and its ideological apparatuses, such as the educational system and cultural apparatuses reproduce ruling-class ideology, and so reinforce existing (exploitative) relations of production. This base – the relations of production – determined the superstructure, including the spheres of culture, but only in the last instance, rather than crudely or deterministically. Ideology was important in its own right, a site of class struggle, rather than simply reflecting the material base (Althusser, 1984).

Without going into detail, for the purposes of this account, what needs to be emphasised here is that Althusser and his fellow structuralists were grappling with similar problems to those which Gramsci had addressed, how to move forward in relation to questions of ideology and culture and the role of cultural strategies and struggles dealing with the ghosts of Stalinism (Davies, 1995). The structuralists produced a valuable critique, it has been suggested, arguing as they did that it was so important not to throw out the baby of an analysis rooted in political economy along with the bath water of crude economistic determinism (Johnson, 1979).

Critics have also suggested, however, that structuralism ran out of steam, and failed to engage creatively with ongoing debates and struggles in the rapidly changing context of the late seventies and eighties. Insofar as these criticisms could be justified, they made it all the easier for such approaches to be rejected in the far more problematic economic and political climate which followed. Free market-led economic restructuring was taking place on an increasingly global scale from the mid-seventies, while the Cold War was concluded, with the demise of the Soviet Union and its former allies in Eastern and Central Europe, at the end of the eighties.

Postmodernist challenges

This changing context and its implications for the changing nature of debates on ideology, culture and cultural struggles will be considered, subsequently, in the summary of Harvey's analysis of postmodernism (Harvey, 1990). Before coming on to the analysis of postmodernism, and its contributions, however, the main outlines of postmodernism need to be set out. This is a particularly difficult task, not least because the term 'postmodernism' covers such a range of approaches. Broadly, as the Introduction summarised, postmodernism has involved the death of the grand 'meta' narratives of modernism, the view of history from the French Revolution onwards, in terms of the development of the Enlightenment, let alone in terms of the potential development of socialism, in the twentieth century and beyond. In place of universalist meta-narratives, and grand plans, postmodernism has focused instead upon diversity and difference.

Rejecting theories of history as the story of human progress, the emphasis shifts instead from time to the study of space and place, the local and the global, in an increasingly globalised world of mass communications technologies which is also a world of increasing fragmentation, and difference (Watson and Gibson, 1995). The all-encompassing identities of class, in the traditional Marxist framework become similarly fragmented into a range of diverse identities, based upon factors such as gender, ethnicity, locality and culture (aspects which are explored in more detail, in subsequent chapters).

For the purposes of this chapter, postmodernists' emphasis upon communications and culture have particular relevance. For some post-modernists, ideology, culture and cultural strategies and struggles have come to the top of the agenda, replacing former concerns with the sphere of political economy. Marxism has been expressly rejected by some for its continuing economism. This fits into a set of criticisms of Marxism from the Left, including a range of critics such as Aronowitz and Giroux, who have drawn upon Marxist insights, but ultimately, as the Introduction explained, rejected Marxism. They criticised Marxism even under its most recent contemporary guises on the grounds of its economism and its devaluing of ideology and culture, both in theory and in practice. Whereas for their purposes of developing transformatory approaches to education including political education for radical democracy, the role of ideology and culture should, they argued, be given primary importance (Aronowitz and Giroux, 1986; Giroux and Aronowitz, 1991). Such conclusions both emphasise the key significance of culture in postmodernist approaches and relate cultural politics to a critical pedagogy (Sholle, 1992). Aronowitz and Giroux's work has particular significance, as a result, for those concerned with social and community education, and the political education aspects of community and youth work, whatever their own perspectives on postmodernism more generally.

Postmodernists have also rejected Marxism for its continuing emphasis upon the role of the working class, rather than the range of new social and cultural movements, including movements based upon identity politics. And they have rejected Marxism for its continuing emphasis upon the possibility of a 'grand narrative' approach to transformation more generally (Smart, 1992) – or, indeed for any combination of these factors. Postmodernism has, in fact, been evaluated positively by the Right, precisely because it has been seen as confirming the end of the old democratic left (Davies, 1995).

Alternatively, however, as the Introduction suggested too, postmodernism has also been evaluated positively by a section of the Left who have seen it as offering new openings. Perspectives have varied considerably on the Left, in fact (as Smart, for example, demonstrated). At one end of the spectrum, there have been those who have rejected postmodernism – as being at heart regressive. At the other end, there have been those who have welcomed postmodernist critiques for their contribution to moving beyond former orthodoxies. As Harvey, for example, has argued from the latter perspective, '(T)he Interrogation of "orthodox" Marxian formulations .... was both necessary and positive in its implications' (Harvey, 1990, p. 355). Harvey went on to cite four areas where the postmodernist critique had been valuable in taking theoretical development forward.

The first of these was the treatment of 'difference and "otherness"', not as something to be added on to more fundamental Marxist categories (like class and productive forces):

> but as something that should be omni-present from the very beginning in any attempt to grasp the dialectics of social change. The importance of recuperating such aspects of social organization as race, gender, religion, within the overall frame of historical materialist enquiry (with its emphasis upon the power of money and capital circulation) and with class politics (with its emphasis upon the unity of emancipatory struggle) cannot be overestimated (Harvey, 1990, p. 355).

The second development which Harvey identified as being of particular significance was postmodernism's recognition of the importance of culture and communications. 'Aesthetics and cultural practices matter, and the conditions of their production deserve the closest attention', he argued (Harvey, 1990, p. 335). Both of these aspects are central to the themes of this book.

In addition, Harvey also valued postmodernist contributions to the development of debates on the dimensions of space as well as time, taking account of the geographies of social action:

> real as well as metaphorical territories and spaces of power that become vital as organizing forces in the geopolitics of capitalism, at the same time as they are the sites of innumerable differences and othernesses that have to be understood both in their own right and within the overall logic of capitalist development. Historical-geographical materialism is an open-ended and dialectical mode of enquiry rather than a closed and fixed body of understandings. Meta-theory is not a statement of total truth but an attempt to come to terms with the historical and geographical truths that characterize capitalism both in general as well as in its present phase (Harvey, 1990, p. 335).

There are three key points here, for the argument of this chapter. The first point is the significance of postmodernist critiques for the development of debates on culture and cultural struggles (as well as for the debates on questions of identity, difference and otherness, debates which are explored in subsequent chapters). As the Introduction argued, postmodernist critiques have to be addressed. Secondly, Harvey's formulation of Marxism as a meta-theory which is open-ended and dialectical, rather than a statement of total truth, would imply that there is no final solution to the problems of moving beyond past orthodoxies. Capitalism is inherently dynamic, contra-dictory and constantly changing (points which, he suggested, some postmodernists underemphasised, in their overall rejections of Marxism as a grand narrative). Marxism, according to Harvey, then, provides a mode of enquiry to analyse social change, not a collection of quotes to offer simplistic answers to complex questions.

This point relates to the third implication of Harvey's analysis – that the development of particular approaches, such as postmodernism itself, need to be understood within their own specific economic and political contexts. Harvey himself analysed the development of post-modernism in relation to changes in the political economy of late twentieth-century capitalism. Key features of these changes included the further internationalisation of production and communications, the growing emphasis upon flexibility, and the fragmentation of the labour market, as capital restructured to maintain profitability in an increasingly problematic period from the seventies and the eighties.

Global changes in the production process provided the backdrop, then, together with associated shifts in the political context, including the increasing marketisation of the public sector and the burgeoning influence of free-market ideologies more generally. Although Harvey provided an analysis of the context in terms of political economy, however, this was absolutely not a mechanistic, deterministic framework for his analysis of ideological and cultural change, including the development of postmodernism itself. He quoted Jameson's thesis that postmodernism represented the cultural logic of late capitalism (Jameson, 1984). Far from being some autonomous artistic movement, postmodernism was rooted, Harvey argued, in material daily life. But postmodernism still had to be taken seriously, as a cultural phenomenon.

There is not the space to develop Harvey's analysis further. The point to emphasise here is simply this – that the economic, political and social context underwent major changes in the latter part of the twentieth century, and so did the nature of debates on ideology, culture and cultural strategies and struggles. These debates have taken on renewed significance, whether they are approached from a Right or a Left perspective. Cultural debates could be seen, for example, as representing a substitute for political debates, in a world in which traditional divisions between left and right were fast disappearing and free-market economics were no longer to be challenged. Such criticisms have been levelled within the field of Cultural Studies (not to be equated with postmodernism, of course, although the debates overlap); the view that cultural studies has failed 'to deal empirically with the deep structural changes in national and global political, economic and media systems through its eschewing of economic, social or policy analysis' (Ferguson and Golding, 1997, p. xiii). Cultural Studies have been criticised, too, on the grounds that this offered a form of 'compensation for the embattled position of the English-speaking left' in the Thatcher/Reagan years (Gitlin, 1997, p. 34). Younger scholars gravitated to Cultural Studies, Gitlin suggested, because '(T)o do cultural studies, especially in connection with identity politics, was the only politics they knew' (1997, p. 34). By the end of the eighties, it has been argued:

> (T)he world had apparently changed dramatically and so had critical theory of culture and society, whereby it scaled down its political expectations and withdrew from commitment to social transformation (McGuigan, 1997, p. 139).

Similarly, identity politics could be seen as representing alternatives to the politics of solidarity, in a post-Cold War world in which class politics had been finally eliminated.

Or alternatively, as it has also been suggested, cultural politics could be seen as key to a renewed politics of the Left – without jettisoning the importance of rooting this in an analysis of the political economy of culture. Within Cultural Studies there have been strongly argued calls for moving beyond the critique of economism and reductionism; 'the project of cultural studies', according to Garnham, 'can only be successfully pursued if the bridge with political economy is rebuilt' (Garnham, 1997, p. 57). Empowerment will not mean much, in Garnham's view, unless it is accompanied by a massive shift in the control of economic resources.

As subsequent chapters will illustrate, an extraordinary range of cultural strategies and struggles have been developed, in practice, in a variety of different contexts in both the First and Third Worlds. In this sense, practice has run ahead of theory. Cultural politics have been developed in practice whether or not progressives have caught up with these developments in theory. And practitioners have found new ways of exchanging experiences, across continents and across cultural differences. The question has been not whether but how, and from which perspective, cultural strategies and struggles have been developing.

Before moving on from this chapter, however, one further contemporary theoretician of culture, the French academic Bourdieu, needs a brief introduction. While much of the debate around postmodernist approaches to culture, and around Cultural Studies more generally, has been taking place within English-speaking contexts (in Britain, North America and Australasia) Bourdieu's work also has been viewed as being particularly relevant. Although coming from a somewhat different tradition, Lash has gone so far as to suggest that, for the sociology of culture, Bourdieu represents 'the only game in town' (Lash, 1993, p. 193).

Bourdieu has been immensely productive and it would be impossible to provide an adequate summary of his ideas, within the space of this chapter. The following points may perhaps encourage the reader to explore his work further, because aspects are so especially relevant to the themes of this book. In particular, Bourdieu's work addresses the problem of understanding how culture (defined both as 'high culture/art' and as 'ways of life') relates to political economy, taking account of structural factors without eliminating the role of human agents, reflecting upon their actions as they shape their social worlds.

In his study of academic life in the period of the ideological and cultural conflicts which took place in French universities around the events of May 1968, for example, Bourdieu explored the extent to which there were underlying patterns in the perspectives of the academics involved. Whether or not academics supported the student movements' demands related – at least to some extent – he discovered, to their positions within the university system (with the more marginally employed, including Althusser and Foucault, tending to be more sympathetic to the students' demands for change). These tendencies were not rigidly determined, however (Bourdieu, 1988).

Although when he started his academic career, he was greatly influenced by Lévi-Strauss's structural approach to anthropology (he described himself as having been a happy structuralist), Bourdieu moved away from this to develop his own theoretical approach to the question of human agency versus social structure. Bourdieu has seen human agency in collective as well as individual terms. And he has explored the relationship between the conscious self, the individual, and the underlying patterns, the unthought predispositions which shape the individual's habits and tastes. Individuals are located in the context of existing practices and meanings – in class society.

Through detailed empirical study, Bourdieu has applied his theoretical approach to the analysis of the processes of cultural production and consumption in ways which mark and reproduce social difference. So, for example, his study *Distinction* explored the processes by which cultural differences relate to and reproduce class distinctions; whether these cultural differences are measured by people's different tastes in food, clothing and furniture, or whether they are measured by differences in taste in music and painting, for example. In each case, it was not only that people's tastes varied significantly, and that these variations related to their social class (which they did); but that social classes reproduce these differences. Elite groups take care to pass 'cultural capital' on to their children, whilst newly emerging social groups take pains to acquire such cultural capital for themselves and/or their children, or at least to redefine good taste in order to legitimate their own preferences (Bourdieu, 1984). The role of education is particularly important here, as a mechanism for distributing cultural capital. Struggles over cultural capital have their own dynamic and significance then. Whilst this needs to be understood in the context of an analysis rooted in political economy, according to Bourdieu, each field has its own semi-autonomous significance. Through the development of his voluminous work, Bourdieu has struggled with these dilemmas – how to analyse the interrelationships between the different fields, and how to understand the interrelationships between the social structure, the cultural order and individual action.

It has been argued that Bourdieu's work has continued to be marked by his structuralist intellectual past. Whilst recognising the influence of his structuralist roots, however, Bourdieu scholars have also pointed to the ways in which Bourdieu himself has moved debates on in the social sciences (Postone, LiPuma and Calhoun, 1993). The particular contribution of Bourdieu's concept of the 'habitus' – exploring the relationship between agents and the social structure – emerges in more detail, in the context of the discussion of cultural strategies in Chapter 6.

It has been suggested too that Bourdieu has been more successful in analysing the ways in which cultural capital is reproduced than in providing a theory of social and cultural change (Lash, 1993). Bourdieu has certainly produced insights which are relevant to this question, though. In particular, he has been concerned with the role of social science, as a means of developing self-awareness. In Bourdieu's view, the reflexive social scientist is able to produce knowledge which can assist human agents in unveiling the ways in which social and cultural inequality is reproduced and legitimated with a view to developing more effective challenges. This potentially emancipatory aspect makes Bourdieu's work particularly relevant, for the purposes of this book.

2
Communities, Identities and Social Movements

The previous chapter questioned the binary approach – the view that culture, cultural strategies and cultural struggles were either top of the social transformation agenda, on the one hand, or a potentially harmful diversion, on the other hand. In place of such over-simplified polarities, it was suggested, the question was not so much *whether*, but *how* culture and cultural struggles were relevant, depending upon which definitions and which perspectives were being applied. This chapter raises a similar set of questions in relation to the analysis of Communities, Identities and Social Movements. The chapter starts by exploring the varying and contested meanings of the notion of 'community', whether 'community' has been defined in terms of geography or in terms of common interests and identities. This leads into some discussion of the concept of 'identity' itself, a concept which turns out to be no less problematic. The concluding sections of the chapter move on to explore varying perspectives on the New (and not-so-new) Social Movements in principle, and differing approaches to the role of social movements and community politics in practice.

Concepts of community

As the Introduction has already suggested, there are definitional problems with the concept of 'community' which has long been recognised for its slipperiness. As Stacey commented, back in 1969, 'It is doubtful whether the concept "community" refers to a useful abstraction' at all (Stacey, 1969, p. 134). Historians, anthropologists and sociologists have used the term in so many different ways, drawing upon competing theoretical perspectives. In the entry on 'community', in his collection of 'Keywords', Raymond Williams identified only one common thread in these competing definitions, that community tended to be used as a 'warmly persuasive word' (Williams, 1976). Insofar as this has actually been the case (and even this has been challenged) this positive glow which has tended to surround the term 'community' may at least help to explain its popularity with contemporary policy-makers, despite the range of critics who have challenged its continuing usefulness (Mayo, 1994).

Given the range of accounts of the varying definitions and usages of the concept of community, it would be superfluous to rehearse these in detail here. (Crow and Allan, for example, have provided a full and critical discussion (Crow and Allan, 1994), and Crow has related these debates to community-based policies and practice (Crow, 1997).) For the purposes of this chapter, it is only the following points which need to be emphasised. Firstly, the term 'community' has featured prominently in debates and in policy initiatives emerging from both ends of the political spectrum. For the New Right, communities have represented alternative foci for addressing social needs. More specifically, the community sector including non-governmental organisations (NGOs) concerned with the provision of social and community care, for example, have been perceived, from this perspective, as offering alternative ways of providing services, and promoting community development, as the state sector has been rolled back as part of restructuring processes. From such perspectives, community participation has been advocated, on a global scale, with support from a range of organisations and agencies including the World Bank, as well as from a variety of national and regional authorities (Mayo and Craig, 1995; Nelson and Wright, 1995).

On the other hand, communitarians such as Etzioni have argued for the importance of strengthening communities and community participation from a somewhat different perspective, as the Introduction explained in summary (Etzioni, 1993). The work of Etzioni has been taken up in the British context, by communitarians concerned to counteract the increasing fragmentation of social capital, social dislocation and excessive individualism which they have identified as the side-effects of increasing marketisation under the New Right in the 1980s and early 1990s (Atkinson, 1994, Atkinson, 1995). Whilst critical of the market-led strategies of the New Right, however, the communitarians have been associated with an emphasis upon people's responsibilities, and with an agenda for remoralisation. This has been consistent with a type of social conservatism – appeals to family and community values – which has generally been associated with the Right rather than with agendas for social transformation.

There are paradoxes both in relation to the Right/New Right, and in relation to the range of politics included beneath the umbrella of the term the 'Third Way'. These varying approaches to the 'Third Way' have included, for example, the agendas of those seeking a more grass-roots-based approach to development, neither dominated by free-market requirements, nor weighed down by controlling state bureaucracies (Jacobs, 1996). Postmodernist criticisms of meta state planning would be consistent with such objections to the paternalism of top-down development strategies. Proponents of the 'Third Way' have argued that it offers a new approach to democratic politics, moving beyond traditional left/right distinctions, combining the dynamism of the market with new forms of democratic dialogue (Giddens, 1994) – and community participation.

How far protagonists of the 'Third Way' have actually succeeded in offering alternatives to state paternalism without reinforcing the dominance of the market has, however, been a matter of contention. Critics such as Mouffe have argued that, on the contrary, far from moving beyond these contradictions proponents of the Third Way have merely blurred the left/right divide, and this, in turn, has actually reinforced the democratic deficit. As left/right political divisions have been obscured, she argued, political discourse has been trivialised, focusing upon sex scandals, for example, rather than focusing upon debating genuinely alternative political agendas (Mouffe, 1998). The politics of the 'Third Way' per se are beyond the scope of this chapter. The point to emphasise here is simply this, that the notion has itself been highly contentious, along with the approaches to community and to the communitarianism with which the 'Third Way' has been associated.

The varying politics of the 'Third Way', have not, of course, represented the only alternative option, however. Communities and community participation have also featured as part of other agendas to develop alternative approaches, to move beyond bureaucratic state paternalism on the one hand, or market domination, on the other. There have been a range of other attempts to move beyond previous orthodoxies, to develop progressive strategies for community-based policies and practice (Hoggett, 1997) as part of wider strategies to revitalise Left agendas, more generally, questions which concerned the Left from the post-Second World War period, as Chapter 1 has already indicated.

The second point to be emphasised, in summarising these debates on the varying uses of the term, is that, for the purposes of community policies and practice, definitions of 'community' have tended to focus upon two aspects – community in terms of place or shared geography, and community in terms of shared interests, whether these are based upon 'race', ethnicity, religion or some other interest which the community in question shares in common. Popple, for example, summarised these differing definitions as being based upon 'locality or territory' or as 'a communality of interest or interest group such as the black community or Jewish community' (Popple, 1995, p. 4) before going on to refine this latter category by adding that communities of interest can be based upon people sharing a common condition or problem, such as alcohol dependency. Both of these categories of definition, communities of locality or place, and communities of interest or identity, are also problematic, however.

Community, as locality, has been used in the context of romanticised notions of the past. Traditional communities, including working-class communities were presented and valourised as tightly knit, characterised by shared values of solidarity and mutuality, based upon face-to-face communication. As a range of critics have pointed out, these romanticised notions of community as locality may have been largely imaginary, drawing upon fictionalised memories of a golden past. As writers such as Gellner (Gellner, 1987) and Anderson (1983) have shown in their discussions of the concept of community in relation to national identities, these have, in effect been 'cultural artefacts' (Anderson, 1983, p. 4,) 'Imagined Communities' – and this has been the case, Anderson argued, for any community which goes beyond the face to face. Similar arguments may be applied, though, even in the context of face-to-face communities.

Insofar as communities of locality have been based upon such shared values, however, this has also been the subject of criticism (Whitt and Slack, 1994). Such uniformity has been criticised for its potential exclusiveness, reinforcing the unity of sameness by marginalising difference, excluding the other, whether the other is defined in such terms as social class, gender, 'race' or ethnicity, for example. Harvey, for instance, drawing upon North American as well as other experiences, has argued that different classes construct their sense of territory in different ways. 'Low income populations, usually lacking the means to overcome and hence command space, find themselves for the most part trapped in space' (Harvey, 1989, p. 265) although they can and do benefit from the mutual aid and self-help which are characteristic means of survival in poor neighbourhoods. As Abrams's research in the British context, demonstrated, traditions of good neighbourliness and reciprocity in social relations characterised the dense interdependence among kin and neighbours in traditional working-class communities, where 'people helped each other because there was no alternative way of surviving (Bulmer, 1986, p. 98).

Conversely, however, for the affluent, as Harvey argued, the construction of community may be more typically related to the preservation of privilege, excluding 'undesirables' to maintain the community's 'tone' – and property values. Examples of such constructions of community by the privileged range from NIMBY (Not In My Back Yard)ism, through to overt demonstrations of racism, in the case of the red lining of neighbourhoods, for instance, to exclude people of colour from particular neighbourhoods in the USA. On the basis of his studies of urban social movements around the world, over a number of years, Castells has made similar observations about local communities. While, for example:

> local communities and their organisations have, indeed nurtured 'the grassroots of a widespread and influential, environmental movement, particularly in middle-class neighbourhoods; these movements are often defensive and reactive, focusing on the strictest conservation of their space and immediate environment, as exemplified, in the United States, by the 'not in my backyard' attitude, mixing in the same rejection toxic waste, nuclear plants, public housing projects, prisons and mobile home settlements (Castells, 1997, p. 62).

Parallel arguments have been applied to women in the community. Women, Fiona Williams has argued, may be trapped in the locality of their communities, place-bound and tied by a range of factors arising from their situations as women, including the ties arising from their domestic and family responsibilities (Williams, 1989). Notions of communities of locality may be based upon male constructs of a romanticised past dominated by male haunts and activities, such as the pub and football. As Massey has pointed out, a 'woman's view would most likely be very different' (Massey, 1994, p. 113).

The question of whose version of the community of locality has dominated, and who has been effectively excluded takes on particular relevance in relation to race. Because, as a number of critics have pointed out, community-based conflicts have been especially liable to become racialised in the competition for scarce resources in deprived neighbourhoods, as well as in the protection of privilege in more affluent neighbourhoods. These questions about 'race', ethnicity, racism and the racialisation of community conflicts are explored in more detail in the following chapter.

The point to emphasise here is simply this – that the notion of communities of locality is itself problematic. There are alternative approaches, approaches ranging from the backward looking, conservative and essentially exclusive, through to the more forward looking, progressive and inclusive, building links with wider movements for social change, as will be suggested in the subsequent section on the New (and not-so-new) Social Movements. The identity of localities, in any case, as Massey and others have argued, is neither fixed nor politically neutral. Places do not have one essential, exclusivist identity – the identity of a place, in Massey's view, 'is formed out of social interrelations' including both local and wider (including global) interrelations and conflicts (Massey, 1994, p. 115). People's perceptions of places and boundaries can and do shift. Massey concluded by arguing for a non-essentialism in the way we think about place. Locality is vitally important, according to such an analysis, but not in any simplistic or essentialist way. By implication then, the notion of communities of locality would need to be viewed in a non-simplistic, non-essentialist way too, taking account of competing interests and perspectives, and the politics of class, gender, 'race' and ethnicity.

Communities of 'interest' and concepts of identity

Does this mean, then, that the notion of 'communities of interest' represents a way out of these dilemmas, a notion which allows for the complexities of difference within communities of locality, taking account of such factors as class, gender, 'race' and ethnic identities? Well no, not really. On the contrary, in fact, on closer inspection, the concept of identity turns out to be problematic and contested too, let alone the notion of 'communities of interests' based upon identities.

As Morris has argued, on the basis of anthropological research, the very concept of 'the person' varies from one culture to another (Morris, 1994). Western capitalist cultures have been seen as placing emphasis upon the individual, in contrast with other cultures, such as Eastern traditional cultures, which have been seen as placing greater emphasis upon the collective. Morris has demonstrated that the reality is even more complex, however, and that differing degrees of individuality can be identified within non-Western capitalist cultures, including, for example, many African cultures. These differing degrees of individuality can be identified, alongside varying emphases upon interdependence and communality. Morris concluded from his cross-cultural study of conceptions of the person that complexity was evident. Cultures varied in their conceptions and these variations could only be understood if they were explored in multi-dimensional ways, to take account of the material as well as the social and spiritual dimensions (Morris, 1994).

The multi-dimensionality of the individual has long been recognised, more generally, in the social sciences. Psychoanalytical theories as developed by Freud and others, have added their particular critiques of the notion of identity as the identity of 'rational man', exploring the significance of the unconscious, as well as the conscious. Freud's account of the formation of the individual was of the individual as a complex being, shaped at both conscious and unconscious levels by interacting with society (Zaretsky, 1994). However controversial, Freud's work has had a profound impact upon the social sciences, as well as art, literature and philosophy in the twentieth century, an impact which continues to reverberate at the beginning of the next. By implication, then, the socialisation of human infants into the norms and values of particular cultures needs to be seen as involving complex processes – individuals are multi-dimensional with their own drives and desires, shifting as they interact with different cultures' systems of social relationships.

Interactionist approaches to sociology have explored these inter-relationships between the individual and society, and the ways in which children developed their social self, their self-consciousness of themselves, by taking account of how others in society see them (Mead, 1934). The work of Mead and others from the inter-war period, has been developed in a number of ways, more recently, in contemporary sociological debates. Labelling theorists, for example, explored the social processes through which individuals may come to internalise the labels which are being applied to them by others – for example, the label of being a delinquent, or a drug addict (Becker, 1963, Lemert, 1972). There are parallels here, with approaches to the ways in which dominated peoples can come to internalise their oppressors' views of themselves, blaming themselves for their own oppression. As the previous chapter pointed out, Freire, the Brazilian adult educationalist addressed precisely this problem when he set out to empower the oppressed to overcome this oppressor within their own heads, this internalised self-deprecation, seeing themselves as lazy, incapable of learning and unproductive.

Giddens has drawn upon interactionist approaches to develop his own approach to the understanding of self-identity in what he has described as 'the post-traditional order of modernity' (Giddens, 1991, p. 5). Modernity, Giddens argues, is a risk culture, not in the sense that life is inherently more risky (which is not the case) but in the sense that risk and risk assessment can be and are addressed in new ways, with greater precision. Individuals face new choices about their lives and lifestyles, choices which have particular implications in contemporary society. He argues:

> The more tradition loses its hold and the more daily life is reconstituted in terms of the dialectical interplay of the local and the global, the more individuals are forced to negotiate lifestyle choices among a diversity of options (Giddens, 1991, p. 5).

The self, Giddens argues in a subsequent paper:

> becomes a reflexive project and increasingly the body also. Individuals cannot rest content with an identity that is simply handed down, inherited, or built as a traditional status. A person's identity has in large part to be discovered, constructed, actively sustained. Like the self, the body is no longer accepted as 'fate', as the physical baggage that comes along with the self. We have more and more to decide not just who to be, and how to act, but how to look to the outside world (Giddens, 1994, p. 82).

The implications of the relationship between the self and the body raise further levels of complexity, issues which have been explored elsewhere too. Pile and Thrift's approach to 'Mapping the Subject', for example, started from the co-ordinates of the body, the self, the person, identity and subjectivity. Each of these co-ordinates, they went on to argue, needs to be understood in the context of their relationship within a system of social relations. So, for example, the body has social meaning, as the body of a male, or the body of a manual worker, in a patriarchal capitalist society, and qualities such as being weak or old, for example, have particular meanings in specific social settings and cultures, just as the sense of self has meaning in the context of particular cultural concepts of masculinity or class consciousness, for example. Such an approach implies that an adequate analysis of agency – human action – in the context of structures and structural constraints would need to explore this in relation to each of these co-ordinates (Pile and Thrift, 1995).

Giddens's view of the contrast between post-traditional, reflexive identities and traditional identities has been the subject of criticism on a number of grounds. Firstly, it has been pointed out that preoccupations with self, and self-questioning have not been confined to modern times, let alone postmodern times. Heelas and others have argued that the notion of detraditionalisation, as sweeping all before it, is too simplistic (Heelas, 1996). Traditions have not been so fixed that there has been no room for human agency, questioning or modification. Even small-scale societies have rarely been complete 'islands', cut off from any contact with alternative ways of life. Anthropologists, Heelas pointed out, 'are also increasingly emphasizing that small-scale societies are internally pluralistic' (Heelas, 1996, p. 8); participants have not necessarily seen things in the same way.

Meanwhile, contemporary societies include examples where individuals and groups attempt to revive traditionalism. For instance, the rise of religious fundamentalism – of whichever religious brand – may be a complex phenomenon, with multiple causes. But from whichever way you look at this, religious fundamentalism would seem to sit uneasily with any all-encompassing notion of detraditionalisation as sweeping all before it.

Notions of agency have been questioned, too, in relation to who has which choices. Giddens himself recognised that 'class divisions and other fundamental lines of inequality, such as those connected with gender or ethnicity, can be partly *defined* in terms of differential access to forms of self-actualisation and empowerment' (Giddens, 1991, p. 6). Lash went on to suggest that 'in today's increasingly class-polarized, though decreasingly class-conscious, information societies' there were 'whole battalions of "reflexivity losers"' (Lash, 1994, p. 120) and to question how far the ghetto mother, for example, had the ability to self-construct her own life narratives. Castells made a similar point when he suggested that reflexive life planning 'becomes impossible except for the elite inhabiting the timeless space of flows of global networks and their ancillary locales' (Castells, 1997, p. 11). Some of these questions re-emerge in subsequent chapters, including Chapter 7, in the context of strategies to address the barriers which inhibit people from making healthy lifestyle choices in general, and more specifically to empower relatively powerless people to make safer choices to reduce the risk of contracting HIV/AIDS.

There is not the space here, to develop these arguments in more detail. The point is simply to emphasise that across a range of social science disciplines, the notion of the individual and individual identity has been and continues to be analysed as a complex phenomenon. There are connections, too, with one of the key questions which was identified in the previous chapter – the question of how far people make their own history, individually and collectively. Or how far are people constrained by structural forces, forces which may shape their very consciousness and their desires, as well as their material situations? These are issues which re-emerge in subsequent chapters, both in theory and in practice (as with the discussion and application of Bourdieu's concept of 'habitus' in Chapters 6 and 7).

In summary, then, the concept of identity is no more straightforward than the concept of community. And if the concept of individual identity is problematic, so too is the notion of communities of identity, let alone the notion of identity politics and New Social Movements based upon these. Communities, it has been pointed out, are not simply the result of shared interests, or shared properties, but about shared meanings (Lash, 1994). And meanings are socially constructed – often on the basis of common struggles (Castells, 1997). If there is no essential individual identity, waiting to be liberated, as a number of critics (including Foucault) have argued, then how can there be 'essential communities' either? What, if anything, does it actually mean, to identify communities of interest based upon identities such as sexual identities or ethnic identities? If there are no essential identities, anyway, how can there be essential 'black' identities or 'gay' identities to be organised around? And what, as the Introduction asked, about multiple identities – identifying oneself as being gay *and black*, for example, or as being an *older woman of colour with disabilities*?

Once again, the issue is not whether but how these questions are addressed. As it has already been argued, in relation to culture and cultural struggles, the politics of identity and difference have become a significant feature of the political landscape, whether particular individuals or collectivities welcome this, or choose to define themselves in such ways, or not. These politics are being developed in varying ways, from differing perspectives. Given the conceptual difficulties that have already been outlined, this makes it all the more important to clarify these varying usages and perspectives. When these terms appear, in subsequent chapters, they need to be read with an accompanying note of caution; like 'community', 'identity' is not simply to be taken as a 'warmly persuasive word'.

The politics of identity

As Colhoun has pointed out in a collection of critical essays entitled *Social Theory and the Politics of Identity* (Calhoun (ed.), 1994), identity politics are not actually a new phenomenon. Ethnicity and ethnic antagonism, he has argued, are very ancient. But contemporary concerns with the politics of identity and difference have taken particular forms. Both individual and collective identities became more problematic with the development of modern capitalist societies, with their increasing emphasis on the individual and individual choice within the nation state (itself a contested and problematic notion, a point which is explored in more detail in Chapter 6). Whilst these changes may have represented progress, in terms of development from feudal societies, there was nothing inherently progressive for the future, he argued.

On the contrary, in fact, identity politics may be pursued in ways which 'undermine the potential for affirming broad commonalities – such as those of class – and achieving collective strength in political action', as the contribution by Gitlin to that particular collection of essays, argued (Gitlin, 1994, p. 5). Identity politics may be divisive, then, turning inwards, rather than turning outwards, to challenge the common sources of oppression, which may be shared by different oppressed and exploited groups, across these divides (Gitlin, 1994). Gitlin's essay questioned the self-declared radicalism of many versions of identity politics, concluding by emphasising the importance of building solidarity while taking account of and respecting diversity (Gitlin, 1994, p. 5). Lash developed a comparable case when he argued that a radical political culture:

> cannot have its core assumptions only in ideas and practices of difference. It must just as much have its basis in the thought and practice of solidarity. That is, solidarity is as crucial in any reconstructed radical contemporary political culture as difference (Lash, 1996, p. 256).

Addressing this recurrent dilemma, Harvey developed similar arguments. Identity politics had a key and progressive role, he argued, in the struggle to break with an identity which internalised oppression. Carried to extremes, as an end in itself, however, he argued that identity politics could lead to fragmentation, undermining the potential for developing solidarity between different oppressed and exploited groups (Harvey, 1993). Once again, then, the point was not whether but how, identity politics were being developed, according to which perspective. Harvey concluded by neither embracing identity politics uncritically, nor denying the importance of addressing issues of diversity and difference within the context of developing strategies for building solidarity for social transformation.

As Colhoun and others have also pointed out, movements based upon identity politics have mirrored some of these differences of perspective within their own movements. So, feminists and those involved in campaigning for lesbian and gay rights, for example, have shared common concerns to reclaim and value identities which have been commonly suppressed or devalued by mainstream culture (to reclaim and value women's identity, or gay and lesbian identities, in these cases). But beyond these common concerns, feminists, or gay men or lesbians have by no means settled their theoretical differences. Feminism has been subdivided, for example, according to the differences of perspective between radical feminists, liberal feminists, black feminists and socialist feminists, to name only a selection of these sub-categories (Williams, 1989).

As bell hooks has argued, 'The concept of "Woman" effaces the difference between women in specific socio-historical contexts, between women defined precisely as historical rather than a psychic subject (or non-subject)' (hooks, 1993, p. 124). The concept of woman, in the abstract, then, obscures the issue of 'race' – the reality that women of colour do not suffer oppression in precisely the same ways as their white sisters. This question of the importance of recognising difference and diversity in general, and specifically of recognising the significance of racial oppression, has been a key issue for debate in the Women's Liberation Movement over the last two decades of the twentieth century.

Hooks's points about difference and diversity within the Women's Liberation Movement raise questions both about multiple identities and hierarchies of oppression. Why or how should oppressed groups be expected to define their identities singly, rather than in more complex ways, as women *or* as people of colour, for example, rather than as *black women*? One of the results of attempts to categorise people's identities in such one-dimensional terms has been to pressurise oppressed people into prioritising their identities, having to choose to identify primarily with one social movement rather than another. As it has already been suggested, such approaches fail to explore the interrelationships between the different dimensions of people's exploitation and oppression – interrelationships with key significance for developing solidarity within difference. The reality, as experiences of particular movements illustrate, is more complex, with overlapping as well as conflicting interests, both within and between social movements based upon the politics of identity.

New (and not-so-new) social movements

Like the notions of 'community' and 'identity', the definition of what constitutes a social movement has been problematic too. As Escobar and Alvarez have pointed out, some scholars (and specifically Melucci):

> even believe that the whole idea of a 'social movement' as a description of collective action should be abandoned because it traps our language in conceptual traditions that have to be discarded (Escobar and Alvarez, 1992, p. 7).

Escobar and Alvarez resisted the temptation to offer their own definition, although they did point to the need for a broad approach, including cultural, as well as economic, social and political dimensions.

In European debates, it has been suggested, debates on social movements in general, and new social movements more specifically, have tended to focus upon questions related to the construction of new social and political identities. In North American debates, in contrast, there has been more focus upon questions about resource mobilisation – understanding the ways in which social movements have organised to gain access to resources and to impact upon decision-making processes (Foweraker, 1995; Della Porta and Diani, 1999). Both approaches have relevance, it has been argued, for developing a critical understanding of social movements: for addressing the expressive questions and the instrumental questions – the *how* questions as well as the *why* questions about social movements (Foweraker, 1995).

While it was still premature, in their view, to speak of an integrated theory, Della Porta and Diani identified four themes which were of key concern to social movement scholars from varying approaches. Social movement theorists focused upon *informal interaction networks*, which were based upon *shared beliefs and solidarity*, engaging in *collective action focusing upon conflicts*, including the *use of protest*. These four elements do not constitute a definition precisely, but they do offer some guidance as to what may or may not usefully be considered as a social movement, new or otherwise. So, for example, in Della Porta and Diani's view, social movements are looser and less formal than political parties or particular religious sects, but social movements such as the environmental movement might *include* a Green political party, along with a range of other groups and individuals. Similarly, fundamentalist religious movements might include specific sects but would not be confined to such particular membership groupings. Through their shared beliefs and solidarity, and their involvement in collective action, social movements can also be distinguished from other forms of alliances – such as alliances of heterogeneous lobby groups.

The final point to emphasise is that whilst social movements are being considered, here, in terms of their shared beliefs and solidarity, these shared beliefs and solidarity are not simply to be taken as givens. On the contrary, in fact, Della Porta and Diani identified two-way processes at work (Della Porta and Diani, 1999). Individuals who become actively involved in social movements, on the basis of their initial beliefs, may develop considerably strengthened beliefs through the process of participating in collective action. To illustrate this point, they quoted a number of reflections from feminists whose perceptions and sense of self had developed through their involvement in collective action in the Women's Movement. As such shared beliefs and values and emotional commitment developed, Della Porta and Diani suggested, participants' involvement became less and less clearly reducible to the type of rational calculations of self-interest which have been associated with resource mobilisation approaches.

It was with questions of values, ideology and culture – rather than with questions of resource mobilisation – that the New Social Movement theorists were predominantly concerned. As the Introduction has already suggested, in summary, the New Social Movements were given enhanced prominence in European debates, in the writings of critics such as Gortz and Touraine, as they set about challenging previously accepted Left orthodoxies about political economy, and political struggles rooted in the leading role of the working class, and industrial struggles at the point of production. In the aftermath of the challenges posed by the students' movement in France, and a number of other countries, at the end of the sixties, critics such as Touraine were seeking new approaches, which would take account of the growing significance of ideological and cultural issues and struggles, and the concerns of students and white-collar workers, in a 'post-industrial' society. Some of these challenges have already been touched upon, in the previous chapter.

While Touraine was not denying any continuing role for traditional working-class politics, he *was* rejecting the orthodox Marxist view that the working class was the key historical agent in the movement towards socialism (Touraine, 1974). In post-industrial society, in contrast, dominated as this was seen by a number of critics to be by changing forms of technology, requiring less emphasis upon mass production and greater emphases upon flexibility, design, knowledge, skill and creativity, cultural and communications issues and struggles over legitimacy, together with demands for greater participation and democracy, would be increasingly important.

As capitalism had developed greater and more sophisticated control mechanisms, it was argued in parallel, intruding further and further into people's personal lives, so New Social Movements had developed, raising counter-demands for participation and personal autonomy, along with demands over questions of lifestyle and values. In short, what the New Social Movements were demanding, their enthusiasts in Europe were suggesting, was the democratisation of everyday life. As the Women's Liberation Movement argued, the proposition that 'the personal is political', in this sense, represented a fundamental demand which went way beyond the programme of any political party programme. What was being demanded, in fact, was the total transformation of social relations (Melucci, 1988).

The implication which was drawn by the enthusiasts was that the New Social Movements represented a novel, and fundamentally more transformatory approach to politics, demanding changes which could not be accommodated within the framework of existing social relations. This was contrasted with the demands of traditional working-class politics, demands around wages and conditions, for example, which could actually be accommodated more readily within the existing social order, whereas the New Social Movements were seen as potential embryos of future societies, based upon networks of self-managed communities. (Lowe, 1986; Scott, 1990).

While debates focused to a considerable extent on movements which were directly concerned with cultural meanings and specifically with identities, movements such as the Women's Liberation Movement, Anti-Racist Movements and the Gay and Lesbian Movement, the New Social Movement theorists were not simply concerned with identity politics, however. Environmentalism, a movement which has had key significance for New Social Movement theorists, provides a case in point not being rooted in identity politics per se; although environmental campaigners have, of course, argued for alternative values, posing fundamental challenges to very basic assumptions about the nature of production and consumption, on a global scale. In this latter sense, environmentalism could be considered as posing questions about future societies in embryo – but not specifically within the framework of identity politics.

Meanwhile the view that the New Social Movements represented a novel and inherently more radical approach to politics did not go unchallenged. As critics pointed out, the labour and progressive movements had long histories of solidarity with struggles which were based around social and community issues, rather than based at the point of production. In Britain, for instance, the histories of tenants' struggles around housing and planning issues, and community struggles around health and welfare issues dated back at least to the earlier part of the twentieth century, histories which had been explicitly linked, in solidarity, with the labour and trade union movements (Cowley, 1979; Mayo, 1994). The first wave of feminism, the movement for women's suffrage, had also included campaigning around economic, social and cultural issues as well as political issues (such as the work of Sylvia Pankhurst and others in East London) (Davis, 1999).

Whether New Social Movements such as the Women's Liberation Movement, and the movements for Gay and Lesbian rights, and Disability rights, from the seventies and eighties, were inherently so different, and so much more transformatory than these previous movements had been, was by no means clear either. Some of their apparently more far-reaching, less negotiable demands may actually have been reflecting the relative novelty of the movements in question, it was suggested (Scott, 1990) – demanding the impossible, before at least some sections of each movement settled down to negotiate around the more specific points of the realistically achievable – mobilising around resources, in other words. Sections of the Women's Liberation Movement, for example, came to concentrate upon campaigning for specific changes such as particular legislative reforms, in just such ways as their predecessors in the First Wave of feminism had campaigned before them. Fainstein and Hirst reached

similar conclusions when they suggested that most urban social movements appear to settle for some form of participation in municipal
decision-making as their ultimate demand (Fainstein and Hirst, 1995).
These are inherent dilemmas facing campaigning and lobbying organisations, dilemmas about when and how far to move inside the policy
process – issues which have emerged more clearly as governments
have developed partnership approaches in the mixed economy of
welfare (see Taylor, forthcoming, for an excellent exploration of
these).

Subsequent histories of the New Social Movements in the harsher
economic and political climates of the 1980s and 1990s, have borne
out the view that there has been nothing automatic about the transformatory nature of their demands. On the contrary, in fact, each
movement has developed a range of demands from the more specific
and potentially accommodatable to the wider and more potentially
transformatory. The contemporary activity of most progressive social
movements, Martin has argued, in a comprehensive review of social
movements in the Scottish context, 'contains both oppositional and
alternative elements, and the balance between them continually
changes' (Martin, 1999, p. 10). Social movements can and do shift
both back and forth – over time; they may raise more or less readily
accommodatable demands, and may themselves become more or less
incorporated into institutional structures and agendas which are effectively determined by others more powerful than they are. In other
words, social movements develop and change across a wide range of
political positions and perspectives. Similar points about the fluidity
and flexibility of social movements have been made, both in general
(Della Porta and Diani, 1999) and more specifically in the context of
Latin American experiences (Escobar and Alvarez, 1992).

In a subsequent work, Castells illustrated this diversity with a typol-
ogy of environmentalism entitled *The Creative Cacophany of
Environmentalism* (Castells, 1997, p. 112). He characterised environmental movements in the following ways as: movements concerned
with the conservation of nature (for example, Group of Ten, USA),
movements concerned with the defence of own space (Not in my Back
Yard), Counter-cultural movements (such as Earth first and ecofemi-
nism), Save the planet movements (such as Greenpeace) and Green
politics, each of which had its own characteristic identity, adversary
and goals. These have ranged from longer-term goals of counter-
power through to more immediate concerns with issues of health and
safety, in the here and now.

There has been nothing automatic, either, about the New Social Movements' potential to coalesce, to form any unified movement for social transformation. On the contrary, in fact, there have been powerful pressures for fragmentation both within the movements and between them. There have been key ideological and political divisions within the New Social Movements, divisions which have emerged more visibly as the movements have developed (Aronowitz, 1992). This point has been argued from a range of perspectives, both within and outside the movements in question, including postmodernists (who would be sceptical, in any case, about either the possibility or indeed the desirability of attempting to unify around such diverse demands and desires).

In summary then, far from representing a new and more transformatory approach to politics, the New Social Movements have covered a wide range of perspectives and political positions, both within and between the different movements. Feminists and anti-racists have identified with international struggles for national liberation and social justice; and feminists and anti-racists have focused upon challenging barriers to individual career progression, within the framework of existing (exploitative) social relations. Gays and Lesbians have campaigned against homophobia. Faith-based organisations and coalitions have campaigned for human rights and challenged the causes of poverty and inequality on a global scale (as the discussions of campaigns for Fairer Trade and Debt relief illustrate in subsequent chapters). And fundamentalists of varying religious affiliations have campaigned to limit the demands of particular social movements, gays' and lesbians' demands for equal rights, for example, and women's demands for control of their own fertility.

On the other hand, while recognising that there is nothing inherently progressive about Social Movements per se, Left critics have argued for the importance of valuing the contributions which the New Social Movements *have* made. Transformatory politics can be enriched with their insights. But this is not to suggest that the New Social Movements could or should substitute for the wider struggles for social transformation. To argue for the importance of building solidarity with the New Social Movements is not necessarily to accept Touraine or Gortz's arguments for the diminished importance of the working class and working-class politics at the point of production. On the contrary, in fact. Class politics remain highly relevant (Aronowitz, 1992). As Left critics have also pointed out, class politics have actually been waged with increasing ferocity by the ruling classes since the late seventies, whether or not the Left has recognised this fact (Aronowitz, 1992). The Reagan administration's New-Right policies have been described, for example, as representing the declaration of a 'new class war on the unemployed, the unemployable, and the working poor' (Fox Piven and Cloward, 1982).

If class politics were being so actively waged by the Right, then, the Left needed more than ever to develop counter-strategies, based upon the widest possible solidarity. Harvey was arguing from such a perspective when he reflected that whatever the limitations and the inherent fragmentation of the New Social Movements per se, they were raising key issues for the development of a more transformatory politics of the Left (Harvey, 1990). Reflecting upon the achievements of social movements, Paterson has argued that they:

> have radicalised left-wing politics in an irrevocable way. They have also indelibly marked our understanding of society and of the political sources of social change. But they have not done away with the universalistic concept of social rights themselves (Paterson, 1999, p. 51).

For Paterson then, the key questions were those which have already emerged in the course of this chapter, how to develop an adequate understanding of identity and difference, how to build unity while genuinely taking account of diversity, how to develop cultural strategies and struggles without losing sight of the political economy of culture.

Social movements and community politics in practice: 'building havens or heavens'?

In practice, meanwhile, social movements have developed community politics in a variety of different ways, reflecting both diversity and commonality. The Women's Movement may have been seen as fragmenting into a range of divergent tendencies, but these tendencies have also included women's struggles around the defence of locality and working-class community (as in the cases of women against pit closures in Britain in the eighties, and women in support of the Liverpool dockers in the nineties) (Samuel, Bloomfield and Boanas, 1986; Seddon, 1986; Loach, 1996). This section summarises examples of such cross-overs in the context of debates about some of the potential strengths, as well as some of the inherent limitations of social movements and community politics, whether these have been defined in terms of locality, or identity or both.

Castells has provided an analysis of social movements which has particular relevance here, because of the range of different types of cross-cultural case materials which illustrate his arguments, over a time span of the past hundred years or so (Castells, 1983). His focus upon urban social movements stemmed from Castells's theoretical starting points, rooted in the political economy of space. For Castells, urban social movements were characterised in terms of whether they focused upon collective consumption issues (issues such as housing and planning, which have featured in community politics over the years) or represented the newer movements in defence of cultural identities (such as gay and Latino identity-based movements in contemporary USA) or whether they could be characterised as movements involved with political mobilisation more generally. Or alternatively, as in the case of the Spanish citizens' movements which he studied, movements might be involved in all three of these aspects.

Some of these movements were characterised by Castells as 'trade unionism' around collective consumption issues (that is, as putting forward very limited, highly specific demands around issues such as rent levels, on a par with the limited demands around pay and conditions, which he saw as characteristic of trade union collective bargaining processes). However important such issues were to the protagonists, by themselves they did not necessarily entail any wider challenges to the status quo. Other movements, such as the Citizens' Movements in Spain in the latter days of Franco's dictatorship, entailed both immediate demands around housing and transport, for example, and more far-reaching demands for political rights to organise. Since opposition political parties were underground, at this period, citizens' movements were able to play a key and relatively autonomous role.

There are interesting parallels here with the role which Civic Organisations played in the latter days of Apartheid in South Africa, organising around immediate issues but also developing oppositional politics as part of the wider struggle for racial equality and social justice (Taylor, 1995). In parallel with the experiences of the Spanish Citizens' Movements which Castells analysed, these autonomous social movements in South Africa also faced a very different scenario, as previously constructed coalitions faced the new challenges of political democracy once the common enemy of the Apartheid regime had been formally removed. In both cases, then, social movements played key roles in the wider struggles for democracy and both opened up new approaches to urban life and culture, based upon participatory forms of democracy – even if these new approaches and the alliances which had been built around them proved subsequently challenging to sustain.

Castells argued that for movements to play such a wider role in creating significant social change at all, let alone to do so on a continuing basis, they needed to be able to combine with other movements. This would involve building alliances geographically between different localities, across cities. And it would involve building alliances between different types of community movements and political movements – without surrendering the autonomy of citizen's movements to become the pawns of any particular political party (even a progressive political party). Castells put special emphasis, here, upon the potential contribution which cultural movements could make, including cultural and identity movements such as women's and youth movements, and cultural groupings such as the groups which organised street festivals, where these were challenging dominant values and norms (issues which re-emerge in subsequent chapters of this book). Drawing upon Melucci's ideas, he argued for the potentially transformative role of movements which questioned previously accepted social roles and structures.

One of the examples which Castells used to illustrate the potential challenge of identity politics, was the case of Gay-community organising in San Francisco. Interestingly, this example illustrated both aspects of community politics. Community organising, here, was based upon the shared identity of being gay. But this had a spatial dimension too as the Gay community organised within a particular locality, Castro Valley, a safe space where gay bars and residences became concentrated. Castells concluded that real gains were made as the gay community built up its own vibrant community culture and alternative life style. But there were also splits within the Gay community. There were class differences and there were political differences – and as others have also pointed out, gay bars and businesses were not necessarily actually owned by gays; many were not; gay managers were producing profits for owners elsewhere (Califia, 1997). Castells concluded that there were wider processes of fragmentation too, between different oppressed groups in the city, characterised by competition between them rather than the development of effective alliances for social change.

Overall, this related to Castells's wider conclusions at that time. He was deeply critical of the traditional Marxist Left, for its economism and for its concentration upon structures at the expense of social action (reducing the analysis of the city, he argued, to the formula of 'the logic of capital') and for failing to recognise the role which autonomous social movements could play in strategies for social transformation. On the other hand, Castells concluded that even if they can develop counter-cultures – posing an alternative global vision – by themselves, social movements would be unable to build an alternative mode of production and development. They cannot, by themselves, tackle the global economy or the globalised communications systems of the late twentieth century. However, he concluded that social movements can be 'live schools' producing new historical meanings and as such their contributions are vital – they are addressing real issues, even if they are unable to resolve these on their own (Castells, 1983, p. 331).

Although this study was carried out in the 1980s, the conclusions would seem to have continuing relevance. In his subsequent writings Castells has pointed to the darker sides as well as to the progressive potential of social movements (although he has explicitly not set himself up as judge in relation to any particular social movement). He returned to the conclusions which he drew in 1983 about social movements' potential for developing new meaning, 'nurturing the embryos of tomorrow's social movements within the local utopias that urban movements have constructed in order never to surrender to barbarism' (Castells, 1997, p. 61, quoting Castells, 1983, p. 331). Since then, he argued:

> local communities, constructed through collective action and preserved through collective memory, are specific sources of identity. But these identities, in most cases, are defensive reactions against the impositions of global disorder and uncontrollable, fast-paced change. They do build havens, but not heavens (Castells, 1997, p. 64).

From some forms of community movements, however, he suggested that it *was* possible that there was some basis for the emergence of new subjects 'that is collective agents of social transformation' (Castells, 1997, p. 67).

These conclusions would seem to apply to more recent examples too. Disabled Peoples' Movements which developed so markedly in Britain and beyond, from the late sixties, have also taken up specific issues such as inadequate services and benefits, and found that this led them into more wide-ranging campaigns to eradicate disabling social attitudes and environments (Barnes and Mercer, 1995). The identity which has been reinforced by prevailing social attitudes towards disability has been a negative one, and the everyday experience of people with disabilities has been summed up as a negative reality (Finkelstein, 1993). Challenging this negative identity has been key, then, to challenging the social basis for the economic and social deprivation and social exclusion which people with disabilities face, and the specific policies which need to be pursued to address these problems.

Disabled Peoples' Movements have developed on a global scale. And since the World Congress of Rehabilitation International in 1980, disabled people themselves have been organising on a global scale through the Disabled Peoples' International (DPI). By the mid-nineties, the DSI had representation from over a hundred countries, with consultative status with the UN, UNESCO and the ILO.

Despite its success in developing a campaigning role for the rights of people with disabilities on a global scale, however, the DPI was no more free from internal tensions and conflicts than other parallel organisations. For example, as Barnes and Mercer have suggested '(F)orging alliances between disabled people in the North and the South opens up possibilities, but is also fraught with difficulties' (Barnes and Mercer, 1995, p. 42). Even within countries, too, there were potential tensions relating to the different needs which needed to be represented within the movement's overall umbrella – the needs of women with disabilities, for example (Morris, 1991).

In any case, as movements address the wider structural causes of their problems, they are confronted by increasingly complex challenges. As far as Disabled Peoples' Movements are concerned, significant structural causes of impairments have been identified, including those of malnutrition (the estimated cause of one in five impairments in the world), industrial accidents, environmental pollution, stress and exhaustion, physical abuse, and war and violence (Abberley, 1987, quoted in Barnes and Mercer, 1995). Such structural causes relate to wider structures of power and conflicts of interest with ramifications which are global.

Disabled people have been struggling to make effective impacts on deeply entrenched prejudice and institutional discrimination, Barnes and Mercer concluded. 'Yet without some major realignment in the balance of economic power between the North and the South, the prospects for further change, particularly in developing societies, remain bleak and many battles remain to be fought', despite the major achievements of the movements so far (Barnes and Mercer, 1995, p. 43).

This emphasis upon the connections between the local and the global can also be illustrated through the case of environmental movements. Environmental activists do not share identities which need to be reclaimed because they have been devalued in the mainstream culture, like feminists or gay and lesbian activists, for example. Nor are environmental activists defined by their common locality in the way that tenants and residents groups tend to be – although environmental activists do, of course, share particular concerns with space and its uses and abuses. Such concerns can and do lead environmental activists to engage in local campaigning on a range of issues, such as campaigning against hazardous waste disposal and the environmental devastation of particular sites through road building, for example, or the construction of other environmentally unacceptable developments. Campaigns of this type have had high media profiles, using a range of strategies and tactics, including the use of community media, representing some of the most visible faces of political action with particular support amongst the young.

In common with the social movements which have been considered so far, as it has already been suggested, environmental movements have been diverse. Ecological perspectives have ranged across the political spectrum with associations of almost every political hue. Environmental concerns can be appropriated by multinational corporations to 'legitimize a global grab to manage all of the world's resources', in Harvey's view (Harvey, 1998, p. 343) contrasting this with the movement for environmental justice and against environmental racism in the USA. As Morris has pointed out, there have been past connections between ecology and Fascist thought, as well as more recent connections between ecology and liberal reformist politics, democratic socialist politics and libertarian socialist thought (Morris, 1996). There have been a range of connections then just as there have been tensions, and attempts to work through these to build alliances and common positions (as in the case of attempts to develop joint Red-Green positions, for example).

Environmental campaigns, like the campaigns of the social movements which have been discussed so far, have ranged very widely in the nature of their demands. Specific campaigns have focused upon particular issues and sites, including the very local within geographical

communities. Ultimately, however, the logic of environmental politics involves challenging an entire way of organising social life, it has
been argued. A qualitatively new vision has been required, of 'how
humans should live together with each other and with the planet'
(Red-Green Study Group, 1995, p. 4). Developing such a vision would
entail questioning some of the most fundamental assumptions of
modern industrial cultures, assumptions about the goals of economic
development for example, and assumptions about the role of
humankind in relation to the rest of nature.

Environmental movements, then, potentially raise some of the
same questions which Castells posed for social movements – that is,
questions about alternative global visions. And environmental movements have also had to address similar issues, and dilemmas,
including dilemmas about how to work with the differences within,
and how to build alliances beyond the specific and the local campaign
– without losing sight of the global context. 'Think globally, act
locally' has been a particularly relevant slogan, not only for environmental movements but also for social movements more generally.

Like the wider demands of other social movements, such as
Disabled Peoples' Movements, environmental demands raise questions of global significance, including questions about economic
power in both North and South. In their study evaluating the potential as well as the limits of local environmental struggles, Gould,
Schnaiberg and Weinberg have argued that neither the local nor the
global can be understood without taking account of the transnational
– meaning by this the political-economic system which is dominated
by transnational capital's requirements for growth. They characterised
this system in terms of the 'treadmill of production' (Gould *et al.*,
1996).

In the North American examples of environmental struggles which
they studied, the requirements of economic growth were typically
taken for granted – assumptions not to be questioned – by governments and local authorities concerned with economic development.
As they demonstrated, similar assumptions were shared by local
people too. This was especially clear in relation to jobs – local people
were fearful about pursuing struggles over industrial pollution, for
example, in case this led employers to shift their investments – and
the associated jobs – elsewhere. There were potential splits within
local communities then, and there were potential divisions between
areas competing for investment and jobs, even if these jobs entailed
environmental pollution. The most significant progress in tackling

local environmental problems was achieved, Gould, Schnaiberg and Weinberg argued, when official schemes to promote citizen participation in environmental protection were built upon autonomous local movements, backed by national environmental organisations (Gould *et al.*, 1996).

The authors concluded, overall, that local campaigning *did* have a key role, even in the context of the transnationals. Local organisations were the 'eyes and ears' of the wider movements. But local campaigns needed to be linked into wider networks, if they were to begin to take on the power interests which were involved in tackling the 'treadmill of production' (Gould *et al.*, 1996).

The problems inherent in addressing global issues have been only too evident. Evaluating the impact of social movements which have sought to challenge rather than to work for global capitalism, Sklair concluded that:

> social movements working against capitalism have been singularly unsuccessful globally, though their prospects of challenging global capitalism locally and making this count globally, globalizing disruptions, seem more realistic (Sklair, 1998, p. 298).

These conclusions have potential relevance far more widely, in evaluating the potential role of social movements whether these are based upon communities of locality, communities of identity, or some combination of both. The concluding chapter (Chapter 8) returns to these key questions.

3
'Race', Racism, Anti-Racism and Identities

As the previous chapter argued, the notion of identity is complex and socially constructed. The individual's sense of self has varied from culture to culture – just as the concept of self has varied over time. More specifically, it has been suggested, contemporary preoccupations with questions of individual identities are themselves rooted in the context of their political economy. Western industrialised cultures have revolutionised our very sense of ourselves; as Rose has argued. '(W)e have become intensely subjective beings' (Rose, 1989, p. 3). This preoccupation with the subjective can be related to the neo-liberal focus upon the individual, and the neo-liberal concept of the individual as freely exercising their right to make choices in the market-place, both as producers and as consumers, urged:

> to shape our lives by the use of our purchasing power. We are obliged to make our lives meaningful by selecting our personal lifestyle from those offered to us in advertising, soap operas, and films, to make sense of our existence by exercising our freedom to choose in a market in which one simultaneously purchases products and services, and assembles, manages and markets oneself. The image of the citizen as a choosing self entails a new image of the productive subject (Rose, 1989, pp. 102–3).

It is a revolutionised view of self, paradoxically demonstrating both extended subjugation, and increasing attachment to the search for individual autonomy and freedom.

The notion of an 'essential' self, it has been argued then, is inherently problematic. Hall, amongst those who have explored the positive potential of identity politics, has also recognised precisely these issues, arguing that 'I do not have an essentialist reading of religious, ethnic or national affiliations or movements *per se* ... They are not fixed and can be transcoded, as the configurations of which they are part shift' (Hall, 1996, p. 12). As Rose has also pointed out, our very concern with self and identity needs to be understood in relation to its political, economic, social and cultural context, at the beginning of the twenty-first century (Rose, 1989). And as Hall went on to argue, in addition, organising around identity has the potential for being exclusive as well as inclusive – 'the very notion of "identity" always involves a certain degree of exclusion' (Hall, 1996, p. 13). Similar arguments may be applied, too, to notions of the 'other' and specifically to notions of 'race' and racism, as these have developed over time in different contexts. Identities based upon 'race' are no less problematic, by definition.

This chapter starts by exploring the concept of 'race', as a predominantly biological notion, as well as in relation to more cultural usages. Having focused upon the contested concept of 'race', as this has shifted over time and space, the chapter moves on to examine differing approaches to defining and organising around racial identities, with varying implications for addressing key dilemmas inherent in the project of developing anti-racist strategies, in the contemporary context. How to challenge reductionist, essentialist stereotypes of the 'other' – while acknowledging the significance of the issues raised through identity politics? How to respect diversity and take account of difference without abandoning the possibility of building broad alliances committed to a common transformatory project? How to take account of the particular without jettisoning the universalist framework? How to move beyond what Raymond Williams described as the militant particularism of isolated local struggles, to construct a more universal alternative (Harvey, 1997)? These debates have implications for the politics of identity more generally, both their significance and their inherent dilemmas.

The problematic concept of 'race'

The concept of 'race' is so often surrounded by inverted commas, precisely because it has been so sharply contested. It is not simply that the concept has been used in so many different ways as to render it relatively meaningless – the charge which has been levelled at the concept of community, for example, as the previous chapter outlined.

The concept of 'race' is not only problematic, however, it is potentially dangerous.

'Race', as the Dictionary of Sociology explains, 'has often been defined as a grouping or classification based upon genetic variations in physical appearance, most notably in skin colour. (M)ost sociologists (and biologists) dispute the idea that biological race is a meaningful concept', the dictionary continues. But the concept of 'race' has had a powerful and most damaging existence as a socially constructed set of categories 'used primarily as a basis for social inequality and oppression' (Johnson, 1995, p. 223). In other words, the notion of 'race' has been invoked in order to justify the unjustifiable, to lend a spurious scientific credibility to the systematically unequal treatment of one social group by another, on the grounds of their supposed biological and/or cultural difference. Miles's use of the inverted commas aimed to highlight the inherently flawed nature of the concept of 'race', together with the dangers associated with even appearing to lend such a concept any continuing credibility (Miles, 1982). Partly in response to such criticisms, the terms 'ethnicity' and 'ethnic group' have come to be widely used, as markers of difference. Based upon such cultural factors as language, religion and life-style, the terms 'ethnicity' and 'ethnic groups' have been utilised to identify difference (sometimes effectively applying these terms as synonyms, in popular usage) without recourse to such inherently flawed terminology as that of 'race'. As it will be suggested subsequently, however, culturally based definitions are not without their inherent problems, either.

Despite such critiques, the concept of 'race' has nevertheless survived. As a number of writers from varying standpoints, have demonstrated, there seems to be considerable agreement with the proposition that, faced with a range of powerful critiques of the validity of 'race' as a biological category, racists shifted their ground towards a more culturally based definition. In the aftermath of the Second World War, it has been argued, as the gruesome evidence of the annihilation of six million Jews in the Nazi holocaust was more publicly revealed, the biological definitions of 'race' which had been invoked to justify these horrors were more emphatically discredited (Kohn, 1996). Nazi claims that the Jews were racially inferior to the Aryans were shown to have no scientific basis, just as similar claims about the supposed inferiority of black people have long since been similarly discredited.

As the report on British Race Relations 'Colour and Citizenship' argued at the end of the sixties 'it is not in accordance with the known facts to speak of one "race" or "breed" as superior in general to another. We have ceased to talk of "race" as a group with a set of constant characteristics' (Rose, 1969 p. 36). It went on to point out that there were in any case, no 'pure' races to be found. 'The processes of mixing (or hybridisation) have meant that every racial group shades off into some other group' (Rose, 1969, p. 37). So any attempt to justify differential treatment of people on the grounds that they belong to one racial group rather than another would, the report argued:

> founder on the fact that there will be many individuals who do not share those distinguishing characteristics of their group which are supposed to justify differential treatment. If there are no 'pure' races, it is misleading to talk of groups of people as though they approximated to some idea of racial purity (Rose, 1969, p. 37).

The evidence from biologists and anthropologists alike, the report concluded, confirmed that 'racial purity' was 'an illusory concept and a delusive ideal' (Rose, 1969, 40). But the argument was actually far from over.

Faced with such difficulties in sustaining crude biological reductionist approaches to 'race', it has been argued, racists turned to more sophisticated, and apparently less socially unacceptable ways of rationalising the unequal treatment of those who were supposedly different. Instead of arguing that black people were biologically inferior, Gilroy, amongst others, has demonstrated how racists such as Enoch Powell shifted their argument to focus upon cultural differences instead (Gilroy, 1993). The issue, according to this more sophisticated version of racism, becomes the issue of difference in relation to culture and identity, rather than of difference in relation to biology. Neither the concept of 'race', nor the racism which invokes it, have been seamless webs. Both have varied, over time and across space.

While this new Racism may have been more sophisticated, however, the concept of 'race' as a marker of cultural difference could be and still was being used in ways which oppressed and excluded. What, after all, was the implication of the so-called 'cricket test' hypothetically posed by former Conservative cabinet minister Norman Tebbit. In an interview in 1990 Tebbit stated that too many Asian Britons failed this 'cricket test' (defined in terms of who black people support in that stereotypically most English of sports, cricket, the English or their West Indian or Pakistani opponents)? When challenged about this statement, Tebbit's response was, in summary, that 'Asian Britons had not become truly integrated into British society' (Smith, 1994, p. 106, summarising Tebbit as reported in the *Guardian*, 1990) effectively concluding that it was problematic to be both black and British. Out of context, such a question as the 'cricket test' may seem merely absurd. In the context of the enhanced nationalism of the Thatcher years, however, such questions could be located within a wider politics of cultural exclusiveness, it has been argued, a politics which focused upon the need to tackle the 'enemy within' – however defined, whether, for example, as black youth or as striking miners, or both. Whether or not such forms of exclusivity are necessarily inherent in nationalism, or whether, at least in some circumstances (such as struggles for national liberation) nationalism can be more generally progressive and emancipatory – or whether nationalism is simply potentially either and both – has been and continues to be a matter of debate (as Chapter 6 considers in more detail). As the previous chapter suggested, there are parallels here, with debates on community, and how far any definition of community, whether in terms of locality or in terms of interest, implies exclusivity?

However flawed the arguments, it has been suggested, Tebbit's views on the impact of post-war migration on British national culture nevertheless illustrated this shift of focus, from biological to more cultural concepts of 'race' and racism. In another contribution, Tebbit contrasted the supposed ease with which previous generations of migrants were allegedly absorbed into British culture, with the greater resistance of more recent waves of immigrants, some of whom were even, he argued 'defiantly claiming a right to superimpose their culture, even their law, upon the host community' (Tebbit in an article in *The Field* entitled 'Fanfare for being British', May 1990, quoted in Malik, 1996, p. 35). Such a response can be located as part of a backlash, a racist response to the politics of black liberation, in general, and to the demands of anti-racist identity politics, more specifically. Tebbit's response could also be located, more pragmatically, within the context of increasingly restrictive official definitions of Britishness, associated with tighter and tighter immigration controls. Cultural forms of racism could, perhaps, have provided less socially unacceptable rationalisations?

The argument, so far, then, has been to suggest that questions of culture and identity took on additional prominence, as cruder biological definitions of 'race' and racial difference were discredited in the post-Second World War scenario. Such explanations have been offered by a number of analysts (including Gilroy, 1993, Malik, 1996). Insofar as this has been the case, this has important implications for identity politics and cultural politics in the context of strategies to combat racism.

Before moving on to explore these, in more detail, however, a caveat is needed. There is a risk of distorting the contemporary picture by over-emphasising this supposed shift towards more culturally based approaches to 'race' and racism. The shifts of the post-war period were also subject to challenge. The boundaries of the socially unacceptable can and do shift in more than one direction. Biological racism did not simply disappear, in any case. Indeed, it has been argued, cultural racism builds upon biological racism adding 'a further discourse which evokes cultural differences from an alleged British or 'civilised' norm to vilify, marginalise or demand cultural assimilation from groups who also suffer from biological racism' (Modood, 1997, p. 155).

As Malik amongst others has pointed out, both in Britain and else-where (quoting from the French context to illustrate this particular argument), 'the discrediting of postwar liberalism has removed many of the taboos against racism that had existed in the postwar period' together with the forms of 'coded language, which cleansed the racist sentiments and recast them in polite, liberal terms' (Malik, 1996, p. 33). In parallel, biological approaches have also proved resilient. Far from disappearing, in fact, racial biology has taken on renewed prominence in contemporary social science debates. Biology, as Gilroy and others have commented, has 're-emerged as the key principle of racial explanation' (Gilroy, 1995, p. 1) as 'the (multi)culture wars have become entrenched' (Gilroy, 1995, p. 1). Amongst the most contro-versial examples of this renewed interest in biological approaches, Herrnstein and Murray's publication *The Bell Curve* (Herrnstein and Murray, 1994) argued that there was evidence to support the view that there were genetic differences in mental ability between black and white, arguing specifically that 'the average white person tests higher (on intelligence and achievement tests) than about 84 per cent of the population of blacks and that the average black person tests higher than about 16 per cent of the population of whites' (Herrnstein and Murray, 1994, p. 269).

The Bell Curve has, of course, been heavily criticised on a number of grounds, for instance that the book relied on evidence from IQ scores which have been shown to be culturally biased. Reducing 'intelligence' to such culturally biased evidence Herrnstein and Murray have been criticised too for defining intelligence without taking account of talent, insight, creativity or capacity to solve problems, let alone with musical, spatial, mathematical or kinaesthetic ability, sensitivity, charm or persuasiveness (Rose, 1997). The point that is being made here is absolutely not that the book's arguments have validity. But it would seem naive to ignore the book's impact. The fact of the matter is that biological approaches to 'race' and racial difference have far from disappeared. On the contrary, in fact, there would seem to be renewed interest in updated versions of these, within the wider context of debates as to whether it is possible to identify specific genes associated with a whole range of human characteristics and behaviour, from the search for a deviance gene to the search for a gay gene. There have been attempts to demonstrate that genes:

> account for every aspect of our lives, from personal success to existential despair: genes for health and illness, genes for criminality, violence and 'abnormal' sexual orientation – even for compulsive shopping. And genes too to explain, as ever, the social inequalities that divide our lives along lines of class, gender, race ethnicity (Rose, 1997, p. ix).

Such approaches to the explanation of diversity raise potentially alarming vistas – going Back to a Future of genetic engineering with a difference – the eugenics of the turn of the twentieth century practised with the technologies of the twenty-first. Whilst the potential dangers have raised alarm bells, however, such approaches have not been unequivocally rejected by the identity groups most directly concerned. On the contrary, for example, some gays have rather welcomed the notion of a gay gene, arguing that this could prove what they already know – that they are in no way to blame for their gay identity. Some of the questions which are raised for identity politics by such debates are discussed subsequently in more detail.

Nor is it the case that such allegedly scientific, biological explanations are necessarily posed as alternatives to more culturally based approaches. It is, of course, possible to subscribe to both biological and cultural versions of racism. Murray himself provides just one such example, having published on both, arguing the case for identifying genetic differences in mental capacity between black and white, as well as arguing for public policies to address the alleged cultural pathologies of the underclass, cultural pathologies which were supposedly particularly, although by no means exclusively, characteristic of blacks of African descent. *The Bell Curve* itself argued that there was evidence 'for those who argue that a culture of poverty transmits chronic welfare dependency from one generation to the next' (Herrnstein and Murray, 1994, p. 199) – although its authors concluded that women who were susceptible to this culture of poverty and chronic welfare dependency were likely to have low intelligence in the first place.

Conversely, too, anti-racist critics of the new biological racism have not necessarily posed their arguments in terms of simple dichotomies, whether differences are to be explained either in terms of biological or alternatively in terms of cultural factors, nature versus nurture. Some of the most challenging criticisms, in fact, have been made precisely by moving on from such dichotomies, to explore the interactions between the two, and the ways in which humans act upon and affect their environment, just as they are affected by their economic, social, political and cultural environment. As Rose has argued, our very knowledge of the living world 'like all other human knowledges, is always provisional, historically constrained' (Rose, 1997, p. 303). 'In living systems, causes are multiple and can be described at many different levels and in many different languages. Phenomena are always complex and richly interconnected' (Rose, 1997, p. 305). As a result, Rose argued, far from being biologically determined:

> for humans, as for all living organisms, the future is radically unpredictable. This means that we have the ability to construct our own futures, albeit in circumstances not of our own choosing, and it is therefore our biology that makes us free (Rose, 1997, p. 309).

A detailed discussion of these vitally important contemporary debates – challenging biological reductionism – is beyond the scope of this chapter. The point to register here is simply this, that biological approaches to 'race' and racism have survived the post-war critique and have even flourished more recently in new forms. Both biological and cultural approaches still need to be addressed. For the purposes of this chapter, however, the key questions centre around the implications for identities based upon 'race' and ethnicity, together with the implications for the politics of identity.

'Race', racism and the politics of identity

Given the problematic nature of the concept of 'race', and the variations in racisms, over time and space, there would seem to be
inherent problems associated with defining identity politics in such
terms. This would seem to be clearly the case where the notion of
'race' is perceived as being about lending spurious scientific
credibility to the systematically unequal treatment of one social
group by another, on the grounds of their supposed biological
and/or cultural difference. In practice, however, as it has already
been suggested in the previous chapter, identity politics have been
developed in the context of challenges to precisely such notions –
challenging negative stereotypes and replacing supposedly spoilt
identities with their positive alternatives – black is beautiful, just as
gay is good. Black, in this context, can become a political rather
than a biological, or even a culturally based definition, a powerful
political definition based upon black self-identification and self-
organisation to confront the negative definitions of racist societies,
and the racist oppressions which such negative definitions have
sought to rationalise.

In the context of the upsurge of black self-organisation and mili-
tancy in North America and in Britain, in the sixties and seventies,
such political definitions may have seemed relatively unproblematic.
There was a black liberation movement with which to identify
(without suggesting that there were no differences of perspective, in
that period, either). There are, perhaps, parallels here with other social
movements, such as feminism and environmentalism, in terms of
initially appearing more homogeneous in their political challenges
than subsequently proved to be the case. Scott, for example, has
demonstrated these points in relation to new social movements such
as environmentalism as well as anti-racism, as the previous chapter
suggested (Scott, 1990). Segal made similar arguments about feminism, showing how, by the late eighties, the women's liberation
movement had become more fragmented (Segal, 1987).

'Race' and ethnicity, Castells has argued, have likewise deeply
altered, as sources of oppression and discrimination, along with the
movements to challenge this, compared with the era of the civil rights
movement in the 1960s. Reflecting upon these changes, in the latter
half of the nineties he concluded that it was still the case that 'race
matters a lot. But, at the same time, the class divide among blacks has
created such fundamentally different living conditions that there is

growing hostility among the poor against those former brothers that left them out' (Castells, 1997, p. 57).

In the current context in Britain, with a less clearly defined black political movement to build upon, and with enhanced emphasis upon cultural definitions of 'race', Sondhi has suggested:

> (B)eing black is now not just politically interpreted, it is being culturally determined to the point that it ceases to have any meaning. 'Black' has gradually been replaced by 'black and Asian' as much in popular language as in the vocabulary of politicians, broadcasters, academics and community activists ... This phrase is in turn proving to be inadequate for some who would wish to make a distinction between say, 'Muslim' and 'non-Muslim' communities ... It would seem that the single issue campaign that set out to combat racial discrimination and gain equal treatment for all black groups is being further divided ever more finely along religious, cultural and nationalist lines (Sondhi, 1997, p. 227).

Modood, for example, has welcomed what he identified as the 'growing calls to revise and update anti-racism by pluralising the concept of political blackness' drawing upon the argument that 'a "black" political identity does not compete with or replace other identities – for example, "Asian"; for, it is argued, different identities refer to different aspects of a person's subjectivity, or are emphasised in different situations – say, one in politics, the other to do with culture' (Modood, 1997, p. 169). Some of the implications of these arguments are explored subsequently in more detail. The point to emphasise here is simply this, that to posit a 'black' identity has become more rather than less problematic.

There has, of course, been a tradition of writers concerned with black consciousness and identity, the 'Negritude' of poets such as Aimée Césaire and Leopold Senghor, which played a critical role in earlier struggles for colonial freedom and for liberated post-colonial identities struggling to remove the colonisers' negative stereotypes from out of the heads of the recently colonised. But as Fanon argued, such a project was also problematic (Hall, 1990). As the movement developed, some of these inherent problems began to emerge more clearly. What might it actually mean to define a movement in terms of black identity? Was it meaningful to postulate an essential black identity in any case, or was this no less problematic than the notion of any other type of essential identity? To argue for the existence of a black identity based upon biology, flesh and blood, would raise the problems inherent in biological approaches to definitions of 'race' and biological racism. How could markers such as skin colour be understood as definers of identity, without setting these in the context of the relations which constitute the social categories of 'race', the processes through which skin colour has come to take on associations with particular – and unequal – social relations? (Guillaumin, 1995).

There has been a long history of black writers who have addressed a range of questions about the complexities of black identity. For example, Gilroy quoted from the work of Du Bois, and his concept of 'double consciousness' to explore the consciousness and identities of black people who were in the West but not of it (Gilroy, 1993). Neither biologically nor culturally was there one essential, unchanging black identity. Gilroy's *Small Acts* (Gilroy, 1993) opens with a critique of what he described as 'racial narcissism', a view of an unchanging black racial purity, just as he was critical of an essentialist approach to black cultural identities. On the contrary, in fact, the black culture of the diaspora was far from representing a single 'essential' identity. In an earlier publication, Gilroy had already pointed out that culture:

> is not a fixed and impermeable feature of social relations. Its forms change, develop, combine and are dispersed in historical processes. The syncretic cultures of black Britain exemplify this. They have been able to detach cultural practices from their origins and use them to found and extend the new patterns of metacommunication which give their community substance and collective identity (Gilroy, 1987, p. 217).

The notion of a kaleidoscope was perhaps a more useful way of understanding cultures which are constantly in the process of changing, as they cross-fertilise each other, back and forth across the Atlantic, from Africa to the Caribbean and the Americas and back again. Culture, Gilroy argued:

> is not a final property of social life. It is a dynamic volatile force. It is made and remade and the culture of the English fragments of the black diaspora is a syncretic, synthetic one. This ought to be obvious but it is not (Gilroy, 1993, p. 109).

Hall has similarly argued that cultural identity is a matter of 'becoming' as well as of 'being':

> Cultural identities come from somewhere, have histories. But like everything which is historical they undergo constant transformation. Far from being eternally fixed in some essentialised past, they are subject to the continuous 'play' of history, culture and power (Hall, 1990, p. 225).

Diaspora identities, according to Hall, are constantly producing and reproducing themselves anew; the notions of hybridity and creolisation capture some of this sense of cultural identities as being processes, rather than as being fixed – frozen in time and space.

The history of black music provides an illustration of these processes of hybridisation. From Africa across the Atlantic, black music developed a variety of forms, forms which have crossed to and fro in a range of ways, from African jazz, for example, through to reggae. And as a number of writers have also shown, black music has been taken up by white youth in alternative ways – both positively as a potential meeting point where dialogues between black and white youth can occur, and conversely, as part of potentially racist skin head style (Back, 1996).

In literature, Salman Rushdie's publication of the controversial *Satanic Verses* provides another form of illustration. On the first anniversary of his 'exile' Rushdie set out his argument on the impurity of identity as follows:

> the *Satanic Verses* celebrates hybridity, impurity, intermingling, the transformation that comes of new and unexpected combinations of human beings, cultures, ideas, politics, movies, songs. It rejoices in mongrelisation and fears the absolutism of the Pure. Melange, hotchpotch, a bit of this and a bit of that is *how newness enters the world*. It is the great possibility that mass migration gives the world, and I have tried to embrace it. The *Satanic Verses* is for change-by-fusion, change-by-conjoining. It is a love-song to our mongrel selves (quoted in Schwarz, 1994, p. 158).

Clifford's essay on 'Travelling Cultures' (Clifford, 1997) provides further illustration of the ways in which cultures travel and interact – even become reinvented. He quoted the case of a Hawaiian band, the Moes, which he learned about from Brosman, a musician and nonacademic music historian, who had been bringing traditional Hawaiian music into the continental United States. The Moe family was a group of veterans who travelled for 56 years performing Hawaiian music on the road – almost never going back to Hawaii. They played Hawaiian guitar and performed song and dance routines in 'exoticist' shows 'all over the Far East, South Asia, the Middle East, North Africa, eastern and western Europe and the United States. And they performed too, the gamut of hotel-circuit pop. Now in their eighties, the Moes have recently returned to Hawaii, where, encouraged by revivalists like Brosman, they are making "authentic" music from the teens and twenties' (Clifford, 1997, pp. 25–6). How, Clifford asked, did the Moe family compartmentalize their Hawaiianness in these different cultures and musical traditions, as they travelled, how 'for fifty-six years in transient, hybrid environments did they preserve and invent a sense of Hawaiian "home"? And how, currently, is their music being recycled in the continuing invention of Hawaiian authenticity?' (Clifford, 1997, p. 26) Clifford wondered. He concluded with the comment that, incidentally, the steel guitar which was known in the twenties and thirties in the USA as the Hawaiian guitar was actually invented by a Czech immigrant living in California. This was an extreme case perhaps, although illustrative of his more general arguments about culture, travel and processes of continuity and change.

Clifford went on to explore issues of race, class and gender in relation to travel, questions about who travelled and how, and how this was perceived, in the context of the privileges of whites, typically white bourgeois males, remembering the relatively invisible local 'guides' without whom white explorers' excursions would not have been possible. As Clifford pointed out, in the dominant discourses of travel, a non-white person cannot figure as a heroic explorer, aesthetic interpreter or scientific authority. He went on to quote the case of the long struggle for recognition for the feat of Matthew Henson, the black American explorer who reached the pole with Robert Peary.

Gilroy's critique of essentialist approaches to black culture and identity also raised questions of class, as well as questions of time and space. Essentialist, 'narcissistic' approaches to black identity were potentially in the interests of the black petite bourgeoisie who stood to benefit from the application of such approaches, through cultural and social policies. So for example, it was the black petite bourgeoisie who stood to benefit, in particular, from opening up employment opportunities in local government, in the eighties, just as they stood to benefit from the promotion of small business through local economic development strategies. Narrowly defined versions of 'political correctness' could be used to justify precisely such outcomes. Funding for black arts was also a potential source of benefit for the black petite bourgeoisie, he argued.

> The most unwholesome ideas of ethnic absolutism hold sway and they have been incorporated into the structures of the political economy of funding black arts. The tokenism, patronage and nepotism that have become intrinsic to the commodification of black culture rely absolutely on an absolute sense of ethnic difference' (Gilroy, 1993, pp. 109–10).

Happily, however, Gilroy concluded, there were:

> elements within Britain's emergent post-nationalist black arts movement that are prepared to move as earlier generations of black intellectuals and artists have done, not into the blind alley of ethnic particularity, but outwards into a global, populist-modernist perspective (Gilroy, 1993, p. 110).

As this final comment illustrates, Gilroy was rejecting ethnic particularism. He was also critical of post-modernist rejections of the possibility of a universalist emancipatory project. Such a rejection smacked of ethnocentrism, he argued, a European crisis of confidence in grand narratives which saw any shift in the centre of gravity away from Europe as meaning the end of reason itself. Those who had been denied access in the past, were just 'beginning to form our own grand narratives. They are narratives of redemption and emancipation' (Gilroy, 1993, p. 108). 'It is worth underlining', he continued, 'that for some of us the "enthusiasm of 1789" relates more to Port au Prince than it does to Paris' (Gilroy, 1993, p. 109). These final comments raise a number of questions for the development of anti-racist strategies, both in general, and more specifically in relation to culture and identity.

Universalism v particularism revisited

If the concepts of 'race' and racial identities are problematic, then, what might be the implications of different approaches, and how might these, in their turn, affect debates on how to develop anti-racist strategies? How might the different concepts of identity relate to such strategies? And how might those concerned with community development, in general, and community arts more specifically, apply such concepts critically, in the development of strategies which aim to respect the particulars of diversity and difference, albeit within the framework of a universalistic transformatory project? By this time, it should already be clear to the reader that this chapter is not going to conclude with any simple answers to such questions. The intention is – rather more modestly – to seek further clarification.

At this point, it may be useful to return, briefly, to some of the dilemmas which were posed in the Introduction and Chapter 1, the dilemmas inherent in the different approaches to universalism and particularism. How meaningful has it been to view the past, at least since the French Revolution in 1789 for the sake of argument, in terms of a single, universal project of human emancipation, of freedom coupled with equality? Or conversely, as postmodernist critics amongst others have argued, is the only meaningful approach to deny such universalities, and to focus instead upon the myriad particular discourses of diversity and difference? The logic of an essentialist approach to racial identity would seem to relate more readily to the latter view, whereas the types of approach to identity outlined by Gilroy and others would seem to imply a more complex range of views.

In his book *The Meaning of Race*, Malik has provided a thought-provoking critique of particularist thinking on 'race' and racial identities which has key relevance here (Malik, 1996). Malik started from a critique of forms of multi-culturalism which freeze identity on the basis of difference, rather than focusing upon working for equality on the basis of shared humanity. He rejected the view that the Enlightenment project was essentially flawed on the grounds of its ethnocentrism and its preference for the universal rather than the particular. The universalist framework, it had been argued could not accommodate differences of cultures (Bhabha, 1990). According to such criticisms, the contemporary focus upon the assertion of difference and diversity embodied the possibility of a fuller and truer democracy, a democracy in which hitherto invisible groups would have the means to speak for themselves. Malik was not convinced of this.

Rather, Malik argued, the Enlightenment needed to be seen dialectically, with the potential for human emancipation, as well as having the potential for being distorted to justify the inherently racist view that it was the West which embodied this progressive project. In racist

interpretations this progressive project which was supposedly embodied in the West could then be contrasted with the supposed
backwardness of the 'other' who could therefore be colonised in the
name of modernisation.

While Malik recognised the significance of the postmodernist
critique, including its critique of any form of essentialism, he rejected
the conclusion that indeterminacy and relativity is all. To put it at its
simplest, '(I)n the context of debates on "race" and racism', he argued,
'a racist and non-racist interpretation of history are not equally valid'
(Malik, 1996, p. 256).

Malik traced key arguments back to debates within anthropology. In
particular, he focused on the work of Boas, and Boas's arguments with
the racist logic of the social evolutionists and their hierarchies of
human difference. As Chapter 1 has already summarised, Boas, in
contrast, was concerned to reject racial theories of human difference
and to replace these with more relativistic approaches which valued
different human cultures by understanding them in their own terms.
Sceptical of Victorian beliefs in universal patterns of human progress,
the relativists viewed society more statically, Malik argued, and as
horizontally rather than vertically segmented. Boas himself, as Malik
underlined, was 'staunchly egalitarian in outlook' (Malik, 1996,
p. 156). But in espousing a relativist alternative, Malik argued, the new
anthropological outlook left key problems to be addressed.

With twenty/twenty hindsight vision, it is possible to trace the
misapplication of some of these ideas in twentieth-century rationalisations of different, separate, if supposedly equal treatment. This, after
all, was the rationalisation of Apartheid in South Africa. The point
which is being made here is absolutely not that respect for diversity
and difference necessarily leads to institutionalised racism, as practised in Apartheid South Africa, however, merely to point to some of
the inherent tensions in the argument.

Guillaumin pointed to similar tensions, when suggesting that in
societies marked by inequalities of class, race and gender '(F)ighting
for your right to be different can mean fighting for your subordination' (Guillaumin, 1995, p. 17). Diversity and difference, from this
perspective, cannot be divorced from their social contexts. Demands
for the 'right to be different' which appeared in the 1960s in international organisations and anti-racist movements amazed her, she
reflected, because they seemed to represent a *'flight of the oppressed'*
(Guillaumin, 1995, p. 243) retreating from the analysis of the relationship between the dominant and the dominated.

The great unfolding of the idea of minority 'cultures' postulates that reggae or preserves, soul music or maternal tenderness are in and of themselves the justifications for our existence. And even more, that they are the virtues, the eternal, isolated virtues of those who produced them, without acknowledging that these supposedly essentialist cultural phenomena did not simply arise in a vacuum. Whereas the reality was precisely that the cultural differences which were described as characterising women, or black people, were developed and reproduced in social contexts – contexts which were characterised by unequal social relationships. (T)here are no preserves without domestic relationships, no reggae or soul music without unemployment' (Guillaumin, 1995, p. 244).

Meanwhile, she suggested, while dominated groups retreated to explore the particularity of their differences, the dominant were 'no doubt content to be general rather than particular' (Guillaumin, 1995, p. 245).

Malik himself concluded by arguing for the right to be equal rather than simply for the right to be different. The logic of his case was to suggest that:

only a dialectical understanding of the relationship between the particular and the universal can allow us to transcend the concept of 'race'. Such an understanding forces us to see the universal and the particular not as separate categories but existing only in a reciprocal relationship. It allows us to see human differences as socially constructed, while at the same time reminding us that humans possess a social essence, arising out of their sociability, which is the basis for human equality (Malik, 1996, p. 266).

To develop such an understanding, he concluded, however, required both an intellectual and a social transformation.

Alternative strategies

Whilst critical of essentialist approaches to identity, writers such as Hall and Gilroy have nevertheless emphasised the potential importance of identity politics. Hall, for example, has discussed the development of identity politics as the constitution of 'some defensive collective identity against the practices of racist society' in Britain in the period of the post-war migrations of the fifties and sixties (Hall,

1991, p. 52). 'In that very struggle is a change of consciousness' he went on, 'a change of self-recognition, a new process of identification, the emergence into visibility of a new subject' (Hall, 1991, p. 54). Culture and cultural politics (from black history to the music of Bob Marley) were central to these processes of the emergence of a black identity, an identity which took on political significance for Asians as well as African Caribbeans for a period. Hall himself went on to recognise the silences of such a single notion of collective black identity – the ways in which Asian identities, in particular, were not being heard. Black women were being similarly silenced. Hall concluded that identity politics needed to be based upon the recognition of diversity and difference within as well as between black and white, taking account of the multiplicity of social identities, gender as well as class.

Such conclusions have varying implications. Hall himself was tentative about the political implications (although he was generally arguing for the politics of 'New Times', which started from a critique of the 'Old Politics' of the Left). Identity politics, as it has already been suggested, have been posed as alternative forms of political practice. When writing in the late eighties, Gilroy, for example, while deeply critical of petit-bourgeois versions of 'political correctness' was far more optimistic about the political potential of other approaches, based upon black cultural and identity politics (Gilroy, 1987).

It was not simply that black struggles around specific issues (such as housing and policing issues) were well developed in their own right. Such struggles were part of a politics which were potentially far wider, Gilroy argued, involving more fundamental challenges to the status quo. The white working class had failed. White working-class organisations such as the trade unions had failed to represent – indeed had actively excluded – black interests from their agendas. And they were failing, more generally, he argued, as agents of fundamental social change. Similar arguments have been expressed by a range of writers about identity politics, contrasting their approach with traditional left focus upon the industrial working classes 'as the privileged agent of revolutionary historical change' (Mercer, 1990, p. 44). This traditional focus, it was argued, had been 'undermined and discredited from below by the emergence of numerous social movements – feminisms, black struggles, national liberation, anti-nuclear and ecological movements' (Mercer, 1990, p. 44). There are resonances here with some of the arguments which were explored in the previous chapter.

Black organisations and struggles, in contrast, Gilroy argued, had the potential to go beyond the limits of previous approaches, with their focus upon agency and struggle, self-realisation, direct democracy and non-negotiable demands. Black movements had the potential to bring the black diaspora together across national barriers, and indeed to transcend the old dichotomy between reformist and revolutionary politics.

While emphasising the vitality and the potential for cultural and identity politics, however, Gilroy, like Castells, also recognised the fragility of such politics, and the ways in which such struggles could be incorporated. They were symptoms of resistance. But that did not necessarily mean that cultural and identity politics would become part of a transformatory project. As Castells has argued of social movements (including cultural and identity politics) more generally 'social movements may be socially conservative, socially revolutionary, or both, or none' (Castells, 1997, p. 70). Mercer made a similar point when commenting that the 'new social subjects have no necessary belonging on either side of the distinction between progressive and reactionary politics, which is to say they could go either way' (Mercer, 1990, p. 45). By the end of the nineties, the fragility and the potential fragmentation and incorporation of black cultural politics had become only too identifiable.

Criticisms of the approaches developed by Gilroy and others (including others based then at the Centre for Contemporary Cultural Studies in Birmingham) have not simply focused upon empirical data – whether subsequent events have borne out one set of arguments more effectively than another. Writing of 'The Death of a Black Political Movement' Shukra started from the incorporation of the black radical activism of the 1960s and 1970s in Britain, into the *race relations* machinery in the 1980s and 1990s. This, she argued, 'produced a layer of black professionals and managers who advocate organisational and policy changes in the pursuit of *racial equality*' (Shukra, 1997, p. 233). (There are connections here with Malik's arguments about the contradictions inherent in campaigning for equality – within the framework of existing and unequal social relations.)

The fact that black politics took this direction rather than the direction of a more transformatory politics, needed to be understood, Shukra argued, in the context of a critical analysis of the underlying theoretical positions involved. Enthusiasts for the transformatory potential of the New Social Movements had contrasted the vitality of their spontaneous consciousness with the more limited, and more institutionalised responses of the white working class, organised through the trade union movement. But all movements 'begin as spontaneities – that is as a social force which includes organisations, activists (sometimes also intellectuals) and a spontaneous consciousness with the objective of effecting social change' (Shukra, 197, p. 235) – a point which has already emerged in the discussion of social movements in the previous chapter.

As Shukra went on to point out:

> Different political strategies and concepts of social change define the direction in which a spontaneous movement develops. It may collapse, maintain a significant level of autonomy from the State, become institutionalised or it might form part of a real-liberatory movement (Shukra, 1997, p. 235).

Black cultural and identity politics, like any other movement could become institutionalised. This institutionalisation could take the form of focusing upon bureaucratic municipal anti-racist procedures, so criticised by Gilroy and others. Or it could take the form of promoting commodification, tokenism and patronage in the black arts. Either way, the end result could be the incorporation of conflict, and the promotion of the interests of individual blacks – without challenging the wider social inequalities associated with 'race', or indeed with gender or class.

Shukra concluded by questioning why separate race and class? Institutionalisation was a weakness inherent in spontaneity, whether this was the spontaneity of black movements or the spontaneity of workplace struggles (struggles in which black workers, including black women workers had, of course, also been actively engaged in pursuing with, and all too often without, the full official backing of their trade union organisations). The logic of posing the New Social Movements as alternatives to the mainstream, was to leave those involved in them on the fringes of wider long-term struggles for a more transformatory politics, she argued. 'The overall effect of the "new social movements" thesis (that is, posing them as alternatives to other forms of politics) is to shrink aspirations for social change to actions on a small scale' (Shukra, 1998, p. 109). She went on to argue:

> In contrast, I contend that 'new social movements' can evolve in different directions: they can forge different alliances and have different outcomes, but their development depends on the result of the dominant politics of the movement. Whilst 'new social

movements' can mean any number of things and be very different from one another, a real movement for fundamental change is one which transcends its spontaneity and is therefore most likely to recognise that it requires a close connection with advanced sections of the working class with a view to politicising all groups to develop a liberatory working-class consciousness independently of the State (Shukra, 1997, p. 241).

Neither the labour movement nor black community politics were lost, she concluded, in terms of their transformatory potential, although this was not, in any way, to underestimate the difficulties of forging an effective alliance between the two. Once again, this was not an 'either/or' question, new social movements versus traditional class organisations, black identity and cultural politics versus workplace politics.

Conversely, however, as it has already been suggested, black community politics, like any form of identity politics, could be developed in ways which were further fragmenting. Identity politics can be developed in ways which increase divisions, not only between new social movements and the organised working class, but also between new social movements themselves, competing amongst each other in hierarchies of oppression – one group competing with another for scarce resources (Meekosha, 1993).

On the positive side, desegregating differences within movements can provide space for groups who had hitherto been effectively silenced to find their own voice. For example, black feminism has provided 'a space and a framework for the articulation of our diverse identities as black women from different ethnicities, classes and sexualities', Parmar argued (Parmar, 1990, p. 106) – a space which had to be fought for and negotiated. Neither black identity politics, nor feminism per se, had been providing this. Black women's experiences could not simply be subsumed within either black identity politics or feminist politics, more generally. Whilst continuing to argue for the importance of the political and cultural articulations around identity, however, Parmar pointed to some of the more negative ways in which identity politics could be developed.

She quoted from the writings and from an interview with the American black feminist, June Jordan to illustrate these arguments, starting from Jordan's view that identity politics 'may be enough to get started on but not enough to get anything finished' ... 'I don't think that gender politics or that race politics per se are isolated from other ways of organising for change, whether reformist change or revolutionary change. I don't think that they will take us where we want to go' (Jordan quoted in Parmar, 1990, pp. 108–9). Ultimately, it was not only that there needed to be unity rather than further fragmentation amongst all those who had been affected by exploitation and oppression, on the basis of the 'isms' of 'race', sex, class, disability and so forth. Both Parmar and Jordan were arguing that there was a need to move beyond focusing upon modes of being, but rather upon modes of doing. Jordan asked:

> What is the purpose of your identity? So what? if sharing experiences of oppression was not the prelude to effective action for social change, encompassing both immediate local struggles and struggles within the wider international context (Parmar, 1990, pp. 111–13).

This emphasis upon action strategies for social change brings the argument back to the point which has been raised from the outset of this book, the point about the importance of understanding how practice has in any case been developing. Whether or not there has been adequate recognition of the potential for progressive practice around cultural and identity politics, activists have rejected false dichotomies of 'either/or politics' in practice – refusing to pose new social movements versus traditional organisational forms, or cultural and identity politics as an alternative to class politics. The question, it has been argued here, is not whether cultural identity politics are developed but how?

There are examples of creative practice of relevance here, developed through critical reflections upon the lessons of the shortcomings of earlier anti-racist strategies. Back's study *New Ethnicities and Urban Culture* started from just such an analysis of the limitations of the 'lapel politics' of anti-racist sloganeering in the eighties (Back, 1996). Drawing upon the insights of debates within cultural studies, Back set out to explore the implications and relevance for new forms of cultural practice and identity formation, and specifically amongst young people, black and white, in multi-ethnic urban Britain. When he began this ethnographic study, Back was earning his living as a youth worker, committed to challenging racism without simply resorting to making a moral dogma of anti-racist sloganeering (such as simply banning racist abuse, and banning young people who use racially abusive language from youth clubs, without also working through the issues with the young people involved). Racist joking, for example, can express ambivalent and contradictory meaning and attitudes amongst young people, and these need to be explored if racism is to be effectively challenged. In the context of football ground verbal abuse, for example, Back and colleagues have quoted the view that all too often 'such race talk' is 'either read as "meaningless play" or taken as "consequential race hate" and the expression of deep felt racial animus' (Back *et al.*, 1998, p. 9) whereas, it has been argued, 'its true significance is found in the ambivalence between these two positions i.e. within a mode of expression that oscillates between the ludic and the literal' (Back *et al.*, 1998, p. 9).

Through his study in South London, Back demonstrated the importance of understanding such complexities in relation to identity and culture formation. Specifically, Back explored the opening up of new identifications – the development of what he termed new 'intermezzo cultures', meaning by this the spaces that linked social collectivities, producing cultures of inter-being and mutual identification (Back, 1996, pp. 225–6). So, for example, he explored the ways in which white youths related to reggae music, and the ways in which south Asian youths developed their own mixtures. Back's study was concerned with the theoretical implications for debates on culture and identity; and he was specifically concerned with the potential implications for working with young people to challenge racism. Young people, he argued 'are attempting to build a culture, and define a space, beyond the circumscriptions of race' (Back, 1996, p. 237). This raised the potential for a vision of unity, although progress towards such a vision was, he recognised, neither simple nor linear.

Despite countervailing pressures, however, and the continuing potential for racism to be invoked, there were spaces where what Gilroy has termed 'kaleidoscopic formations of "trans-racial" cultural syncretism' – a new racial hybridism – could grow (Back, 1996, p. 245). Such a view has major implications for moving beyond previous debates about culture and identity, diversity and difference. There are key implications too, for developing new ways of reaching young people, black and white, through cultural work – from music to sport (starting with campaigning against racism in football for example).

Music and drama can reach young people and engage them in differing ways, emotionally as well as rationally. As the previous chapter suggested, there has been increasing awareness of people's complexity, encompassing both conscious and subconscious levels. Racism is not simply or even predominantly a rational response to 'the other'. Cultural strategies have the potential to appeal to people at other levels too.

Both football and drama have been combined, for example, in a play about racism in football, produced by the ARC Theatre Ensemble for Secondary Schools – 'Ooh Ah, Showab Khan' (ARC, 1999). Through watching the play, young people have been stimulated to question racism, moving from the initial feelings which the play aroused through to some more reflective discussions about the nature of racism and how to challenge it. 'When the kids hear the racist language on stage most of them don't identify with the abuse – they laugh out of embarrassment or think it's not their problem' (ARC, 1999). But the play very subtly suggests that 'it's everyone's problem. Football is used as a backdrop but it's really about society. Asking young people to think about who they are choosing to be for the rest of their lives' (ARC, 1999).

Having raised these questions, the play aimed to stimulate critical discussion. The intention was not 'to come up with a Hollywood ending' but to leave the audience with the space to explore further questions for themselves (ARC, 1999). Engaging young people's feelings was absolutely not a way of substituting for rational discussion – on the contrary, this provided a way in, a way of working at both emotive and rational levels. There are parallels here with the potential contributions which cultural strategies can make in other contexts – the use of dance and drama, for example, to open up group discussions on emotionally charged issues – as subsequent chapters of this book explore in further detail.

The use of cultural strategies has been central to the 'New Unionism' which the Trades Union movement has launched, to recruit those who have been hard to organise, young people and women, especially young people and women from ethnic minorities who have been disproportionately likely to be working in unorganised workplaces. Drawing upon North American and Australian experiences, the New Unionism programme launched the Trade Union Academy in 1997, to train young people themselves to be organisers, based upon the principle that 'like' can be effective in recruiting 'like'. The aim was to use a range of approaches to attract young people to trade unionism – in the context of an increasingly casualised and fragmented labour force, research had identified that young people were proving hard to organise because they lacked information about and contacts with trade unions, rather than that they were hostile to trade unionism per se (TUC, 1996, Mayo, 1999).

The issue of racism was seen as particularly important to address, if young members were to be recruited and retained in membership. The New Unionism has built upon initiatives such as anti-racist summer 'Respect' festivals launched in the mid-nineties, with music as central to the festivals' appeal. In this, the strategy has drawn upon previous experiences; the use of music has been a feature of organising in the past, including the use of rock music in campaigning against racism in the late seventies ('Rock Against Racism' achieved considerable successes in involving a range of young people in anti-racist campaigning at that time) (Gilroy, 1987).

To emphasise the potential significance of these developments is not, of course, in any way to underestimate the scale of the task. As has already been pointed out in this chapter, there are formidable difficulties in the way of building alliances between the labour move-ment and the new social movements, just as there are formidable difficulties in the way of involving young people in traditional organ-isations at all. The point to emphasise here is simply this – that there is evidence of renewed interest in approaching these questions – as questions of *how* rather than questions of whether – such strategies need to be developed. The specific contribution of culture and community media to the development of such a strategy is one of the key themes which is to be explored in more detail in the chapters which follow.

4
Community, Culture and Cultural Strategies: Alternative Approaches in Community Development

This chapter sets out to build a bridge, to connect the debates on competing perspectives on cultures, communities and identities outlined in the preceding chapters, to debates on alternative approaches to community development policies and practices. 'Culture' in the broad anthropological sense – of culture as a design for living – has been central to community development agendas as these have been developed in both the First and Third Worlds in North and South. And 'culture' in the more specific and restricted sense of community arts and media, has featured in community development programmes across the range of practice settings.

The roots of community development, community and youth work and community education can be traced from the nineteenth century, if not earlier. In the first part of the nineteenth century, initiatives to promote adult education focused upon providing working-class men with 'Useful Knowledge' – defined in terms of its usefulness in maintaining social order whilst increasing economic productivity. The first Mechanics' Institute, set up in 1823 by Lord Brougham, an aristocratic philanthropist, aimed to:

> increase men's scientific knowledge in the belief that such learning would contribute new inventions, and to serve as a safety valve offering a controlled context for debate, in order to deter more politically motivated attacks on the *status quo* (Wolfe, 1993, p. 7).

Perhaps unsurprisingly these Mechanics Institutes did not succeed in attracting large numbers of unskilled workers (although they did attract some skilled workers and lower-middle-class participants). The Institutes were criticised from the reactionary right (who feared that any attempt to educate the working class could be destabilising). And conversely, the Institutes' patronising approach was criticised by progressives, such as the Chartists. Early British socialists established their own educational initiatives, as part of wider strategies to Educate, Agitate and Organise, strategies to promote 'Really Useful Knowledge' – knowledge for empowerment and social change. From these early beginnings, then, through the nineteenth and twentieth centuries, there have been varying and contested approaches to adult education, social stability and social transformation (Kelly, 1970; Johnson, 1988; Mayo, 1997).

The Settlement Houses such as Oxford House (founded in 1883) and Toynbee Hall (founded in 1885) in Britain were more directly central to the history of community development, along with the youth movements such as the Boys Brigade and the Boy Scouts. In their varying ways, these initiatives were concerned with culture as a design for living, as well as with culture in terms of the arts and recreation. In the context of late-nineteenth-century Britain, the Settlement Houses aimed to improve the living and working conditions of the poor. The Settlement Houses also provided educational and recreational services such as art and music classes. The university graduates who lived in these Settlements had a mission which, as Canon Barnett, a key mover and contemporary theorist argued, included both combating material poverty and sharing the universities' cultural riches (Popple, 1995). 'Nothing that can be learnt of the University is too good for East London', Barnett reflected, adding that the learning would also be a two-way process, as the settlers learned about the lives of the poor (Briggs and Macartney, 1984, p. 5). There needed to be a search together for social improvement.

Right from these early days, there were inherent tensions and contradictions here. The origins of community and youth work in Britain included a 'civilising mission'. In a letter to *The Times*, supporting a proposed gallery in Whitechapel, East London, Watts testified to the 'humanising and even encouraging [effects] works of art can have upon those whose lives are a round of dullness'. . . 'It is no wonder the weary and joyless should too often seek and find relief in gambling and drunken-ness. Art and music, which I should like to see enter the gallery scheme, would be found possible auxiliaries of the pulpit' (quoted in Briggs and Macartney 1984, p. 58). This 'humanising' mission could be paternalistic and patronising. In the case of the uniformed youth movements, for example, the goals could be ethnocentric and explicitly imperialist – inculcating the cultural values associated with empire. Baden-Powell's 'Scouting for Boys' has been described as 'essentially a book of right-wing political propaganda' (Morris, 1996, pp. 61–2) 'a crude and insistent expression of Tory imperialism' (Hynes, quoted in Morris, 1996, p. 62) with Baden-Powell' s model of the backwoodsman being the 'pioneer civilising a savage country so that it becomes a colony for our empire' (quoted in Morris, 1996, p. 65).

But this is not at all to imply that the origins of community and youth work in Britain were unequivocally imbued with imperialism, or even that the civilising mission in general was uncontentious. Barnett himself reflected, in 1905, that 'Settlements had been inclined to become too much like the "missionary" they were designed to supplement' (quoted in Briggs and Macartney, 1984, p. 59).

The point to emphasise is that 'culture', both as a way of life and, more specifically, in terms of recreation and the arts, has a long and contentious history in relation to community and youth work and community education. This chapter focuses more specifically upon competing approaches to culture and community development since the Second World War. Community development, in the post-war period, has been associated with the development theories which were prevalent at that time, modernisation theories which placed consider-able emphasis upon cultural factors. As this chapter outlines in summary, the dominant development paradigm which emerged at this period (Escobar, 1995) presupposed that 'Western cultures consti-tuted ideal examples of what a modern society should be. The Third World nations could achieve the same results as the Western coun-tries, but this meant dismantling all the non-Western traditional structures' (Melkote, 1991, p. 48). In other words, cultural change was prescribed as the essential prerequisite for self-sustaining economic growth.

As this chapter will go on to outline, the modernisation theorists' emphasis upon the key significance of cultural factors was challenged from the late sixties and early seventies by dependency theorists, who were, themselves, then challenged, both from the political left and increasingly from the New Right. In this more recent period, the role of culture and the media have re-emerged, in the context of post-modernist debates.

There are parallels between these debates on development in general, and debates on community development and culture, in both Northern and Southern contexts. And there are important differences. Both in theory and in practice, the role of culture in community development has been and continues to be contentious. Having set the scene, in terms of these debates, the second part of this chapter goes on to illustrate the potential for participatory and empowering approaches to community development through community theatre and community video.

Modernisation, culture and development

In the post-Second World War period, the dominant development paradigm was based upon the assumption that Third World countries would be able to follow the industrialised West's path to self-sustaining economic growth (Rostow, 1960). But successful economic take-off was not automatic – a number of preconditions were required, including the development of modern, rather than traditional cultural attitudes and values. Max Weber's classic study on the Protestant Ethic and the Spirit of Capitalism (tracing the links between the protestant ethic of individual achievement and the rise of capitalism) was quoted, in this context. A number of influential studies explored the social and psychological characteristics which were associated with modernising cultures (Lerner, 1958, McClelland, 1967). For example, individualism, achievement motivation, secularism and the desire to consume were contrasted with supposedly traditional attitudes, such as familialism, low achievement motivation and limited aspirations.[1]

The implications of such approaches were to emphasise the importance of culture in development. Values and attitudes needed to change if free-market economic growth strategies were to succeed. Communication was key – including the mass media of radio, television, films, newspapers and magazines. As Melkote's study argued, in the fifties and sixties, there was considerable optimism about the mass media's potential for modernising cultures, in general, and more specifically for conveying particular development messages (Melkote, 1991).

There are parallels with the history of community development, although there are also contradictions. Community development emerged in the post-war period as 'a process designed to create conditions of economic and social progress for the whole community with its active participation' (United Nations definition, 1955). The roots of community development, as this had been developed by the British in

1   How far such stereotypes actually corresponded with realities in supposedly 'traditional' societies was, of course, more problematic, as Chapter 2 has already suggested.

their colonies, lay in programmes for basic education – subsequently called mass education – to provide literacy training, and to stimulate self-help initiatives in agriculture, health and other social service areas.

Colonial peoples were also to be educated, as part of colonial strategies to transform attitudes and behaviours. Cultural change was seen as key to economic development. And this was also linked to political development, the British aiming to 'encourage democracy and local initiative' and to establish solid foundations with approaching self-government (Brokensha and Hodge, 1969, p. 164). Community development could be seen, in fact, as part of wider strategies to win the hearts and minds of the colonised, during the Cold War period, to keep as much of the Third World as possible safe for (capitalist) democracy.

The United States of America was similarly supporting community development programmes to contain subversion at this time, it has been suggested, especially in countries such as Thailand and Vietnam, which were considered to be most threatened by communism (Brokensha and Hodge, 1969, Midgely *et al.*, 1986). Miniclier summarised the rationale for US foreign aid for community development in the sixties in somewhat less explicit terms as follows: 'The project of successful Community Development is not only wells, roads, other community facilities and new crops; it is, more properly, the development of stable, self-reliant communities with an assured sense of social and political responsibility' (Miniclier 1969, p. 9). This could, of course, be seen as a form of cultural imperialism, persuading rural people to provide unpaid self-help labour for development projects which were disproportionately of benefit to the relatively powerful and their colonisers/former colonisers.

The community development agenda cannot simply be equated with the modernisation agenda which was so prevalent in the development literature of the time, however. Both focused upon cultural change as a key prerequisite for development. But whilst the modernisation agenda emphasised aspects of Western industrialised, urbanised cultures – aspects such as individual achievement motivation for example – community development was more ambivalent, being concerned, too, with co-operation and collectivism, with an emphasis upon rural development. Populist and anarchist ideas about mutualism have been identified amongst the roots of community development, along with nostalgic notions about the virtue of simple people in rural communities which were being disrupted by wider processes of economic and social change (Midgely *et al.*, 1986).

As Chapter 2 outlined, the very use of the term 'community' can be associated with romantic views of an idealised lost past – a past which needs to be saved, or reconstructed as an antidote to the social dislocation which results from urbanisation and industrialisation (the 'community lost' approach to community – see Bulmer, 1987; Crow and Allen, 1994; Mayo, 1994). Community development came to be applied to urban areas, too, on the basis of such contradictory assumptions – the assumed need to modernise traditional cultures in general, and to tackle 'cultures of poverty' more specifically, versus the assumed need to reinforce the collective ties which supported social solidarity and self-help. The challenges to such notions as 'the culture of poverty' – cultures of social pathology, which were supposed to characterise the poor in deprived areas – featured significantly in critical community development debates in the sixties and seventies (Lewis, 1968; Loney, 1983).

Before moving on to the critical debates of the late sixties and seventies, however, there are further contradictions to be highlighted about the post-colonial community development heritage. The practice as well as the theoretical underpinnings contained inherent tensions. The 'Dual Mandate' which has been associated with British colonialism has been criticised as the mission 'to civilise whilst exploiting' (Midgely, 1986, p. 17). The British approach to colonialism's 'civilising mission' differed somewhat from the approach which was adopted by rival colonial powers such as France. British colonial strategy put more emphasis upon working through local structures and cultures – the basis for Indirect Rule – rather than simply defining 'civilisation' in terms of the cultures of the colonisers – becoming culturally French.

Community development turned out to be potentially contradictory in practice, too, with some space, at least, for differing agendas. Key theorists and practitioners of community development such as Peter Du Sautoy, in the former Gold Coast (now Ghana) were clearly far removed from being colonial cultural attachés. On the contrary, in fact, the mass education and community development work which Du Sautoy developed in the then Gold Coast, was seen as potentially challenging by the colonial regime. Rather than simply 'civilising' the natives, whilst encouraging them to increase cocoa production, community development initiatives were seen as raising critical consciousness and hence supporting political campaigns for independence. This mass education and community development work included the use of cultural tools, particularly the use of drama, building upon the local history of drama in West Africa. Du Sautoy found himself practising these approaches to community development away from the capital, out of the colonial eye, precisely because these uses of drama were found to be so critical, and potentially so subversive, by the colonial regime. (My attention was drawn to this potentially more subversive aspect, by a drama lecturer who had taught in West Africa: James Gibbs in a personal communication.)

This example illustrates some of this inherently contradictory potential then, right from community development's colonial origins. In my concern to explore the self-interest of the colonial agenda which underpinned the history of community development in the past, I myself, amongst others, have underplayed these contradictory aspects, thereby presenting too simplistic a critique (Mayo, 1975). Community development, even in the colonial context, had the potential to facilitate processes of challenge as well as processes of incorporation. This example is also significant as an early illustration of the uses of community arts and media for development.

From this period onwards, there are examples of the use of community media, typically, although by no means invariably, to discharge development messages from the top down. Melkote has characterised such approaches more generally as the 'magic bullet theory' of communication (Melkote, 1991). Specific development messages have been conveyed through traditional community media such as puppets and drama, as well as through modern media such as radio and television. And attitudes have been challenged, as part of strategies to promote cultural climates which are more favourable for development. Writing about the uses of traditional drama forms to introduce community development messages in Nicaragua, Weaver explained that plays were developed to include didactic points, 'subtly yet tellingly introduced into the dialogue. The evils resulting from alcoholism, or the shame of being illiterate when one has the means to learn how to read and write, are brought out by "good" characters. Virtue is rewarded' (Weaver 1970, p. 45). These are morality plays updated to promote social change in varying directions.

Drama has, of course, been used for such didactic purposes, from the morality plays of medieval Europe, through to the very different uses of agitprop theatre, to promote working-class culture and social change in post-revolutionary Soviet Russia – to organise, to educate and to agitate. (Whether or not didactic plays actually carried their intended messages effectively and unambiguously in practice was another question.) In the context of community development programmes, the didactic traditions of theatre, together with song and dance, were adopted in a range of countries (including a number of African countries) for the purposes of conveying development messages, including health, hygiene and literacy messages (Mlawa, 1991, McGivney and Murray, 1991).

The point about the example of the uses of drama in the former Gold Coast is that even in that colonial situation, this was not simply a case of the use of drama to convey 'magic bullets' of development information. The reality was more complex. Gibbs's view was that community drama, in that context, was seen as potentially challenging precisely because the approach was more participatory (Gibbs, personal communication). This connects with alternative approaches to the use of drama and community media in community development, approaches which have been more interactive (Mlawa, 1991; Zakes, 1993; Mayo, 1997).

Etherton has distinguished six different stages in relation to drama and development in fact, starting with traditional performances ('preserved' by arts councils and ministries of culture and tourism) through commercial theatre to programmes to take theatre to the people, folk theatre and development projects, the use of theatre to promote self-help and finally the use of theatre as part of a wider process of raising political consciousness (Etherton, 1982). As the second part of this chapter suggests, community arts and media can also be and have been developed, then, as part of bottom-up and transformatory approaches to community development. Melkote's study of communication and development in the Third World explores a range of examples of such more open-ended approaches. Before moving on to the discussion of these, however, a summary of some of the critiques of earlier approaches is required. This sets the context for a critical understanding of the relative marginalisation of cultural questions, in community development debates, in the following period.

Critiques from the sixties and seventies

The dominant development paradigm of the post-war period was increasingly challenged from the late sixties and early seventies. According to the theorists of underdevelopment, development for some was being accompanied by underdevelopment for others, in the Third World (Frank, 1969). Whether or not critics shared this particular analysis, there was, overall, increasing focus upon structural rather than 'cultural' reasons for the disappointing persistence of poverty in both Third and First World contexts.

The mid- to late sixties and early seventies was a period of challenge, both in terms of economic theories and in terms of social, political and ideological debates. This was the era of mobilisation against racial discrimination in the United States, the development of the student movement and second wave feminism. Community development debates were significantly influenced by these challenges, albeit with some evident time lags (feminist approaches to community work only really emerging from the late seventies, Mayo, 1977; Dominelli, 1990).

There had, in fact, already been a number of challenges to community development approaches within the then predominant paradigm. Back in the fifties, Worsley, for example, had argued that the Indian Community Development programme, a major initiative launched in 1952, represented an ideological offensive within the context of Cold War objectives. Community development was being launched in India to promote rural democratisation and development through education and extension work, but the underlying structural factors which were inhibiting development – structural problems related to inequalities based upon caste, class, landownership and labour relationships – were not being tackled (Worsley, 1984, p. 146).

This was the context within which UN representatives from the former Soviet Union and Eastern European states began to argue that community development, as it was then being promoted, was marginal if not actually diversionary. Their criticisms have been paraphrased as follows:

> You are dealing with marginal questions in community development ... Aren't you avoiding the basic problems of social reform – land reform, administrative reform – the people on the bottom are never going to benefit from what you are trying to do (Dunham, 1970, p. 88).

As community development programmes were increasingly applied to the problems of the cities of the metropolitan powers, from the sixties, through the War on Poverty in the United States and the so much smaller government Community Development Projects in Britain, critics focused upon the need to address the structural causes of poverty and inequality (Loney, 1983). Cultural factors were particularly discredited, according to the critics. Because theories of cultural poverty had been used, at least in part, in official attempts to explain

the causes of poverty – in terms of the pathological values and attitudes which were supposed to be prevalent in deprived areas. The poor
could thus be blamed for their own poverty – blaming the victim for
the negative cultures which were being associated with factors such as
inadequate parenting – 'the inadequacies of, or inabilities of poor
families rather than on the structures of a society which tolerates or
even requires poverty' (Loney, 1983).

CDP inter-project publications such as *Gilding the Ghetto* and *The
Costs of Industrial Change* challenged such explanations based upon
theories of cultures of poverty, emphasising instead the importance of
addressing structural causes rooted in economic restructuring. *Gilding
the Ghetto*, for example, started by challenging the assumptions which
underpinned the CDP brief, including the assumptions that 'it was the
"deprived" themselves who were the cause of "urban deprivation"' or
that 'the problem could best be solved by overcoming these people's
apathy and promoting self-help' (CDP, 1977, p. 4). On the contrary,
in fact, radical adult and community educationalists working with the
Liverpool CDP, for example, developed alternative approaches in
adult education for social action (Ashcroft and Jackson, 1974; Lovett,
1975). *Gilding the Ghetto* concluded in similar vein, emphasising the
need to move away from programmes about managing poor people,
to:

> fighting against the diversion of resources away from the public
> services but also acting collectively to change the structures
> through which these services are provided so that both workers and
> consumers have a service which is geared towards their needs and
> over which they have control (CDP, 1977, p. 64).

The point to emphasise here, is that these critiques formed part of
wider pressures to shift the focus of community development
programmes. There was a shift away from issues of culture towards an
increasing focus upon issues of production and distribution, together
with issues of public service provision – issues such as employment
and income generation, as well as issues of health and housing, in
the metropolitan contexts. As Dunham had already pointed out, it
had also been argued, in the context of Third World development
that, 'Unless community development contributes substantially to
economic development it is doubtful whether it will be given
much weight in future national development programmes (Dunham,
1970, p. 89).

Squeezed to the margins of community development agendas in the eighties and nineties?

Did this shift of focus mean that questions of culture – whether defined in terms of ways of life, designs for living, or whether defined more specifically in relation to community arts and media – were effectively squeezed to the margins of the community development agendas, then? The answers to these questions, it will be suggested, are not so straightforward.

Questions of culture – however defined – have been treated with some wariness, since the seventies, by those who have been convinced by structuralist analyses of the causes of social problems such as poverty and social deprivation. As previous chapters have suggested, whilst 'cultures of poverty' theories seemed to have been critiqued in the seventies, aspects of these approaches seemed to be re-emerging in the eighties, this time as theories of the cultural pathologies of the underclass in the USA – typically young unemployed men and unmarried mothers who were disproportionately likely to be black (Murray, 1990). More recent versions, including versions linked to communitarian approaches in both the USA and Britain, have focused upon the importance of strengthening the sense of community, replacing the culture of welfare dependency with a new public moral order (Field, 1995). As the Citizen's Commission on the Future of the Welfare State made abundantly clear, service users *do* want to be supported to live independently rather than in dependence (Beresford and Turner, 1997). But this is very different from accepting the logic of cultural explanations of welfare dependency – explanations which continue to be regarded with suspicion on the political left, despite their continuing appearances in contemporary policy debates.

This has been the context, then, for some of the wariness towards 'cultural' approaches in community development – at best, bordering on the marginal – at worst, linked to contemporary versions of victim blaming. Meanwhile, cultural aspects of community development – in the more specific sense of 'culture' in relation to the arts and media – may have been potentially further marginalised and/or appropriated for more directly economic purposes, in the harsher economic climate of the eighties and nineties. Cultural development may have been perceived as relatively peripheral to community development from the political right, as well as from the structuralist left.

New Right approaches to the role of the community sector in Britain from the 1980s, placed increasing emphasis upon the importance of specific outputs – value for money, in the contract culture (Mayo, 1994). In this scenario, funding for community initiatives tended to become increasingly tied to measurable performance indicators. Community participation was a requirement, built into a range of government interventions such as City Challenge and Single Regeneration Budget programmes, to promote economic and social regeneration in the eighties and nineties – but with relatively specific regeneration objectives in mind. There tended to be less space, in this context, for community initiatives with less readily quantifiable aims and objectives. So initiatives to promote 'cultural development' tended to be relatively marginalised – except insofar as they could be seen to be contributing significantly to the creation of confidence-building and opening up opportunities for economic and social development.

Community arts have 'been seen as marginal to the real issues within communities – health, housing, unemployment', it has been suggested, from New Right perspectives too, and this marginalisation has only shifted as policy-makers have seemed to accord the community arts a little more status since the eighties. This apparent policy shift, Orton has suggested, has been related to a growing realisation of the community arts' potential for contributing to economic regeneration, rather than because of a more fundamental acceptance of democratic participation within the arts per se (Orton, 1996). (Alternative perspectives on culture and economic development in general, and the role of cultural industries more specifically, are addressed in more detail, in the following chapter.)

However understandable the potential marginalisation of, if not active hostility towards cultural issues in community development, though, this has simply not represented an adequate response, either in theory or in practice, whether from the political left or from the political right. Earlier chapters of this book have already argued that crudely deterministic structuralist approaches, as these were developed and caricatured in the seventies, could be seen to have invited the attacks which were then mounted by postmodernist critics. The arguments for re-evaluating the significance of cultural politics have already been set out, in general, in Chapter 2, so there is no need to repeat them here.

For the purposes of this chapter, the points to emphasise relate more particularly to the history of cultural issues in the context of community development, because community development has continued to be concerned with cultural issues, both in the broader sense of culture as a way of life and consciousness, and in the more specific senses of the community arts and media. And just as there have been market-oriented approaches – to the potential role of the cultural industries for example – so, alternatively, there have been more transformative approaches, drawing upon the ideas of theorists such as Gramsci and Freire, as these have been developed and applied in both the First and Third Worlds. Cultural politics have been pursued, and continue to be pursued, from varying perspectives.

Just as there was an upsurge of questioning, with the emergence of social movements which influenced the development of critical thinking about community development in the sixties and seventies, so there was an upsurge of questioning on the role of community arts and media. This upsurge has been described as signalling:

> an oppositional movement to what were seen as sterile and elitist views of traditional art. Community arts, in this account, contrasted with high art in that it placed emphasis upon participation and process, and reflected a view of arts as part of a wider development of cultural renewal and communication between people, where the end product was valued either less, or merely as much as, the process itself (Orton, 1996, pp. 173–4).

Community arts had a restorative element too. Whether in the Third World or the depressed inner cities of the First World, there were cultural heritages which had been destroyed by processes of change. 'Much of what community arts did was to recreate and reinvent this heritage and give it a positive value' (Harris, 1999). In the UK, this heritage had included the Music Hall, singsongs and street parties, for example. Through community arts this re-created heritage developed new roots, roots which are evident in contemporary pub theatres, music venues and local festivals for example. Wider recognition of the value of arts activity, expression and fulfilment, can be seen as the legacy of the cultural development movement of this period.

This dynamism and creativity was reflected, for example, in an account of community arts work at the Albany Settlement in Deptford, South East London in the early seventies. The arts programme was central to the Settlement's work – a programme of democratic popular participation. Community arts were to be enjoyed – painting, murals, photography, jazz, pop, theatre – 'Everyman is an artist.' 'Authentic art does in fact tend to mirror and extend political awareness', it was argued, but entertainment was key as well. 'We are Deptford's entertainers, not missionaries of Art' (Collins *et al.*, 1974, p. 175). The differences between this approach to culture, and that of the settlement houses' earlier and more 'missionary' style approach, in the nineteenth century, is striking; art as bringing civilisation – 'sweetness and light' in Matthew Arnold's terminology – valued for its contribution to the improvement and enlightenment of the deprived.

The community arts movement of the seventies has been charac-terised in terms of a combination of radical libertarianism, social concern and innovative arts practice, which demanded:

> a direct and collective relationship between artists and people; egal-itarian in giving the opportunity for everyone to have a cultural voice and to be able to represent themselves; relevant art in a social sense; participatory rather than consumable; challenging and raising questions about the role of art in particular and the domi-nant ideas of society in general (Orton, 1996, p. 177).

The reality of community arts practice was not without problems, however. There were uneasy experiments, such as projects to put artists 'in residence' in communities, for example, whether or not the artists and the communities in question actually shared common understandings of what all this was to be about (Braden, 1978). The very term 'community arts' has been a contested one. 'Confusion existed over the language and the meaning of "art" itself', according to Orton, 'whilst the purposes of community arts and artists' inter-ventions in communities were increasingly contested' (Orton, 1996, p. 179).

'It was perhaps the fusion of this emerging community arts move-ment with the growing interest in community development, prevalent within many communities in the 1970s which offered the most radical opportunities', Orton concluded, evaluating the legacies of this period of dynamism and debate (Orton, 1996, p. 179). She identified a number of strands which have particular relevance here. The Craigmillar Festival Society provided a well-known case study of community development using community arts (a case study which became known and quoted far beyond the peripheral Edinburgh housing estate where the Craigmillar Festival Society – the CFS – developed.) The role of community festivals such as the Craigmillar Festival is explored in more detail in Chapter 6.

Community arts, in the CFS's view, were not simply about asserting democratic rights of access to the arts in deprived communities, or challenging the elitism of establishment art. Community arts were seen by the CFS as:

> a way of raising individual community and cultural confidence which complemented their other activities such as campaigning on housing, social welfare, education and economic development issues. The CFS argued that, in this form, community arts were instrumental in building up skills and powers for expression within individuals, enabling local people to feel and develop a sense of worth, identity, pride and confidence which transferred into other areas of individuals' lives (whether it be standing up to doctors or negotiating rent rebates). At a broader level it also crucially provided the foundation for collective action around issues of concern within the community (Orton, 1996, p. 178).

The approach adopted by Craigmillar and other such community organisations was a source of inspiration for workers who were attempting to build links between community arts and community development, from the seventies.

Orton identified a relatively small number of community arts workers in the Scottish context who were influenced, more specifically, by the radical analyses developed by the Community Development Projects. This led to a number of attempts to address the structural causes of poverty and deprivation through making links and building alliances between community organisations and the trade union and labour movement, seeking to develop community arts within the framework of a radical community work practice. Scottish examples to illustrate these approaches included the Pilton Video Project (Edinburgh) and the Cranhill Arts Project (Glasgow) which produced an arts resource, both for the local community and for trade union and political campaigns in the 1980s. Without minimising the difficulties of working in these ways – linking movements with very different organising traditions to build alliances which could, she suggested 'at best be described as uneasy', Orton concluded that projects such as Cranhill had pioneered ways of working which can, nevertheless, provide lessons for community arts work with the newer social movements.

The women's, gay and lesbian, disabled, anti-racist and environmental movements have, each in their own way, challenged

ts of cultural hegemony and made creative use of the arts and
*i*a in promoting their respective causes (Orton, 1996, p. 182).

She drew connections here with Gramsci's ideas on cultural hegemony, the cultural domination of the many by the few. Community
arts has the potential to assist working people to challenge this
cultural hegemony, she argued, by enabling them to create representations of their own realities, in image, form and language. Such
approaches to the use of community arts and media, drawing upon
the ideas of theorists such as Gramsci had been and were being
promoted, she pointed out, not only in Scotland, but in a range of
contexts, internationally, from Argentina, Brazil, Chile and Peru and
back to Europe. Community arts and media could be used to challenge
the power relations of the market, rather than simply for producing
cultural commodities, she argued, assisting individuals, groups and
communities to envisage and to represent alternative scenarios and
agendas. Subsequent chapters will explore some of these differing
potentials, in relation to community economic development, as well
as in relation to personal and community identities, health and well-
being and political consciousness.

From Gramsci and Freire to the ideas of Boal and the 'Theatre of the Oppressed'

Before moving on to explore such alternative approaches to the uses
of community arts and media, in different contexts and practice
settings, this chapter concludes with a brief summary of the key ideas
of one of the theorists whose work has strongly influenced the development of participatory drama. This sets the scene for the subsequent
discussion of participatory uses of community media in community
development, in both Third and First World contexts.

As it has already been suggested, community arts and media have
been used in varying ways and for different purposes, to convey a
range of community development messages from the top down, as
well as to facilitate more empowering processes of community representation and participation from the bottom up. Freire's approach to
adult literacy and community education has provided a key theoretical reference point for the development of the latter. Mlama, for
example, has drawn parallels between Freire's criticisms of the
'banking approach to education', on the one hand, and the use of
theatre to convey development messages from the top down (Mlama,

1991). In both cases, the audience/adult learners are being treated as empty vessels which need to be filled up with information, however much these messages may be 'for their own good'. Just as 'banking' approaches to community education have been problematised by Freire, so have their counterparts in the uses of the media for community development.

Drawing upon the work of Paulo Freire, his fellow Brazilian Augusto Boal developed alternative and more interactive approaches, as he applied critical theories of drama to experiments with people's theatre in Latin America. Boal's ideas have been taken up and applied in very different settings in Africa as well as Latin America and elsewhere. Boal's approach, as he explains this in 'Theatre of the Oppressed' (Boal, 1979) started from the critique of Aristotle's view of the purposes of classical drama, as this critique was developed by Brecht, from a Marxist perspective. The argument developed by Boal can be summarised as follows.

Although Aristotle was not arguing that the theatre should be political, classical tragedies did have a social purpose in a very broad sense – in this case, to inspire the audience with pity and fear. The tragic hero was to be pitied for the fatal flaw in his character – the excessive pride which leads Oedipus to his downfall, for example – but the audience is also to be inspired with fear. This is because the hero's fatal flaw represents a human characteristic – a trait such as pride – which members of the audience may also share. The spectators are to keep in mind the terrible consequences which follow those who commit the same mistakes – out of excessive pride or whatever. The classical tragedy concludes, then, with a moral ending – the tragic hero comes to grief and the spectators go home terrified by the spectacle of the catastrophe and purged of their own leanings in a similar direction. According to this view, the play does not need to preach morality directly. Through the spectators' empathy with the tragic hero, they come away cleansed, and, by implication, more appropriately socialised, even if the play did not spell this message out to them explicitly.

Aspects of this Aristotelian system have survived into the twentieth century, in Boal's view. Although the form has varied – from the medieval morality play through to the contemporary 'Western' film, antisocial elements can be purged as the audience empathises with the characters whose lives are played out before them. Vicariously, Boal suggests, we do evil when we empathise with the villain's tragic flaw, only to re-emerge purged when the hero gains the advantage, the villain gets his/her come-uppance and morality is restored. Ultimately, this type of drama is profoundly political, in Boal's view, in that its basic task is 'the purgation of all antisocial elements' (Boal, 1979, p. 46). This system, he argues 'appears in disguised form on television, in the movies, in the circus, and in the theaters' (Boal, 1979, p. 47). 'It appears in many and varied shapes and media. But its essence does not change: it is designed to bridle the individual, to adjust him [sic] to whatever pre-exists.' This is precisely why, Boal argues, if 'on the contrary, we want to stimulate the spectator to transform his society' then alternative approaches to drama are required (Boal, 1979, p. 47).

Boal drew upon Brecht's notions of alienation, to develop an approach to people's theatre in which the audience was not simply empathising with the characters. The aim was to stimulate the spectators into standing back from the characters, engaging in critical reflection as the basis for transformatory action. The spectators may indeed be moved to tears in Brecht's plays, for example, when Mother Courage loses her sons, one by one in the war, in *Mother Courage*. But the playwright's aim is that, at the conclusion, the audience is moved not simply to tears, but 'rather with anger against war and the commerce of war, because it is this commerce that takes away the sons of Mother Courage' (Boal, 1979, p. 103) and it is this which has been exposed through the play. Brecht aimed to provoke precisely such reflections – as the prelude to action for social change, rather than simply wanting to inspire empathy with his characters.

Boal developed his own experiments with people's theatre through literacy work in Peru in the early seventies, drawing upon previous work elsewhere in Latin America and using Freire's methods. The aim was not only to teach literacy in the first language and in Spanish, but also to teach literacy 'in all possible languages, especially the artistic ones such as theater, photography, puppetry, films, journalism, etc':

> We tried to show in practice how the theater can be placed at the service of the oppressed, so that they can express themselves and so that, by using this new language, they can also discover new concepts (Boal, 1979, p. 121).

The main objective here, was to change people from being passive spectators into active subjects, transformers of the dramatic action. (Boal distinguished 'spectators' from Spect-Actors.) The Spect-actors reserve the right, here, to think for themselves. Their critical reflections provide the basis for exploring alternative outcomes. The 'spect-actors' in Boal's 'forum theatre' assume the protagonist's role, try out solutions and discuss plans for change as their critical consciousness awakens (Boal, 1992).

Boal's account of his experiments in Peru included descriptions of examples of his approach in practice. For instance, some actors were working with the residents of a barrio in Lima. The actors started by inviting the audience to suggest a theme for a short play – a 10- to 20-minute-long scene which would explore an issue of local concern. One of the women suggested that they tackle a controversial local issue – the case of a woman who had been deceived by her husband. The actors worked through a scene which ended with the woman discovering her husband's deception. The action was then interrupted, and the women in the audience entered into a lively discussion about what she should do next. Several solutions were proposed, each of which were then tried out by the actors and evaluated by the audience. For example, one solution that was proposed involved the woman leaving her husband. But when this was acted out, it was rejected by the audience, because in punishing her husband she ended up punishing herself since she had nowhere else to live. Through discussing these different solutions, a critical exploration of gender relations ensued. In this particular case, the audience – both men and women – unanimously agreed with the fourth solution which was acted out, as the most realistic outcome which could be negotiated in the circumstances. (In this version, the woman beat her husband with a stick to make him recognise that he was at fault and feel repentant, before making up the quarrel and forgiving him.)

This type of theatre, using a range of different techniques to develop a critical dialogue between actors and spectators, can be applied to a variety of issues and situations. The starting point can be any local issue such as the lack of water in the barrios. Or it can be a more abstract issue such as exploitative employment relations, oppressive land-tenure systems or imperialism itself. In addition, Boal has developed a range of approaches to address more personal aspects of oppression and unhappiness, aspects which are explored further in Chapter 7 (Boal, 1995).

Boal's ideas have influenced the development of people's theatre and community media across continents. As Boeren has argued:

> Influenced by the politically oriented thoughts of Paulo Freire and Augusto Boal on liberation and development of the poor, many

development workers in the world came to see the role of communication and media to stimulate critical analysis, and to develop self-confidence, participation, awareness and the organisation of groups and communities. In line with the goals of participatory projects, media had to be produced in collaboration with the people and preferably by the people. This required the employment of media that were congruent with modes of communication of the (ethnic) group, small-scale and dialogue-prone (Boeren, 1992, pp. 47–8).

Some of the African influences have already been referred to. Boeren referred to a number of examples, from the community education work developed by adult educators such as Kidd in Botswana in the seventies, through to a range of similar activities in a number of countries, including Swaziland, Zambia, Zimbabwe, Nigeria, Malawi and Cameroon. Boal's ideas could be traced in a number of these – although Boeren also commented that over the years (in the tougher economic and political climate of the eighties) approaches have tended to become 'less radical, less confrontational and more pragmatic' (Boeren, 1992, 48) with increasing emphasis on the natural environment.

The following example provides an illustration of some of the ways in which such interactive approaches can be applied in different settings, in this case through the use of participatory video in community development in South-East Asia. Subsequent chapters illustrate some of the ways in which these types of ideas have also had influence in other settings.

Participatory approaches – a case study of community video in Vietnam

Like theatre, film and video have histories in relation to community development, both for the dissemination of development messages and for the promotion of more participatory approaches. The UN report on Popular Participation in Development: Emerging Trends in Community Development included, for example, references to the work of the National Film Board of Canada's 'Challenge for Change' programme of educational films relating to community development. In addition to producing films on community development and social change, the National Film Board had also carried out an experimental project in Newfoundland which was described as a unique attempt to use film 'as a direct means of communication and as a catalyst for social change' (UN, 1971, p. 121).

This project placed film-making technology at the disposal of the local people, who used the process of making the film to explore and face their problems, and then communicate their views directly to the provincial cabinet. Replies from a cabinet representative were then filmed and sent back to the local communities in question. Through these processes, communication was improved as attitudes and awareness changed – 'a dialogue was started between the islands and the Government' (UN, 1971, p. 122).

This example, from the early seventies, includes features which have become characteristic of more recent uses of film and video for community development. Braden's account of a pilot project to explore the prospects for participatory video with Oxfam in Vietnam in the nineties, also started from video's potential for retrieving and reflecting back the voices of under-represented people, to enable them to communicate more effectively, both amongst themselves and with others. Through these processes, video could provide a tool, it was anticipated, to help develop dialogues between communities and decision-makers, as well as with other grass-roots communities.

The Vietnam project to explore participatory uses of video for community development drew upon Freire's work on critical peda-gogy – the process of dialogue between experts and learners as these ideas had been applied via Participatory Learning Approaches (PLA) and Participatory Action Research (PAR). PLA/PAR methods, as these were developed by Chambers and others, were designed to promote critical thinking and reflection, as local people worked alongside outside experts to research their own problems (Chambers, 1983, 1997). Through sequences of learning and reflection between local people and outsiders, new insights could be elicited, which would set the framework for the development of appropriate community development strategies. Chambers's methods included the use of three-dimensional models and diagrams constructed using locally available materials. In this way, local people without literacy skills could participate, actively researching their own areas, using sticks, stones, pebbles and beans to indicate the location of particular crops, wells and irrigation channels, for example.

Community video could be used, not only to record the PLA/PAR process, but to become part of the process itself. Video, as Braden explains 'can enable under-represented and non-literate people to use their own visual languages and oral traditions to retrieve, debate and record their own knowledge' (Braden, 1998, p. 19). And these record-ings can then be used to enable excluded people to enter into negotiations with those with power over them (including those with the power to allocate key resources via international development agencies).

Community video can also be used to challenge the representations of others, whether these others are outsiders or whether they are different groupings within the locality. This last point is an important one as PLA/PAR approaches recognise that, because local communities are not expected to be homogeneous, there are typically differences of interest and perspective relating to differences based upon factors such as caste, class and gender. This raises questions about whose voices are being represented, and whose voices are being heard, or not being heard – key questions for community video practitioners to take into account. Community video, like PLA/PAR methods more gener-ally, are only as participative, in practice, as their practitioners can ensure.

The Oxfam-supported pilot project (developed, incidentally, through the initiative of Michael Etherton, the Oxfam representative who had previously researched and written about the use of theatre in Africa (Etherton, 1982)) set out to train community communication and development workers in the use of participatory video. They worked with local people in three villages in a commune in North-Central Vietnam, making videos on the issues of key concern to the villagers in question.

The issues which emerged as the subjects for the videos were not unusual topics for community development, although they were not entirely as expected. The villagers were concerned about irrigation issues, salination and water supply, examples of issues which had been anticipated. But instead of requesting a secondary school for the commune, as expected, the villagers also raised rather a different problem – non-attendance at a local primary school. The video teams accordingly focused upon the reasons for this problem, as well as upon the irrigation and income-generation issues.

Video tapes were made, played back, discussed and edited, all with the villagers' active participation. Women, men and children all took part in lively discussions. Through the process of making and discussing the tapes, the villagers were, indeed enabled to record and retrieve their own information, and so to expose a critical view, in the case of the water-storage and irrigation problems. This led one group to use video as a means for presenting their own solutions – in the hope that this video would then be presented to the authorities and used to advocate on their behalf with potential funders. Through the discussions which ensued during play-backs in another case, additional material was included to take account of women's concerns about income-generation. Meanwhile, the process of making the video about non-attendance at the local primary school enabled villagers to identify and then to enter into negotiations around previously unresolved conflicts between the parents and the headmaster of the school in question. Video had been used as a tool to facilitate communication. And this, in turn, led to processes of conflict-resolution, as officials were held more accountable. Video had clearly contributed to community development, facilitating participative approaches to addressing the issues of central concern to the local communities in question.

The case study makes a powerful case for the relevance of video, then as a tool for participatory community development. Braden's study is of such wide relevance, however, because she evaluates both the creative potential of community video, and key potential limitations, limitations which emerge in participatory approaches to development more generally. The questions which the study raises – the lessons learned – are questions which need to be addressed in relation to participatory approaches to community development, per se, whether or not community video is being used to facilitate the process.

From the follow-up visit, a year later, it emerged that those who had participated had actually been assigned to do so by the authorities in question, which raised issues about whose voices were actually being represented – and conversely whose voices were not being represented? It would be too simple, however, to suggest that some voices were just being excluded – for whatever reason. On the contrary, in fact, one of the villagers commented on the fact that the poorest found it difficult, if not impossible, to find the time to participate. 'Had we not been assigned, we would not have participated, because it was so time-consuming, it was hot, and we lost several days' work' (Braden, 1998, p. 77). To what extent, then, might demands for community participation, however well-intentioned, come to represent yet one more hoop which has to be jumped through, in order for communities to qualify for development/regeneration funding?

Community participation has been described in terms of a new prevailing orthodoxy (Craig and Mayo, 1995) a 'quiet revolution' which has accompanied the increasing popularity of participative approaches to development more generally (Holland and Blackburn, 1998). A note of caution is needed then. Participative approaches, from the bottom up can, after all, be pursued for varying reasons, as part of alternative policy agendas, from the right as well as from the left of the political spectrum.

Participation then, as Braden's study demonstrates, is not necessarily a desirable end in itself. The villagers, in this case, did not just want to express their views or even to articulate their needs – they wanted to be effectively heard. Was it all worth it, some wondered, when a year later, they were still waiting for funding. Who was actually listening?

In fact, in this particular case, funding *was* being actively pursued, via international development agencies. The problem here was the lack of transparency – the villagers had not been kept informed. But the wider questions about representing the voices of the under-represented, from the bottom up, remain to be answered, more generally – who is really listening, and how much difference can this make?

From the perspectives of theorists such as Freire and Boal, participatory approaches from the bottom up, however desirable, are not by themselves sufficient for transformation. In the context of participatory processes such as PAR more specifically, Braden quoted Mosse's view that these are not being matched in the structures and practices of implementation. Reports 'sit on office shelves, and charts and maps provide attractive wall decoration and public statements about participatory intentions' (Mosse, 1995, quoted in Braden, 1998, p. 96). This takes the discussion into the wider policy framework which needs to be tackled, and the structural issues which community development also needs to address, whether using participatory community media or not – issues to which the concluding chapter will return.

5
Cultural Strategies and Community Economic Development

'During the last twenty years', Bianchini pointed out at the beginning of the nineties, 'cultural policy has become an increasingly significant component of economic and physical regeneration strategies in many west European cities' (Bianchini, 1993, p. 1). This potential contribution to the urban economy was certainly becoming increasingly recognised in Britain, as the Arts Council's report of the creative future for the arts, crafts and media in England argued. The arts, according to this report 'can help to keep cities alive' economically as well as socially and aesthetically (Arts Council of Great Britain, 1993, p. 110). 'And not before time', will be the response of many artists and others active in community-based arts development, according to Matarosso (Matarosso, 1998, p. i) although he was not underestimating the continuing need to convince an even wider section of politicians, policy-makers and professionals in other fields (Matarosso, 1998, p. i). There needed to be even greater recognition of the potential contribution of the cultural industries – including community media – to the processes of urban regeneration and local economic development. These potential links between culture and the economy have been the subject of increasing interest too, in relation to Third World development. As the previous chapter suggested, there has been a long history to build upon here. As the UNESCO Report 'Our Creative Diversity' argued in 1995, the economy is part of people's culture and culture, defined as 'the flourishing of human existence in all its forms and as a whole' represents the end aim of development (World Council on Culture and Development, 1995, p. 24). The report went on to explore and to critically evaluate a number of ways in which cultural strategies might, or might not contribute to economic, social and community development. These ranged from the benefits and pitfalls of international agencies' support for the cultural heritage and tourism industries through to a variety of grass-roots approaches including community-controlled museums and fair trading for craft industries. The key point to emphasise here is that this increasing interest in culture and community media, in relation to urban regeneration and economic development, was emerging in both the First and Third Worlds, from the seventies and eighties.

This chapter starts by exploring the context for this growing interest. As the chapter will go on to argue, there have been varying explanations and competing aims and objectives. Just as questions about culture and community development in general have been contentious (as the Introduction and preceding chapters have already argued) so have questions about culture and local economic development more specifically.

As the case study examples go on to illustrate, these differences of perspectives have significant implications in practice. Cultural industries can be and have been promoted as part of New Right market-led strategies for urban regeneration. And in contrast, cultural industries can be and have been central to alternative approaches, including social and community movement strategies based upon alternative and more transformatory aims and objectives. Whatever the underlying aims and objectives, however, as the case material will also illustrate, community-based initiatives still operate within the contexts of wider constraints. Local craft co-operatives, for example, like other small to medium enterprises, tend to be highly vulnerable to market pressures, however strong their community roots or however effectively they express local cultural aspirations and identities.

Having explored a range of approaches in varying contexts, the chapter concludes by raising questions about ways of exploring the potential connections between these, across the First and Third Worlds. How might the cultural industries and community media contribute to developing a wider and fuller understanding of varying perspectives on these connections, on a global scale? In what ways could film, video, and drama, for example, be used to promote critical debates about the issues involved in 'Fair Trade'? And how might such enhanced understanding contribute to the development of more effective policies and practice, across national boundaries?

Alternative perspectives on the significance of culture for urban regeneration and community economic development

Economic justifications for cultural development strategies have a history which pre-dates the market-dominated preoccupations of the New Right, from the late seventies onwards. As the UNESCO report 'Our Creative Diversity' pointed out, historic preservation was one of the first cultural domains to be considered 'bankable' (World Council on Culture and Development, 1995). Already in the 1970s, for instance, both UNDP and the World Bank began to devote funds to the preservation of the built environment and for crafts development, both of which could be justified in purely economic terms.

As the report went on to point out, the heritage industry slogan 'preservation pays', developed in the UK, soon found adherents across the globe. And in both urban industrialised contexts and in Southern contexts, there have been inherent tensions here. Market-dominated appropriations of this heritage for cultural tourism can end by harming the very cultural assets on which the cultural heritage industry feeds. 'Top-down' bureaucratic approaches to conservation can lead to 'a profound hiatus between ordinary civic life and public concern for the cultural past embodied in an officially listed monumental heritage', especially when these state institutions were established during the colonial period and 'tailored to the needs of empire' (UNESCO, 1995, p. 183).

The report contrasted these bureaucratic legacies with various alternative grass-roots approaches to culture and tourism, approaches which 'have brought about community development and the upgrading of living standards at economically realistic and technically appropriate levels' (UNESCO, 1995, p. 183). Local communities have benefited economically from such grass-roots strategies, although the most durable return, it has been suggested, has not been financial but educational and social. Spending in fields such as cultural heritage 'remains difficult to justify in the midst of poverty, and the deficiencies of infrastructure and local governance encountered in decaying inner cities throughout the South', the report recognised. '(Y)et non-govermental efforts are beginning to challenge governments to move in this domain as well from centrally conceived and administered programmes to schemes that are based on community participation' (UNESCO, 1995, p. 183).

The living heritage of crafts for instance, provide examples of grass-roots-type initiatives which can be tailored to differing social needs or cultural preferences, offering opportunities for generating income with relatively low levels of investment. While citing examples of positive practice in relation to the development of income and employment in craft industries, the report also draws attention to some of the inherent constraints which need to be addressed if local producers are to receive a more equitable deal for their products on the global market; hence, the report argues, 'the need to strengthen the notion of "fairly traded crafts"' (UNESCO, 1995, p. 192).

As the UNESCO report suggests, there have been both parallels and contrasts with experiences and debates around these varying experiences in the industrialised cities of the West. Cultural policies in urban regeneration have differed between Western European cities, depending upon local economic, social and political as well as cultural contexts (Bianchini,1993). Despite considerable variations, however, according to Bianchini a common trajectory in the development of cultural policies can be identified. One contributory factor, he argued, was the decentralisation of powers to local and regional government in a number of countries, including Italy, Spain and France in the eighties. This then raises the question as to why a number of these cities and regions chose to use their extended powers and resources to promote cultural policies for regeneration.

In Britain, during this period, there was a contrary trend – towards greater centralisation. The Thatcher government's policies for increasing centralisation included the removal of a tier of government with the abolition of the Greater London Council and the six metropolitan councils in 1986. Cultural policy was a partial exception to the trend towards increasing centralisation, however, with some significant shifts in the control of resources for the arts, as proportionately more of the Arts Council's expenditure went to Regional Arts Associations, and their successors, the Regional Arts Boards.

These apparently contradictory trends in Britain can be related to varying political and economic factors. There were left agendas for cultural policies, within the framework of the social, economic and political strategies which were being pursued by municipal socialist authorities such as the Greater London Council (GLC). And there were New Right agendas including Margaret Thatcher's avowed intention to make Britain safe from precisely the type of political ideas which underpinned the cultural policies of the GLC – an aim which she pursued to the extent of abolishing that authority.

Municipal socialist cultural policies emerged in innovative and high profile forms in the early seventies, it has been argued, in the rise of post-1968 urban social movements – femini. revolts, environmentalism, gay activism, racial/ethnic min. activism and community activism. In Bianchini's view 'the new urban social movements saw cultural action and political action as inextricable' (Bianchini, 1993, p. 9). And cultural events, such as arts festivals formed part of wider strategies to promote public participation in new and imaginative ways, building 'Rainbow Coalitions' in support of municipal socialist agendas, across a broad range of interests, from women's groups, black and ethnic minority communities, gay and lesbian groups, environmentalists and community activists. The GLC, in the early eighties, for example, prioritised cultural policies to meet the needs of the unemployed, women's groups and gay men's groups, and the elderly together with Black and ethnic minority communities. Local participation in the arts – including community arts and media – was to be resourced, as well as the more established recipients of arts funding in the capital, such as opera and classical music, the visual arts, theatre and literature (Mulgan, 1986).

In addition to these political objectives, cultural policies included economic and employment objectives. In cities such as London, the traditional manufacturing and transport industries were shedding jobs during this period, as part of wider processes of economic restructuring. These job losses weakened the traditional constituencies of the Left, in the organised labour movement (hence the increasing interest in building new constituencies and forming 'Rainbow coalitions'). But local authorities such as the GLC, in the early eighties, were not only concerned with the political implications for the Left; alternative economic and employment strategies were high on the agenda in any case. And the cultural industries were identified as having a key role to play.

The cultural industries offered the potential for developing employment and training opportunities, both city-wide and as part of more locally based community economic development strategies. These employment and training opportunities ranged from community bookshops and publishing ventures, to local radio and recording studios, from photo co-ops to community theatre projects, from Black music co-ops to women's film distribution projects. And in addition, cultural events such as the GLC's 'Jobs for a Change' Festivals, provided mechanisms for stimulating public discussion and building support for these alternative economic and employment strategies (Mulgan, 1986). These were hugely popular events, attended and enjoyed by Londoners from across a wide spectrum. The GLC prised open the South Bank space (adjacent to County Hall) more generally, opening up the concert halls and public spaces to popular events as well as to more traditional forms of cultural expression. There were a million visitors in 1983, the first year of this open foyer policy.'When Ranking Ann was toasting free on the stage of the Queen Elizabeth Hall, Misty was making the County Hall car park shudder, ragas tintinnabulated through the Purcell Room and ice-cream vans sounded outside, one began to hear what a socialist city might sound like' in the view of one contemporary commentator (Widgery, quoted in Hewison, 1995, p. 239).

The GLC 's strategy for the Cultural Industries started from the fact that some quarter of a million people were employed in the sector, if the definition included electronic as well as traditional, popular as well as 'elite' forms. The sector included both large and powerful producers and distributors and numerous small independent producers (GLC, 1985). In particular, the GLC was concerned to support the latter (which was more realistic in terms of what might be achieved via municipal intervention) together with 'the communities of interest such as those of the women's movement, black culture and working class experience' (GLC, 1985, p. 170). The aim here was to enable them to be more successful economically (for example, via assistance with distribution to improve their viability) both to improve economic and employment opportunities and to promote cultural diversity.

The GLC identified aims and objectives which could be pursued at the city level, to promote local economic development as part of cultural strategies to maintain and enhance cultural diversity and popular participation. The London Industrial Strategy set out to achieve these employment and training goals within the framework of the GLC's overall aim to 'restructure for labour' – that is, to safeguard the pay, conditions and organisational strengths of the workforces in question. This was contrasted with market-driven approaches to restructuring, geared towards the requirements of profitability for capital. The London Industrial Strategy's aims were of course easier said than done, as a number of critics pointed out both at the time and subsequently (Gough, 1986). The chapter on the cultural industries in the London Industrial Strategy itself concludes by pointing to the limits of what could be achieved by local government action, also arguing the need for action at national policy level. Rather than putting the case for a 'free market in culture' – a free market which was, in any case a myth, it was argued – the government should 'be playing an enabling role' expanding public provision whilst ensuring 'genuine diversity and real choice' (GLC, 1985, p. 189). This was, of course, precisely not what the free-market policies of the Thatcher era aimed to do.

The GLC's policies for the cultural industries were relatively high profile in Britain, and to some extent at least, beyond. The arguments were presented as part of alternative economic and political strategies, in face of the growing dominance of New Right, free-market strategies in the eighties. By 1986 (when it was abolished) the GLC 's strategy towards culture and the arts was 'seen as the leading edge of a radical social and economic agenda' (Hewison, 1995, p. 238) combining agendas for economic as well as social, political and cultural transformation.

The GLC was not, of course, unique in its approach though. A number of municipalities developed comparable strategies to promote local economic and community development via cultural policies, as part of a transformatory agenda. In Britain, for example, Sheffield City Council developed a cultural industries quarter (Oatley, 1996). Building upon the strategy which was developed in the eighties, the cultural industries quarter, in a formerly run-down central location, was housing 125 businesses by the mid-nineties. The cultural industries quarter included projects such as 'Red Tape' providing recording facilities, together with training in recording and music technology, with the aim of meeting employment and training needs as well as contributing to cultural diversity in the city. There were a range of examples of creative strategies to promote both local economic development and to contribute to cultural creativity and diversity, elsewhere in Western Europe (Bianchini and Parkinson, 1993).

The increasing influence of market-led strategies approaches in Thatcher's Britain

Meanwhile, cultural policies were being developed as part of very different agendas, as part of free-market strategies for economic development in general and urban regeneration more specifically. And cultural policies were increasingly being promoted as part of image strategies – to construct urban images which might attract inward investors and tourism.

Prestigious arts festivals, major sports competitions and other high-profile cultural events were organised by urban policy-makers to

support 'internationalisation' strategies, and to enhance the cosmo-
politan image and appeal of their cities (Bianchini, 1993, p. 14).

In some cases, the overall impact of these ventures, in terms of
wealth creation and employment, was relatively small. In others, the
impact was actually negative, as cities were left to pay off the costs of
borrowing to invest in facilities for events which had failed to break
even (for example, the Olympics in Montreal, the Youth Olympics in
Sheffield – which made an operating loss of £10 million). Since the
Montreal Games, the Olympics have been far more profitable, a factor
which contributed to the intense rivalries and allegations of corrup-
tion surrounding the choice of locations, at the turn of the century –
the Olympics as big business. But that would presumably have
provided little comfort for those left to pay off the costs of previous
miscalculations.

Critics have also pointed to the use of cultural policies as distrac-
tions from the growing social polarisation and conflict within cities,
as a result of the economic restructuring processes of the eighties.
Harvey pointed to the use of cultural events as carnival masks, 'a spec-
tacular event (the Youth Olympics in Sheffield), or a palace of culture'
as part of a formula for urban regeneration, 'the serial reproduction of
the same solution' which generated 'monotony in the name of diversity' (Harvey, 1989, p. 21).

> Much of the imagination derived from the 1960s spirit of cultural
> revolt. In the very different context of the market-led (re)develop-
> ment strategies of the eighties, with unemployment and increasing
> homelessness, disempowerment and despair, of crime and social
> decay, these strategies appeared as an appalling social and political
> diversion. If a project generates employment it is almost certainly
> not for those already living there, if it brings money it almost
> certainly flows straight out again, and if it brightens the urban
> scene then it does so in the vein of a carnival mask that diverts and
> entertains, leaving the social problems that lie behind the mask
> unseen and uncared for. The formula smacks of a constructed
> fetishism, in which every aesthetic power of illusion and image is
> mobilised to mask the intensifying class, racial and ethnic polarisa-
> tions going on underneath (Harvey, 1989, p. 21).

Harvey's critique of these types of cultural event can be applied to
free-market approaches to the cultural industries, more generally.

Increasingly, in Britain, in the early to mid-eighties, public policies to support the cultural industries were needing to be justified in terms of market criteria, with less focus upon the wider social and cultural agendas. There was growing pressure to show value for money. The arts were more generally 'caught in an irresistible tidal change' it has been argued – in the words of the then Arts Minister, Richard Luce, 'the culture of wealth creation' (Hewison, 1995, p. 256). This applied to the cultural industries directly, as well as to the potential knock-on effects of the arts and culture – for example, in promoting tourism and improving the environment for inward investment more generally. 'The arts are to British tourism what the sun is to Spain' commented the Arts Council Chairman in a lecture entitled 'The Political Economy of Art', in 1985 (Hewison, 1995, p. 258).

Politicians' interests in the wealth-creating potential of the cultural industries were reinforced by the findings of an audit of the arts in the UK. Commissioned in 1985 and published in 1988, 'The Economic Importance of the Arts in Britain' concluded that overall the cultural industries had a turnover of ten billion pounds, amounting to 2.5 per cent of spending on goods and services. The cultural industries were key in generating invisible exports, the report argued, as well as for generating employment, both directly and indirectly, through the multiplier effect (including spending on food and drink and accommodation associated with tourist events for example) (Myerscough, 1988a).

The research included a detailed case study of Glasgow – a city which had experienced major problems of urban decay and rising unemployment as a result of industrial restructuring. In the eighties, policies to promote cultural revival were key to overall regeneration strategies. Glasgow offered a test-bed, then, within which to evaluate the potential contribution of the cultural industries to economic regeneration.

Myerscough concluded that the arts sustained over 14 000 direct and indirect jobs in the regional economy. The arts and tourism were closely linked. The study of Glasgow concluded that '(T)he attractions of Glasgow's arts facilities drew significant levels of spending into the regional economy from day and evening visitors and especially from tourists' (Myerscough, 1988b, p. 111). The arts, the overall report on the economic importance of the arts in Britain concluded, 'are a cost-effective means of cutting unemployment and they have a cost advantage over other forms of public sector spending' (Myerscough,

1988a, p. 7). In addition, the report argued, the arts have less tangible but no less real economic benefits, including benefits in terms of the city's image and hence attractiveness for business investors.

This last point is one which has been endorsed more widely by others, including others who have expressed reservations about some of the study's more ambitious claims. Hewison quoted Bianchini and Parkinson's conclusions to illustrate the point.

> The direct impact of eighties cultural policies on the generation of employment and wealth was relatively modest in comparison with the role of culture in constructing positive urban images, developing the tourism industry, attracting inward investment, and strengthening the competitive position of cities (quoted in Hewison, 1995, p. 278).

Myserscough's study of the 'Economic Importance of the Arts in Britain' has been criticised more particularly for being over-optimistic in relation to the economic role of the cultural industries themselves, and specifically in relation to the multiplier effects on employment generation.

There were, in addition, further questions raised by critics. If some cities were to gain competitive advantage would this, in any case, imply that others would be losers? And what about potential losers within cities? Birmingham City Council's strategy to promote cultural industries in the eighties was criticised, in the early nineties, on precisely such grounds – that the emphasis upon prestige cultural projects as a focus for urban regeneration was diverting scarce resources from much-needed social spending in key services such as education (Hewison, 1995). Beazley, Loftman and Nevin similarly concluded that although Birmingham's strategies to promote business tourism, leisure and culture had been acclaimed by the media and some academics, key criticisms had emerged as to who had actually benefited. Many of the jobs which had been generated were of low quality (for example, in catering and cleaning), and relatively few of the benefits overall had trickled down to the city's most disadvantaged groups, including those from black and ethnic minority communities. Finally, Beazley, Loftman and Nevin also pointed to the criticism that scarce public resources had been diverted away from basic services such as public housing and education. The authors concluded by drawing parallels with experiences of cultural strategies for urban regeneration in North American cities, which had been 'even more brutal and socially regressive' in terms of their social effects (Beazley *et al.*, 1997, p. 192).

Similar questions were raised about Glasgow's 'Miles Better strategy' – miles better for whom? Glasgow succeeded in becoming the European City of Culture in 1990. But were the benefits really reaching the bulk of Glaswegians, from the inner city outwards to the outlying housing estates? The city did succeed in attracting considerable numbers of additional tourists (Booth and Boyle, 1993). But how far did this impact upon the commercial and manufacturing sectors? Much of the employment growth which was being achieved has also been characterised as relatively low-paid and temporary, 'increasing the proportion of the population who have only a tenuous hold on the labour market' in the view of critics (Mooney and Danson, 1997, p. 85; Booth and Boyle, 1993).

Reflecting upon the overall impact of the Year of Culture, Booth and Boyle concluded that whilst Glasgow's image was successfully marketed, there was 'little evidence to support the argument that Year of Culture 1990 made a clear contribution to local economic development' (Booth and Boyle, 1993, p. 45). 'Can Year of Culture 1990 be described as "urban spectacle"' (to use Harvey's phrase). 'The answer is surely yes', they concluded (Booth and Boyle, 1993, p. 45). In the long term, they suggested, the real test would be the extent to which local groups could sustain the momentum and develop community-based roots.

Similar arguments have been applied to heritage and tourist industry strategies for local economic and community development in the Third World. As a special issue of the *Community Development Journal* in the early nineties asked after the carnival, what scope was there for community development? What were the local consequences – whether positive or negative – of the twelve-fold increase in tourism, over the previous three decades? How were the effects being measured – 'by more facilities and bars for tourists, or by more local children being able to enter school because their parents can afford it?' (Lovel and Fuerstein, 1992, pp. 337–8). 'What part do communities play in determining growth or control of tourism in the areas where they live and work? ' And how, the authors questioned, 'are gender relationships and roles, such as the employment of rural women as commercial sex workers in the tourism industry, affected by tourism?' (Lovel and Fuerstein, 1992, p. 338). This last question poses a further set of questions in turn, questions around culture, communities, identities and sexual health, which are explored more fully in Chapter 7.

As in the European context, there were questions as to who was actually reaping what economic gains, at local level. What types of jobs were being created, for whom and with what knock-on effects? Were local people being effectively confined to low-paid seasonal work? And were there negative impacts, such as the decline of traditional activities? Were local people being squeezed out of tourist areas by rising prices? And were there negative effects on the environment, effects such as water pollution, wild life harassment and the destruction of archeological remains? When tourists note such negative changes, they can move on to other tourist locations, the authors commented, leaving local communities to cope with the results – the smog which frequently covered the sacred mountain above the tourist resort of Chiang Mai in Thailand, for example (O'Grady, 1990, quoted in Lovel and Fuerstein, 1992). The UNESCO report on culture and development made the same point. Whilst tourism was fast becoming the biggest industry in the world and cultural heritage provided much of its lifeblood, cultural tourism had sometimes harmed the assets on which it fed (UNESCO, 1995).

Of particular relevance to the concerns of this book, the editors of the *Community Development Journal* Special Issue concluded their introduction by posing questions about the impact of tourism on local cultures, 'trinketisation' on the negative side, versus growing respect, on the positive side. What were the lessons for the development of tourism based upon just and sustainable interaction with local communities? And how might alternative approaches to tourism fit into wider strategies for community economic as well as social development?

Examples of cultural strategies for community economic development from both the First and Third Worlds

Whilst academics and policy-makers have been debating the varying implications of different strategies, communities and those who work with them, have been developing their own approaches in practice. Without underestimating the nature and extent of the challenges which they face, in the current context of the global predominance of the market-led paradigm, these community initiatives can, nevertheless, provide pointers towards alternatives. This section summarises examples of such alternative approaches, from both First and Third World contexts, together with a number of key caveats.

Alternative approaches to tourism have emerged in response to a number of concerns about the negative impact of mass tourism, including environmental concerns. Broadly defined, alternative tourism represents 'forms of tourism that are consistent with natural, social and community values and which allows both hosts and guests to enjoy positive and worthwhile interaction and shared experiences' (Eadington and Smith, 1992, p. 3). This all sounds fine, except that it is easier said than done. As critics have pointed out, 'Alternative Tourism means all things to all people' (De Kadt, 1992, p. 50) – 'an ideological concept, reflecting a contemporary social movement' (Nash, 1992, p. 224). Despite the criticisms, however, there has also been considerable agreement about the need to address the negative as well as the positive aspects of tourism, and to involve communities in all aspects, from planning to implementation stages (Marien and Pizan, 1997; Fennell, 1999).

At best, community participation may increase the local benefits, with profits accruing locally instead of flowing outside and ecotourism could have environmental benefits. But communities are not generally homogenous, and as a number of critics have pointed out, the benefits may accrue disproportionately to local elites (De Kadt, 1992; Fennell, 1999). And if it is not properly managed, the impact of ecotourism may be just as serious as the impact of mass tourism, if not even worse, it has been argued (Cater, 1994, p. 5).

How then have local community-based initiatives attempted to grapple with these challenges? *The Community Development Journal* Special Issue on Tourism and Community Development provided examples of alternative approaches, even within the constraints outlined in the editorial introduction. In Belize, for instance, the 'Programme for Belize' experiment set out to integrate environmental concerns with a form of planned tourism which ensured that 80 per cent of the revenues generated would be controlled by the government and local people (Wilkinson, 1992). The unique ecosystem and the Maya temples would be preserved, whilst local people would benefit economically, rather than the benefits going mainly to international hotel chains.

The case of Belize has been quoted in a number of contexts, both for the approach and aims and for the difficulties in implementation. Mowforth and Munt, for example, have questioned the extent to which local communities were actively involved, or the extent to which benefits were actually being spread beyond particular groups (Mowforth and Munt, 1998). And Fennell raised similar points

(Fennell, 1999). In their chapter in the *Earthscan Reader in Sustainable Tourism*, Munt and Higinio argued that ecotourism in Belize had actually gone awry. Whilst Belize 'basks in the warm praise it has received from the international community for being eco-friendly' (Munt and Higinio, 1997, p. 101) the reality was that 'much of the tourism industry is already in the hands of the country's small, but powerful expatriate community, estimated to number 1,500' (Munt and Higinio, 1997, p. 100).

The UNESCO report on Culture and Development provided another case study to illustrate the potential for local communities to benefit directly from projects which were promoting local economic development without undermining the local cultural heritage. This report cited the case of the indigenous people of Peru's Lake Titicaca, for example, where the islanders organised themselves to respond to the upsurge of tourism in ways which would improve local economic opportunities whilst preserving their local culture (World Council on Culture and Development, 1995).

The story of the islanders of Taquile, Lake Titicaca has been described in more detail in an account of 'Taquile's Homespun Tourism' (Healy and Zorn, 1993). This account – provided by Healy (a development worker) and Zorn (an anthropologist) who were themselves involved in supporting the islanders' initiatives – offers their perspective on the islanders' achievements – whilst recognising their projects' limitations and the wider constraints.

In response to growing numbers of young travellers in search of the 'unspoiled', from the seventies, the Taquilenos managed to develop their own facilities. The aim was to maintain local control and ensure that the potential economic benefits accrued to the local community. Although the islanders were relatively poor, they did have some homegrown assets to counterbalance their disadvantages. First, they had a tradition of community mobilisation. During the thirties they had organised savings to purchase the land from the landowners, and in the forties, they had mobilised collectively to build fishing boats. Secondly, in addition to this co-operative tradition, they also had handweaving and knitting skills within the community, skills which Healy and Zorn described as becoming widely recognised as 'superb'. In the late sixties, with the support of a Peace Corps volunteer (one of the authors, Healy) the islanders had drawn upon both these assets to create a co-operative to market their weaving. Despite some early hitches (including the problems which arose when a local manager embezzled the funds) the islanders soon discovered that there were indeed markets for their weaving, markets which included foreign buyers.

By the mid-seventies, Taquile began to attract foreign tourists, generally backpackers. In response, the islanders pooled their savings and bought motors for their boats, going on to set up co-operatives to transport tourists to and from the island. By 1982 the islanders' 13 co-operatives had displaced the private boat owners on the mainland. Although profit margins were low, at least the benefits were staying within the local community which was also benefiting from the improved transport to the mainland.

By the early eighties, in addition to the benefits from providing transport, the islanders were also providing accommodation for the tourists. Effectively every one of the two hundred or so families on the island was involved in having overnight guests, thereby benefiting from tourist spending, even if the sums involved were still very small.

As tourism grew over this period, so did the opportunities for generating income from the local textile crafts. The weavers set up a community-run store. In addition, the islanders went on to organise a community museum to display their older, better textiles. In these ways, tourism, Healy and Zorn argued, had reinforced rather than undercut the local culture, and the economic benefits had gone to the local community via co-operatives and community-run projects (Healy and Zorn, 1993). The island's very isolation enabled the islanders to keep outside entrepreneurs at arm's length and to control the flow of tourists, but their success was also partly due to their co-operative organisational experience and skills and their traditional craft skills. Taquiles's 'homespun tourism' could not necessarily be replicated elsewhere.

The story was, however, not one of unqualified success. Healy and Zorn pointed to the differential benefits which were accruing, arguing that 'women have not reaped a fair share of benefits from the tourist boom nor has their relative status on the island improved' (Healy and Zorn, 1993, p. 143). Tourism had both reinforced and undermined the communal tradition, they argued. Economic stratification had increased as some individual restaurant and store-owners and some individual boat owners had benefited from new opportunities.

In the longer term, Healy and Zorn questioned how far the community would be able to continue to benefit from tourism without being swallowed up by it. There were external pressures from private competitors, in the transport business, for example. 'Tourism is still controlled by the community, but as the stakes rise, that control cannot be taken for granted indefinitely', Healy and Zorn concluded (Healy and Zorn, 1993, p. 145). I have not visited the island personally (although I have had discussions with someone who visited in the late nineties) so I am not in a position to comment further.

Although the remote island location of Taquile made their experiences relatively specific, there are features which are far more widely spread. Crafts have provided the basis for community economic development more generally, including elsewhere in Latin America. In Colombia, for instance, there has also been a tradition of crafts production to build upon; and in Colombia there have been opportunities to support crafts in ways which benefit local community economic development and promote co-operative development (Goff, 1993). In Colombia too, the limitations and ambiguities of such strategies have also been apparent. The relatively high costs of raw materials and the relatively low prices for finished products were identified as a key problem; how to develop viable projects and sustainable livelihoods. As one potter commented in relation to the level of financial rewards involved, 'What I do is more like a sport than a job' (Goff, 1993, p. 130).

Programmes which set out to promote economic development through craft activities were facing major challenges, both external and internal, Goff concluded, as they struggled to build strong, empowering and self-sustaining organisations in local communities. They were striving to achieve economic viability, to compete effectively in wider markets, whilst paying fair wages. And in addition, the local craft development projects in Colombia which Goff was evaluating were also having to address conflicting cultural pressures. The local potters at the craft museum in Raquira, Colombia, for example, were apparently disconcerted to find that the coffee there was being served in locally made clay mugs, rather than in factory-made mugs. The potters themselves preferred the factory-made mugs, for their own use. Even those who were producing the crafts were not 'seeing the beauty they had made with their own hands', Goff concluded (Goff, 1993, p. 132). It was to address these negative attitudes towards the local culture that school programmes were set up, to encourage young people to develop more positive concepts of their culture and personal identities.

This, in turn, raises further questions and dilemmas. Who, after all, is to define these concepts and where should the boundary be drawn between the protection of local cultures and identities on the one hand, and their enforced fossilisation on the other? The points to emphasise here are simply these; that cultural strategies for community development are not necessarily confined to their economic aspects, nor are they necessarily confined within the framework of local opportunities and constraints. Both of these factors apply to the following examples of cultural strategies to promote community economic development in the UK.

Examples from Northern Ireland

From the late eighties and early nineties in Derry, Northern Ireland, a number of community based co-operatives were developed, as mutual aid and self-help responses to the problems of unemployment and social deprivation. The area had a history of high unemployment (then over 30 per cent in the city and over 60 per cent in the worst affected areas), a history which had been compounded by the effects of religious discrimination and civil unrest during the 'Troubles' from the end of the sixties. In Nationalist communities in particular, self-help and mutual aid were seen as essential, because of the State's perceived partisanship – the State being seen as providing for the needs of the Unionists rather than the Nationalist communities. This view of the State, as being unwilling or at least unable to provide long-term economic solutions was reinforced by the limited, short-term nature of those employment creation schemes which were being provided (Robson, 2000).

In this context, the Community Studies Unit at Magee College, University of Ulster (with European Union support) offered a course in Community Economic Development, to support local communities in developing their own community-based initiatives. The course won the 1990 Shell UK Prize for Open Learning in recognition of its innovative approach. As the video 'Between Street and State: Derry and the Co-operative Movement' demonstrated, community organisations used this facility to support the development of co-operatives. The aim was to generate local jobs and training through producing socially useful goods and services (that is, defined by local people as being needed by them). The course set out, as the video explained, to support local people in this by giving them 'the space and access to knowledge and access to resources to allow them to make new jobs for themselves' (University of Ulster video).

The community co-operatives in Derry and the surrounding area included a number of cultural projects such as a craft co-operative (Templemore Crafts Co-operative which embroidered Irish dance costumes) and a young musicians project (the North West Musicians Co-operative). The video provided the space for those who were directly involved to set out their own perspectives on what the co-operatives were each seeking to achieve, their strengths and potential and the challenges which they faced.

The Templemore Craft Co-operative, for example, was developed at the end of the 1980s by a group of women who had been on a temporary employment creation programme at a local community centre. Since this employment terminated at the end of the one year of the employment programme, they decided to explore ways in which they might build upon their existing skills to create jobs for themselves – in ways which would contribute to the community. They identified that they had skills in sewing and embroidery, skills which could be put to use in making Irish dance costumes. Having done their research, they were convinced that there was a market for these dance costumes – interest in Irish folk dancing was part of a wider and growing interest in Irish culture and the Irish language – and multinational companies were not interested in competing in this area. In this estimation of the potential market for Irish dance costumes, they were proved correct; there was indeed a market for these costumes, including an international market (especially in the USA). The women had the skills, then and they had determination. But as they themselves recognised, they had all the problems associated with any small business: they lacked capital and the necessary business skills.

For three years, their skills and determination won through, against the lack of capital and business training. 'I am very optimistic', reflected their spokeswoman, in the early part of the video. There was lots of commitment, she commented, and confidence that was spreading in the local community. 'If we can do it, others can.' The co-operative was succeeding in providing local jobs for the women, whilst contributing to local cultural developments.

Although there was support from the Community Studies Unit course, this could not, however, substitute for the support which they also needed in terms of capital investment and specific aspects of business training. Reflecting subsequently upon the experiences of these three years, the spokeswoman was still confident that the project could have been viable. The co-operative had won prizes and been featured on television as a success story, both in relation to community economic development and in relation to the contribution to local cultural development. But in the end, they were unable to sustain the co-operative. Despite the craft skills being there in the community, they had not been sufficiently supported, the women felt, either in terms of access to capital, or in terms of access to business training. Although particular initiatives thrived (largely through the skills, creativity and determination of local people) overall, state institutions were failing to provide appropriate back-up.

As a result, the spokeswoman argued, tourists in search of crafts were passing through the city of Derry and going across the border to Donegal, where crafts were being more effectively developed and supported by development agencies. Although she was disappointed at the Templemore Craft Co-operative's failure to survive, however, she was undaunted, concluding her comments by suggesting that government was now becoming more supportive, and by advising other co-operatives to 'hang on in there – keep going' (University of Ulster video).

The Templemore Co-operative's criticisms of government's (including local government agencies') lack of effective support were echoed by other commentators in the video. 'They have not put their money where their mouth is. There is lots of grand talk about co-operatives' it was argued, but the reality was somewhat more modest (University of Ulster video). The maximum grant at the time (early nineties) was £5000, which was described as a joke. There were also criticisms of the lack of resourcing for support agencies such as the Northern Ireland Co-operative Development Agency. At the time, this agency had only one accountant available to assist the different groups to develop their business plans. This was quoted as an example of the overall shortage of back-up services. Even the co-operatives which were surviving spoke of their struggles in the face of this lack of effective support.

But the positive side of this was precisely the 'tremendous sense of power' that these struggles had given the groups. This was certainly the view of the spokesman for 'Bookworm' the co-operative bookshop (an earlier co-operative development which had succeeded in surviving for 12 years). And there were clearly benefits over and above the benefits to those directly involved economically. The bookshop, for example, was also providing social and cultural benefits to the community. Similarly, the North-West Musicians Co-operative was providing the young people involved with opportunities to develop their musical talents, offering access to facilities which had previously been lacking. The Musicians Co-operative was an important success, with an international reputation as a multi-media co-operative. As one commentator reflected, in the past young people had felt forced to emigrate if they were determined to pursue their musical interests, because of the lack of facilities in the area. Now there were local opportunities.

Once again then, despite all the difficulties, these community economic development initiatives were demonstrating potential in terms of social and cultural objectives. Without in any way minimising these aspects, however, or minimising the potential in terms of local jobs and training opportunities, it is important to recognise the limitations of these initiatives, limitations which emerged only too clearly in both contexts, in the North as well as in the South. Even with increased government support, these co-operatives in Northern Ireland would still have had to address the range of challenges facing other small and medium-sized enterprises within the market economy. Achieving both economic viability and the provision of sustainable livelihoods for co-operative members was similarly problematic in both contexts.

Even so, community arts initiatives have continued to contribute to local economic development. In the context of Northern Ireland a study of the community arts in Belfast, published in 1998, provided evidence of this impact for community development and regeneration (Matarosso, 1998). This report, 'Vital Signs', was based upon a study of a sample of more than fifty projects covering the range of activities in the community arts sector in the city. The study found ample evidence of the positive contribution made by the community arts, a contribution which was clearly increasing, when the findings were compared with the results of a baseline study, carried out some eighteen months earlier. The community arts sector emerged as 'not only varied and vibrant, but vital' (Matarosso, 1998, p. ii).

The community arts sector provided employment and training directly. And in addition, participation in community arts was identified as a factor in increasing participants' subsequent employability, through skill development and as result of increased self-confidence. In addition to economic and employment effects, participation was also associated with spin-off effects such as increased involvement in other community development activities. Participation in community arts was especially valuable for, and valued by, young people. 'We are the young people of Belfast and we can change its future' (Matarosso, 1998, frontispiece).

This positive view of the potential contribution of the community arts sector to local economic development was reinforced by evidence from group discussions. Whilst the sector was very small in terms of employment in the city's economy as a whole – and the report was realistic about these limitations – there was consensus about its positive impact on the development of community enterprise. There was also widespread agreement that community arts activity assists the local economy by helping to strengthen people's employability. This was seen in terms of improving confidence and skills as well as encouraging people to take up further training and education opportunities.

Participants commented that their involvement in community arts projects had also made significant differences to their personal lives. People had developed new friendships and two-thirds said that participation in community arts projects had also enabled them to gain a better understanding of other people's cultures. Over 90 per cent of those surveyed commented that they felt more confident about what they could do, since being involved. The overwhelming majority felt that they had gained new skills including improved communication skills. Over half of those surveyed had gone on to some further form of training or education.

There were key benefits here, then, both in terms of potentially improving people's employment prospects and in terms of people's sense of themselves, their own lives and their personal sense of fulfilment. As one respondent commented 'It has increased my awareness of my identity in the joint community and (I'm) more aware of my rights as an individual.' 'I now know that I'm not just a number in the dole office', commented another (Matarosso, 1998, p. 20). In the context of Belfast, with its history of communal divisions, it was also potentially particularly significant that the report concluded that the community arts were contributing opportunities for cross-community co-operation.

Working on the wider scenario

The importance of making wide connections emerges as a key theme. Whether in the cities of Northen Ireland or the remoter islands in Peruvian lakes, cultural strategies for local economic development operate within the wider context of the market economy. This sets the overall framework within which community economic strategies operate, as they strive to balance the requirements of economic viability against local demands for living wages and sustainable livelihoods. Although remoter areas like Taquile may have remained relatively insulated, ultimately these wider factors do more generally have to be faced.

But this is absolutely not to conclude that there is nothing to be done. On the contrary, in fact, there have been growing pressures to challenge the inequities inherent in this wider framework, pressures which have included the Jubilee 2000 Campaign, launched by an alliance of non-governmental organisations including faith-based organisations, to tackle the debt crisis. Jubilee 2000 has made a major impact on public awareness of the issues in Britain, using imaginative campaigning tactics such as massive demonstrations in Birmingham in 1998 and in London in 1999. Similarly, Christian Aid's Ethical Trading Initiative has been campaigning to persuade British supermarkets to guarantee fairer conditions for overseas suppliers. Several major supermarkets have already responded to the call for a better deal for the people who produce food in the Third World, for consumption in the First. There have been a number of initiatives around these issues, demonstrating the capacity of non-governmental organisations and faith-based groupings to campaign to challenge the international causes of poverty and social inequality.

Amongst such initiatives to promote fairer trade, have been those to enable Third World producers of craft products to obtain fairer terms of trade. NGOs such as Oxfam, and a range of others, combine campaigning with practical initiatives, selling Third World craft products at fair prices in their shops and through their catalogues. And organisations such as Oxfam have also been organising alternative approaches to tourism, such as tours for their volunteers to enable them to visit Oxfam-sponsored community development projects in the Third World. This is tourism with a difference; the visits can result in deepening levels of understanding and commitment – a 'bridge of people' on both sides (Barraclough, 1992, p. 401). As a tour leader commented on her return, 'We must have more exchange; learn from experience on both sides. This is what an overseas tour is for; strengthening the bridge of people. I don't think there is any substitute for it' (Barraclough, 1992, p. 401).

This is in no way to underestimate the scale of the task to be addressed on a global scale. It is absolutely not being suggested that the initiatives of NGOs, by themselves, could offer effective long-term solutions. But they have already demonstrated the capacity to challenge prevalent orthodoxies, raising the possibilities of economic and cultural alternatives. The final Chapter 8 returns to some of these issues, and to the potential contribution of community arts and media to advocacy and campaigning at the global level.

6

Nationality, Ethnicity, Identity and Displacement: Cultural Strategies to Find Ways of Feeling 'at Home'

The previous chapter on cultural strategies and community economic development included some discussion of tourism, with a focus on the varying implications for the local host communities. This chapter shifts to focus upon those who travel, and more specifically upon those who travel in response to wider pressures, rather than predominantly as a matter of individual preference. Leaving the homeland raises potential questions about culture, community and identity and processes of change, both for those who leave and for their children, second generation migrants, raised in another place. How might cultural strategies for community development address the issues faced by migrants, refugees and asylum seekers, those who have left home, whether as a result of wider economic, social or political pressures? And how might such strategies take account of diversities within as well as between these communities as these develop and change over time including differences relating to gender, age, class and political perspective?

This chapter starts by summarising debates on nationality, ethnicity, culture and identity, in the context of globalisation. This sets the scene for the discussion of community development and cultural strategies drawing upon examples from community festivals and carnivals and from dance.

Nationality, ethnicity, identity and displacement in the context of globalisation

As Smith argued in the introduction to his study *Nations and Nationalism in a Global Era*, 'We are constantly being reminded that the globe we inhabit is becoming smaller and more integrated ... In short, our world has become a single place.' Yet 'we are witnessing a rebirth of ethnic nationalism, of religious fundamentalisms and of group antagonisms which were thought to have been long buried'. 'For many people a "narrow", fissiparous nationalism has become the greatest source of political danger in the contemporary world, while everywhere ethnic and national identities remain highly charged and sensitive political issues' (Smith, 1995, pp. 1–3). Smith himself went on to explore this apparent paradox of global interdependence and fissiparous nationalism from a socio-historical standpoint, with the aim of illuminating the underlying roots, symbolism, emotional depth and consequent continuing social hold of nationalism at the end of the twentieth century.

The world has become a single place (in terms of increasing communication as well as in terms of mobility on a global scale) and places, it has been argued, are no longer so clearly linked to peoples' identities (Morley and Robins, 1993). Yet despite this wider context of globalisation, for many peoples, the homes and associated identities lost through enforced exile or chosen migration remain vitally significant. They 'continue to resonate throughout the imaginations of displaced communities' (Carter, Donald and Squires, 1993, p. vii). If places are no longer the clear supports of identity (Giddens, 1990) and if the continuity of identity is broken, there may still be a need (perhaps even a greater need) to find ways of being '"at home" in the new and disorientating global space' (Morley and Robins, 1993, p. 5).

As Morley and Robins go on to demonstrate, however, this search for the home can also be exclusive, finding ways of being 'at home' which are rooted in intolerance of those who are not included – the 'other'. At the beginning of the twenty-first century, scarred as the past century has been by mass murders 'rationalised' on grounds of ethnic difference, the potential dangers of exclusivity and xenophobia have been only too evident. Exclusivity and xenophobia have made their own contribution to the magnitude of twentieth-century human displacement, through ethnic, racial and religious persecution, political turmoil and wars, causes as well as effects of displacement and 'homelessness'.

As Pieterse and Parekh have argued, in the context of debates on decolonisation, cultural pluralism and the existence of multiple identities can be viewed from several perspectives – as a situation which increasingly reflects the global human condition – a potentially creative situation, offering the possibilities for hybridisation and a cultural politics of global democratisation. Or conversely, from a racist perspective, cultural pluralism has constituted a 'social problem', a person with multiple identities being perceived as someone without place 'who did not belong, failing in terms of racial purity, or in twentieth-century terms, failing in authenticity' (Pieterse and Parekh, 1997, p. 15). Twentieth-century history provided illustrations to demonstrate that those who have been labelled in such terms can apply such labels to others and displace them, in their turn.

The sheer scale of human displacement is often not fully realised (Cernea, 1996). The number of refugees alone has been growing. In the early eighties there were some 11 million cross-border refugees according to United Nations High Commission for Refugees (UNHCR) estimates, a figure which had grown to some eighteen and a quarter million by the early nineties and was continuing to rise in the mid-nineties. In addition, by the late nineties it was estimated that between 20–22 million people were displaced internally, as a result of conflicts within the borders of their own countries, one of the world's most acute and growing problems (Hampton, 1998). In the eighties, the numbers of refugees and the numbers of internally displaced people grew rapidly, but then the pattern began to shift, partly due to the increasing difficulties which asylum seekers experienced when crossing international borders. (In Britain, for example, legislative changes have sought to reduce the entry of allegedly 'bogus' asylum seekers, and asylum seekers have been detained.) The underlying problems were not being solved, however, and huge population movements have continued, especially in Africa and more recently in Europe too, as a result of conflicts in the Balkans.

Even these figures exclude forcible displacements due to factors such as development projects – projects such as the construction of dams or transport systems which involve the resettlement of people living in the project area. All of these forms of human displacement would need to be taken into account along with economic migrations, the movement of peoples within and across national boundaries in search of livelihoods, in order to arrive at an estimate of human uprootedness. The United Nations estimated that the world's stock of international migrants rose from 75 million in 1965 to 119 million in 1990 (United Nations, 1997).

This is absolutely not to suggest that the experience of migrating in search of work, or being born to migrant parents in the second generation, is to be equated with the experience of being ousted by a development project, let alone with the experience of seeking political asylum, fleeing from ethnic, religious or political persecution. As the subsequent discussion demonstrates, there are significant differences, including significant differences in the ways in which governments and other agencies define the status of those concerned, labelling which then affects the allocation or withholding of resources (Cernea, 1996). And migration and displacement may be experienced very differently, depending upon social factors such as gender and other social differences (Chant and Radcliffe, 1992). The point is rather to emphasise the sheer scale of human displacement as a result of these varying economic, political, social and cultural factors.

The experience of 'homelessness' (in this broad sense of the term) has been associated with the experience of modernity itself – the project of modernity to make oneself somehow at home in the maelstrom of perpetual disintegration and renewal (Berman, 1983). Hall has written of the centring of marginality – the realisation that the experience of marginality and difference has been becoming more typical (Hall, 1987). From this standpoint, the question becomes not whether but how to make oneself 'at home'.

For those who have moved, whether as migrants or refugees, from choice or necessity or some combination of both, there are more specific questions too, including varying degrees of choice – or lack of choice – in relation to national identity and ethnicity, continuity and change, inclusion or exclusion, integration or cultural pluralism. There are implications here, for community development policies and programmes, and particularly so in relation to cultural programmes. Before moving on to explore specific examples of cultural strategies and practices, however, it may be useful to summarise alternative approaches to nationalism, ethnicity and culture, in order to clarify their varying implications for community practice.

As it has already been suggested, national identity and ethnicity are terms with contested meanings, relating to competing perspectives. A nation has been defined as a society that 'occupies a particular territory and includes a common identity, history and destiny' (Johnson, 1995, p. 188) and nationalism as the social process 'through which nation-states are formed by bringing national identities and political control into alignment' (Johnson, 1995, p. 188). But far from providing definitive answers, these formulations raise further questions in their turn, as the definitional summary goes on to point out, through the case of Yugoslavia, formerly one nation-state under communism and subsequently partly fractured, in relation to ethnic conflicts. How far the causes of this fracture can be understood in terms of ethnic conflicts, without reference to underlying economic, political and social factors (including factors related to the interests of external powers) has been contested. Western public opinion, in Chussudovsky's view, has been misled by the representation of the plight of the former Yugoslavia as the result of deep-seated ethnic and religious tensions. The break-up of the Yugoslav federation, he has argued 'bears a direct relationship to the programme of macro-economic restructuring imposed on the Belgrade government by its external creditors' (Chussudovsky, 1998, p. 243) contributing to the collapse of the national economy and the piecemeal dismantling of the welfare state. 'Secessionist tendencies feeding on social and ethnic divisions, gained impetus precisely during a period of brutal impoverishment of the Yugoslav population (Chussudovsky, 1998, p. 244). Meanwhile, the possibility, let alone the desirability of attempting to redraw the map of nation-states in the Balkans along ethnic lines has been the subject of tragically lethal contestation.

Nations do not necessarily coincide with nation-states, nor is this necessarily either possible or desirable. As Yuval-Davis has pointed out, membership of 'nations' can be sub-, super and cross states (Yuval-Davis, 1996).

> There are always people living within particular societies and states who are not considered to be (and often do not consider themselves to be) members of the hegemonic nation, there are members of national collectivities who live in other countries, and there are nations which never had a state (like the Palestinians) or which are divided across several states (like the Kurds) (Yuval-Davis, 1996, p. 11).

Most modern states are not nation-states in fact, in the sense that only some 10 per cent of United Nations states are without ethnic diversity (Smith, 1995). Smith quoted the cases of Belgium, Lebanon, Nigeria and India as examples of states with deep divisions in terms of such factors as language, religion and culture, or China, Mexico, France, Spain and Britain as examples where the whole society is not so deeply divided, but where there are still significant minority issues.

If nations cannot simply be defined in terms of nation-states, then how might they be defined? Here too there are varying approaches – in terms of such factors as language, territory, economic life, shared myths of common origin, culture and common destiny, factors which are not necessarily to be equated. Anderson approached the notion of nations in terms of 'imagined communities', although none the less powerful for being socially constructed, rather than being universal or eternal. Smith, in contrast, while recognising the relatively recent origins of nationalism, put greater emphasis upon the significance of earlier ethnic myths and symbols (Smith, 1995) historically embedded in the nation. Despite the capacity of nationalisms to generate widespread terror and destruction, in Smith's view, 'national identity, based upon these shared myths and symbols, continues to have positive relevance in the modern global context, satisfying peoples' needs for cultural fulfillment, rootedness, security and fraternity' (Smith, 1995, p. 159).

There is not the space here to develop debates on the 'nation' and nationalism, however defined, from whichever perspective. Nationalism has been seen as a progressive force linked to the development of nation-states and industrial economies in the nineteenth century, and the development of anti-colonial and national liberation movements in the twentieth. And conversely, nationalism had been seen as a reactionary force, a backward-looking movement, merely a protest against the status quo, 'or more precisely against "the others" who threaten the ethnically defined group', in the late twentieth century, as Hobsbawn, for example, has suggested (Hobsbawn (quoted in Smith, 1995, p. 9)), and nationalism has been seen as facing in both directions simultaneously, with varying possibilities, a modern Janus, in Nairn's view (Nairn, 1981); Nairn questioned the view that nationalisms can be separated out – positive and negative, 'good' and 'bad' nationalisms.

For the purposes of this chapter, it is important, simply, to emphasise the complexity and the contentiousness of these notions – the nation, nationality, nationalism and ethnicity – and to bear in mind their potentially exclusionary implications. The challenge, as it has been suggested in the context of Scottish debates around the time of devolution, is 'to avoid the kind of national pride that is associated with racial intolerance' (Arshad, 1999, p. 287) and to develop a more inclusionary approach to national identity. The Scottish National Party leadership's definition of who is to be regarded as Scottish – 'whoever lives in Scotland and feels Scottish' – may contribute, it has been suggested, to increasing opportunities 'to enable a meaningful dialogue to take place about racial justice in Scotland' (Arshad, 1999, p. 287).

There are perhaps, particular issues for the English to address, in relation to Englishness, given the historic associations with imperialism, and the continuing associations with racism, xenophobia and the Far Right of the political spectrum. There has, of course, been an alternative history, a history of democratic patriotism as well as reactionary patriotism: as Hill's essay 'History and Patriotism' pointed out, English revolutionaries in the seventeenth century referred to themselves as the patriots, just as French and American revolutionaries did subsequently (Hill, 1989). Down to the nineteenth century Chartists were radical patriots. But as Samuel pointed out, in the same collection of essays, patriotism has been a site or arena in which competing thought idioms contend (Samuel, 1989). By the late nineteenth century, by and large, the term had been captured by the Right, associated with empire and jingoism, not to forget sexism (women as the reproducers of empire) – despite efforts to pursue alternatives by the Left attempting to recapture the flag for more progressive agendas.

The possibilities for constructing a progressive post-colonial version of English nationalism – in the wake of devolution in Scotland and Wales – remains contentious. Others, meanwhile, have raised the possibility of focusing instead upon the plurality of national allegiances:

> the diversity of regional differences; the plurality of racial and migrant strains; the importance of gender loyalties; the complexity of religious affiliations; and the conflicting allegiances of class (Barnett, 1989, p. 149).

In similar vein, while recognising the inherent difficulties, Howe suggested that rather than focusing upon an alternative version of 'us' the one nation, the Left might more usefully begin 'with the fact of a mosaic of subjectivities; of gender, ethnic, regional, occupational and a myriad of other identities' (Howe, 1989, p. 137).

Focusing upon difference, though, raises further questions in turn; how to recognise differences of gender, ethnicity, region or class without categorising identities in essentialist, unidimensional terms – disregarding the differences *amongst* women, for example, or *amongst* ethnic communities, in terms of class, age and other social factors – and without undermining the possibililities of mutual support and solidarity across such differences. The notion of 'transversal politics', as an alternative approach to addressing these questions, was explored by Yuval-Davis in the concluding chapter of her study *Gender and Nation* (Yuval-Davis, 1996). 'Transversal politics', she suggested, offers an alternative to universalist approaches to politics which obscure difference on the one hand, and to identity politics which inhibit the development of solidarity across difference, on the other hand.

'Transversal politics', in contrast, addresses the questions of 'how and with whom we should work if/when we accept that we are all different' (Yuval-Davis, 1996, p. 125) recognising rather than obscuring differences such as those of gender, ethnicity and class (and accepting that there may be conflicting interests so that solidarity is not always possible).

For the purposes of this chapter, these are key questions – the notion that national identities are unidimensional needs to be challenged, together with the notion that national identities are essential, natural and historically given rather than socially constructed over time. Yuval-Davis has argued that '(T)he myths of common origin or shared blood/genes tends to construct the most exclusionary/homogeneous visions of "the nation"' (Yuval-Davis, 1996, p. 21). While approaches based upon the cultural dimension 'in which the symbolic heritage provided by language and/or religion and/or other customs and traditions is constructed as the "essence" of the "nation"' allow more scope for assimilation, she went on to argue, this still tended to have little tolerance of 'non-organic' diversity. The reality, in any case, is that national identities can and do change across time and space. Ethnic minority cultures need to be understood, as Chapter 3 suggested, not as frozen entities, but as processes, developing to and fro between the diaspora and the homeland.

Macdonald illustrated some of these processes of change in his study of Iu-Mien refugees from Laos, settled in the USA (Macdonald, 1997). The Iu-Mien migrated originally from China some two hundred years ago, forming a minority in Laos. Following the Vietnam War (during which many of them had supported the Royal Lao government rather than the Pathet Lao) some thirty thousand Iu-Mien migrated as refugees to the USA, although there were still minority communities in other areas including Burma, Thailand and Vietnam (exemplifying an ethnic group which had definitely not been a nation in the sense of a nation-state). Although Macdonald's study demonstrated that – as with so many first generation migrant communities – there was an initial 'myth of return' the Iu-Mien began to take on hybrid identities, with second generation Iu-Mien increasingly identifying with the USA. Many Iu-Mien became Christians, rituals changed, and the written language became romanized, although cultural links with South East Asia were maintained, and cultural exchanges developed. Far from being frozen as a culture, Macdonald referred to processes of cultural revival and cultural recreation amongst the Iu-Mien (Macdonald, 1997).

In her studies of Greek Australians, Bottomley has also explored the ways in which cultural beliefs and practices (including those pertaining to class and gender as well as ethnicity) are both reproduced and reformulated as they are handed down from parents to children (Bottomley, 1992). Here, Bottomley used the concept of 'habitus' – Bourdieu's formulation of the relationship between structure and agency as a dialectical relationship, between the structures which underpin people's circumstances, and people's own perceptions and actions. As Bottomley demonstrated, the 'habitus' of the second generation has been made up of the cultural beliefs and practices handed down from their Greek parents, in the social context of Australia, as these second generation Greek Australians have perceived this context and acted within it (taking account of changes such as shifts in social policy and increasing multiculturalism from the mid to late 1970s, changes which she related to increased self-respect among the offspring of immigrants). Second generation migrants have developed a variety of responses, from rejecting the parental culture to playing ironic parodies, 'celebrating their attributed "wogginess" in their own way', 'taking on a negative epithet as a symbol' (Bottomley, 1992, 135). Bottomley went on to explore other cultural responses and strategies, including an exploration of the role of dance, as potentially empowering for elderly Greek women, coming as they did from a culture in which elders danced, and dance was a communal activity. This raises issues for culture and community development, the focus of the following section.

Culture and change in the context of community festivals and carnivals

Community festivals have a history of contributing to cultural strategies for community development. The previous chapter referred to the case of the Craigmillar Festival, a well-known example, based in Craigmillar, a peripheral housing estate near Edinburgh, Scotland. Community development was seen to have been founded on the Festival, and community art was the foundation and spur for community development within Craigmillar (Craigmillar Festival Society, 1978). The Festival Society began from the frustration of a mother whose son wanted to learn the violin – in an area which lacked facilities, an area struggling with an image problem, associated with the negative stereotypes of social disadvantage. The community-based initiative which developed the Craigmillar Festival Society set out to provide opportunities for children to develop their talents and to give them a sense of their own history, tradition and culture, a sense of belonging and a pride in their own environment (Craigmillar Festival Society, 1978). The aim was also to combat what was regarded as an unfair bad image given by the press to Craigmillar as an area.

From these voluntary initiatives, the Festival Society obtained funding at the beginning of the 1970s, moving on to develop a range of other community activities, in addition to the annual festival. As well as other arts events, sub-committees organised continuing activities for children, the elderly and people with disabilities and other adults in the community. The Craigmillar Comprehensive Plan for Action, drawn up by the late 1970s included, in addition, sections on housing, planning and the environment, education and employment. Community arts, for the Craigmillar Festival Society was about asserting the democratic right of access to existing arts (including challenging the inaccessibility of much of Edinburgh's establishment art, and about participating in creative processes. It was also seen as 'a way of raising individual community and cultural confidence which complemented their other activities such as campaigning on housing, social welfare, education and economic development issues' (Orton, 1996, p. 178). The Craigmillar Festival Society has been famed for its achievements, 'providing the foundation for collective action around issues of concern within the community' (Orton, 1996, p. 178).

Festivals have been linked to the development of a sense of worth, confidence, identity and pride amongst communities of interest, as well as amongst communities based upon shared localities. Gay Pride marches in Britain, and the Gay and Lesbian Mardi Gras carnival in Sydney, Australia provide examples here. From a gathering in Sydney of some two hundred in drag in the sixties, and harassed by violence in the early days in the seventies, this carnival developed into a parade of six thousand by the end of the nineties, representing the diversity of the gay and lesbian communities standing up for their rights and celebrating their identities (Landon, 1999, p. 8).

This is not, however, to suggest that such cultural events have been unproblematic within the communities of interest in question. The London Gay Pride march, for example, has been contested, with varying views on the extent to which Pride should be a march, or a carnival-type event, the critics arguing that Pride risked becoming too commercialised – potentially downgrading the political aspects in the search for profits (Morris, 1999, p. 108). This point about festivals and carnivals being contested events has particular relevance in relation to the Notting Hill Carnival.

The Notting Hill Carnival

The roots of carnival – as a feast of 'topsy-turvydom' – have been traced from the Saturnalia of Roman times, through medieval times to the contemporary context. On the basis of studying carnival in contemporary Andalusia, Spain, Gilmore has described this as being 'above all a license for the expression of powerful feelings and impulses normally kept in check by a repressive moral code' (Gilmore, 1998, p. 3) – a licence for the exploration of roles and relationships such as those relating to status and gender. In Andalusia, for example, mock transvestism provided the space to explore and reaffirm gender roles (temporarily exchanging roles like masters and slaves in the Roman Saturnalia) whilst the 'coplas' – gossipy rhymes – mocked the existing status order. There are parallels here with the calypso, the creole musical form which was developed in Trinidad; calypsos attacked injustice and made fun of the powerful (Besson, 1989).

Carnival has been viewed as a form of sublimated class (and gender) struggle, challenging the existing social order (Scott, 1985) class conflict in the realm of the imagination. And conversely, carnival has been seen as ultimately culturally conservative: after the parody and farce of carnival, when the steam of social discontent has been released, traditional order is then reaffirmed and restored. This latter view was the interpretation which was offered by structuralist-functionalist anthropologists – carnival as a great 'joking' relationship which ultimately legitimizes the existing social order. Gilmore, in contrast, argued that Spanish carnival was 'both revolutionary and reactionary, subversive and conservative at the same time' (Gilmore, 1998, p. 4). Like the medieval carnival in its time, Spanish carnival was ambivalent and nuanced, challenging and contested.

This view of carnival as the site of continuing contestation can be applied to the Caribbean experience, both at home and overseas, including the contested history of carnival in London's Notting Hill. The Trinidad carnival, a key root, was itself the product of change and contestation, shifting from being a white settler event to becoming a celebration of ex-slaves' freedom. In the late nineteenth century carnival was associated with mass protest against the authorities and the white upper class, sometimes leading to organized confrontations between the police and lower-class blacks (Alonso, 1990). Since political independence, carnival has been seen as a state-dominated event, a means for promoting national integration and encouraging tourism, a view which has also been criticised in its turn for failing to recognise carnival's continuing openness and ambivalence (Van Koningsbruggen, 1997). From his study, Van Koningsbruggen concluded that carnival was still 'an arena in which contesting values and ideas are dramatised' (Van Koningsbruggen, 1997, p. 269) expressing both alliance and enmity, consensus and conflict at one and the same time. Carnival, in his view, had a life of its own, as a cultural event. For the numerous black Trinidadians who come home from North America for carnival, this offered an enjoyable way of renewing social ties, reaffirming a community identity which had itself been subject to processes of change.

So how did the contested arena of the Trinidad carnival come to London's Notting Hill? The Notting Hill Carnival was first staged in 1966, as a white event, initiated by a local community leader and former community worker. The original aim was to stage a series of cultural events and street processions, based on the notion of an English 'Fayre', to bring different cultural groups together in an area where there had been racial tensions (with riots in 1958). In the words of one of the original organisers the intention was to 'bring some colour, warmth and happiness to a grim and depressed neighbourhood' and to 'correct the image of the Notting Hill area, which had been unjustly castigated by the national media as a den of prostitution, drug addiction and political extremism' (Cohen, 1982, p. 25). This would be a revival of a traditional annual fayre, with events such as drama, folk singing, dancing and masquerades, including characters from the novels of Charles Dickens. The first procession was led by an Englishman masquerading as Queen Victoria.

From these origins as an English community festival, the Notting Hill Carnival became linked to community struggles particularly around housing, exorbitant rents for poor housing and racial discrimination. This was a key issue for West Indian immigrants in the area, the majority of whom had come from Trinidad (immigrants from Jamaica and other islands tending to settle initially, in other areas, such as Brixton). Cohen's account describes the housing situation in the area as a 'nightmarish jungle' (Cohen, 1982, p. 28) which affected black people particularly badly, although working-class whites were also affected. Joint black–white associations were formed to work together on these issues, including the London Free School, which aimed to promote co-operation and understanding through education and cultural activities (including those associated with preparation for carnival), while also working together on shared socio-economic problems. These latter activities included a household survey to reveal the extent of housing problems in the area, and to develop collective housing struggles, in response (O'Malley, 1977).

The first carnivals represented the ethnic diversity of Notting Hill, albeit within a predominantly British framework. In the words of one of the original organisers, local people 'regardless of race, colour and creed, have a common problem: bad housing conditions, extortionate rents and overcrowding. Therefore in this misery, people become one' (quoted in Cohen, 1982, p. 31). The carnival itself, however, was about enjoyment rather than misery. The housing problem emerged via song, dance and musical parody – which is not, of course, to imply that community campaigning was not also promoted through these connections with carnival.

By the 1970s, Cohen described carnival as having become almost exclusively West Indian, with Trinidadian features such as steel bands and calypso lyrics of social comment and criticism. In this period, black political consciousness heightened locally, as well as more widely, in response to a number of factors including police confrontations in the area. In this context, Cohen pointed out, carnival songs were often used to express criticism and discontent against the police and public racism. While these lyrics could be humorous, they were expressing serious underlying tensions (tensions which were expressed in a particularly serious and bloody confrontation between the police and young black people in 1976). The steel band has been associated with sounds of protest against injustice and oppression as well as with sounds of pleasure. Thus, it has been argued:

> The Notting Hill Gate Carnival in London has come to reflect the love–hate relationship that patterns the conflict between young Afro-Caribbean blacks and the established order in Britain' (Pryce, 1990, p. 130).

From the start, then, the Notting Hill Carnival exemplified processes of challenge and change, demonstrating carnival's potential for promoting social integration, a vehicle for social control, on the one hand, and conversely for articulating political opposition in varying forms, whether in relation to community housing campaigns and/or anti-racist struggles against discrimination, oppression and police violence. Moving from an English August Bank Holiday fayre,

to a Trinidadian carnival, the Notting Hill Carnival went on to express
the culture and politics of other Caribbean groups and especially of
second generation Afro-Caribbeans, Black British youth with more
interest in Reggae (building upon cultural forms developed in
Jamaica). Carnivals in the latter part of the seventies included both
steel bands and reggae-music, with reggae-music being employed, as a
symbol to express resistance against the police, who were seen by the
youths, in Pryce's words, 'as enforcers of institutional class rule and
social control' (Pryce, 1990, p. 130). Cohen has also pointed to challenges from women, as well as from young men, at this period. 'Lion
Youth' for example, was a small masque group, first organised in 1977
by two women who argued that carnival was too dominated by
men, despite the fact that it was women who were actually doing
most of the preparation and work. 'Lion Youth' challenged this male
domination.

Summarising these experiences Cohen concluded that carnival had
been transformed through the participation of a new generation of
British-born youth who had developed new themes and new artistic
forms, in response to the economic and political realities of contemporary Britain (Cohen, 1980). 'The Notting Hill Carnival, like all other
carnivals, has been changing throughout its history and will continue
to do so as long as it lasts' in Cohen's view (Cohen, 1993, p. 8).
Carnival was both cultural and political, although the balance
between the two – and the extent to which carnival might be taken
over and/or commercialised if external financial support was provided
– was contested, as the split of the carnival committee into two separate committees in the second half of the seventies illustrated. In
Cohen's view, the debate focused not so much about whether carnival was expressing political issues, but more about the extent to which
political messages should be more or less explicit – although other
accounts of this split include a number of factors, to explain these
divisions in the leadership, focusing too upon the gap between both
leaderships and black youth (Pryce, 1990).

Carnival takes place over two days in the year, but these two days
have developed as the culmination of a whole year of activities in
preparation. Cohen referred to these events as a 'series of gatherings
in fetes, launching balls, seminars, exhibitions, calypso tents, gala
performances and educational sessions for the young in, as well as out
of school' (Cohen, 1993, p. 5). These linked into political and community activities more generally, networks based around carnival
activities which served as communication systems between the

various parts of the community (in different neighbourhoods) facilitating the exchange of information and the discussion of political problems and strategies.

To illustrate these interconnections, Cohen referred to the wide community influence of leaders such as the La Rose brothers, who were actively involved in carnival (with a sound system 'Peoples War'). For some time Michael La Rose was vice-chairman of the Carnival Development Committee. He was also manager of New Beacon Books (a bookshop specialising in Black, anti-racist and Third World books). He was associated with the Black Youth Movement, the Black Students Association and the Black Parents Association. Cohen summarised the immense contribution which the La Rose brothers made both to carnival and to Black Politics, community activities and education more generally as combining 'art and politics to educate as well as to guide youth forces' (Cohen, 1993, p. 118).

For Pryce, there were inherent contradictions in the Notting Hill Carnival, tensions between carnival leaderships which were pro-youth whilst also being involved in controlling young blacks. In the mid-seventies, he argued, carnival expressed 'two opposing tendencies within a unity of form; one towards a symbolic affirmation of the status quo, and the other towards expressions of mass resistance, protest and violence' (Pryce, 1990, 145). Since that period, Pryce argued, despite some lingering anxieties, the event has been more containing of young blacks, with an absence of 'vocal utterances by the leadership reflecting the hidden ideological and structural contradictions of the event' (Pryce, 1990, p. 130) a view which led him to question at what cost this had been achieved.

The thirty-fifth carnival, at the end of the nineties, illustrated these continuing tensions. Media reports remarked upon the range of musical activities (with 75 bands and 40 sound systems) and the range of political issues which were raised (floats included Caribbean banana farmers protesting about the negative impact of international trading policies). The continuing struggles against racist policing were marked by the tribute to Stephen Lawrence, the black teenager whose murder by racist thugs had been so inadequately investigated by the police (the subject of a public inquiry which had reported earlier that year). And the whole event was watched by more than seventy closed-circuit television cameras; as the *Guardian* commented in an article headlined 'Police Cameras Ring Notting Hill', 'Few of the revellers would have realised that almost every move was being watched a few miles away at Scotland Yard's central London headquarters, via the

CCTV cameras' (Dodd, *Guardian*, 1999, p. 9). The Carnival had been anticipated to have exceptionally large crowds of some two million people in 1999, as a result of another cultural event – the huge success of the film 'Notting Hill', ironically a film which had been criticised for portraying the area as effectively all-white, with no significant black characters, let alone positive references to carnival, the largest street festival in Europe .

For the author, as a white person, the Notting Hill Carnival has also been significant in varying ways, changing over time. As a social policy student in the sixties, the housing survey which was organised via the London Free School provided student volunteers with a formative introduction to new approaches to community development through collective action. In more recent years, in the nineties, attending carnival has been a remarkable experience, a cultural event which has also been offering white people opportunities to renew friendships and re-establish contacts, to network informally and share information and ideas, including information and ideas about community and workplace strategies. But what does this say about the current state of carnival as a changing and contested event?

Dance

Like carnival, dance has also been associated with power relations and with challenges to these. Dance in the Greek theatre was linked with cults of Dionysos, cults which were regarded as subversive (Bottomley, 1992). Plato disapproved and banished it from his Republic. Christian churches too have issued various prohibitions over the centuries – although people have continued to dance, despite these prohibitions (Bottomley, 1992). In Britain, rave has provided a contemporary example of a dance culture which has been perceived as subversive. The Exodus Collective – an alternative community and social development collective which developed out of raves near Dunstable has been highly contentious, despite its community benefits (Malyon, 1998). The comment attributed to the libertarian socialist Emma Goldman 'If I can't dance, I don't want to be part of your revolution' posed this potential connection between dance and the subversion of the existing social order, in a previous era (quoted in Bottomley, 1992, p. 71 and Yuval-Davis, 1996, p. 132).

And conversely, dance can represent a ritual of social solidarity. As O'Connor has pointed out, 'anthropologists and dance historians have pointed to the important role which group dancing plays in generating community solidarity' (O'Connor, 1997, p. 157). She referred to the work of Radcliffe-Brown and Rust, for example, amongst others, to illustrate this point (Radcliffe-Brown, 1964; Rust, 1969). Dance has potential significance then, in terms of social power.

Potentially subversive or potentially contributing to the release of tension and the promotion of social harmony – or both – dance has nevertheless been relatively marginalised as a cultural theme, it has been argued. With the significant exception of anthropological studies, dance has been 'largely silenced in industrialised societies' (Bottomley, 1992, p. 73). Dance has also been described as 'invisible', not in the sense that it is actually unseen, but in the sense that non-verbal forms of communication such as dance do not fully register in the general consciousness. In a culture in which verbal forms are prioritised, non-verbal forms are relatively marginalised (Ward, 1997). Such attitudes to dance, it has been argued, form part of a broader cultural framework in which the body has been disregarded, even despised (Seidler, 1989). But dance offers alternative ways of communicating, non-verbally and expressively. As previous chapters have already argued more generally, cultural strategies have this potential for communicating at different levels, recognising the significance of the sphere of emotions as well as the sphere of reason.

Whether visible or invisible to academics, for the purposes of this chapter the focus is upon the ways in which dance actually has been, and continues to be significant in relation to questions of community and identity, both changing and contested over time and space. Just as dance has been seen as a means of reinforcing community identities, dance has also been seen as a means of reaffirming and renewing a sense of community for those who have been displaced. O'Connor's study of Irish Set Dance in urban Ireland provides an illustration (O'Connor, 1997).

The increasing popularity of the rural set dance in urban Ireland may be explained by a number of factors, O'Connor suggested, including the increasing popularity of dance more generally, and the specific interest in the revival of indigenous cultural forms in a country which was until relatively recently colonised. This interest in the Irish language and cultural forms has already emerged in the previous chapter in relation to local economic development (such as the development of co-operatives making Irish dance costumes). In the contemporary city, these traditional rural dances were also being enjoyed for the group nature of the activity, working as part of a team, 'communicating with the people that you are dancing with' whether verbally or not (O'Connor, 1997, p. 156). As one of the women in O'Connor's study commented, the dance creates a great feeling of community.

This focus upon 'community' did not necessarily represent an attempt to re-create some romanticised version of rural community in the contemporary city, however. Although some women did refer back to connections with the rural past (and their own families' rural connections in a country in which rural–urban migration has been a relatively recent phenomenon), the reality seemed to be more complex. The rural connections also carried more negative associations, including connotations of being 'square', drab, out of date and culturally conservative. For women in urban Ireland, set dancing offered a safe space for women to socialise in an inclusive and friendly environment, 'rural space' in the city, but without demanding 'the continuous duties and obligations attached to being members of a rural community based upon local residence' (O'Connor, 1997, p. 168). As O'Connor concluded:

> (P)erhaps there is a little irony in the fact that a dance form which is associated with tradition and rurality is a source of pleasure, freedom and individual expression for women in the city in conditions of high modernity (O'Connor, 1997, p. 168).

Similar ambivalences emerge from Bottomley's exploration of the role of dance amongst Greek-Australian women. Greek folk dancing has been seen as having been integral to rural life – an important ritual of solidarity which had also been associated with national independence and freedom. In the contemporary context, the film of Kazantzakis's novel *Zorba the Greek* has been taken to symbolise the free individualist, liberating the uptight Anglicised rationalist through dance, a myth which has been taken up to promote tourism. Whilst traditional Greek dancing has become commercialised – a tourist attraction – tourism has also resulted in the mushrooming of discos, offering young Greeks what they have seen as a more glamorous and sophisticated alternative (Bottomley, 1992).

Amongst Greek migrants to Australia, however, traditional group dancing has had continuing relevance, and this has been particularly so for older women. Elderly migrants stand to benefit from group activities which counter their isolation and marginalisation. This is particularly at issue, Bottomley argued, in a consumer society like Australia in which the elderly are more marginalised than they have been traditionally in Greece. Dance has other obvious benefits, including the health benefits of movement and group exercise.

In Greece, dancing was not traditionally confined to youth; children learnt to dance by following their elders. Whilst modern disco dancing in Greece is increasingly confined to the young, Bottomley pointed out, older Greek-Australians do still dance at family and community festivities. This, she argued, can have particular significance; dance can have cathartic effects.

> In personal terms, the euphoria of dance can help to dissolve some of the tensions and contradictions that arise from the experience of migration. It can also help in reasserting identity – as a Greek, or as someone from a particular region or village.

What Erikson calls the 'psychosocial identity' is constructed in a particular place and time. Although identities develop and change, a stable basis is important as a touchstone for such changes (Erikson, 1968). 'Collective participation in activities such as Greek dance can reactivate the earlier bases of identity formation. In fact dance can stimulate memory in a particularly evocative way' (Bottomley, 1992). This offers important advantages for older people's health and well-being. Bottomley went on to provide an example of such memory stimulation from an older Limnian woman who told her that when she was dancing she felt that she was not in a Sydney dance hall at all – she was back at home in her village; she could 'even smell the pine trees' (Bottomley, 1992, 141).

This kind of embodiment of memory, Bottomley concluded, could 'work powerfully against the silencing that marks both migration and ageing' (Bottomley, 1992, p. 142). Dance, in this context, offers much more than exercise to elderly migrants, affirming their socio-cultural identity, 'formed in their pre-migration habitus, but also affected by the experience of migration and of minority status' (Bottomley, 1992, p. 142). For these reasons Greek community workers in Sydney were encouraging elderly people to dance. The celebration of their cultural memories by older Greek-Australians who formed dance groups, in response, was 'by no means a retreat to ethnicity', Bottomley argued, but 'a positive statement of another way of becoming old' (Bottomley, 1992, p. 143).

Change and hybridity emerge as key themes too, in relation to Indian dance in the Western city. Classical Indian dance, it has been suggested, may and often does:

fulfil a 'community' function by providing Indian migrants with a positive sense of belonging, not only by symbolising a valorised heritage to which they can lay claim, but also by providing occasions when they can meet in an 'Indian' context, where a sense of community and identity can be participated in, constructed and affirmed (Roy, 1997, p. 74).

But Indian dance forms have not remained frozen in the Western city. In Roy's view, dance can also express hybridity; a new form is created from the constituent cultural parts. And through this hybrid dance, differing groups may come to express and work through their varying experiences of life as British Asians.

As it has already been suggested, minority communities do not simply share a common culture, to start with. Despite differences of class, religion and previous histories in their areas of origin, however, Subramanyam found ways of working with South Asian women, using South Asian dance forms – classical, folk, creative and contemporary forms – to address their experiences of isolation and depression in Britain (Subramanyam, 1998). Drawing upon the familiar to provide women with collective experiences which are comfortable and culturally acceptable, traditional forms have been reinvented.

The use of myth, song and dance and other forms of non-verbal expression has a therapeutic history. Stories and myths, it has been argued, provide powerful metaphors to facilitate personal development (Bartal, 1997). Until recently, however, disabled people in the South Asian community were not usually involved in dances associated with community festivals. This represented lost opportunities, it has been argued, because people with disabilities, including women with learning disabilities, could benefit greatly from participating in such experiences of dance (Subramanyam, 1998). On the basis of her work providing dance movement therapy with South Asian women in Britain, Subramanyam concluded that offering opportunities for women with learning disabilities to perform such dances was enriching and empowering, providing 'a sense of community and a sharing of one's cultural forms with others' (Subramanyam, 1998, p. 186). Here too, there are ironies in the use of traditional cultural dance forms, recreated to address aspects of contemporary life in modern Britain.

Dance and movement therapy has also been used in working with those of the displaced who have been most severely traumatised, including those who have sought asylum, after experiencing political torture and organised violence. Despite the passing of several covenants including the 1984 United Nations Convention against torture, human rights abuses including torture continue to be practised on a global scale. In addition to the physical effects, the survivor who flees into exile is then at risk of experiencing further traumas, experiences of loss, isolation and loneliness. Some find support in their communities; others have no communities to turn to in exile. Torture survivors may find themselves in an alien society where they may not speak the language, without friends or family, living in a state of legal limbo as they await the outcome of their asylum application – a cause of yet more suffering in Britain (Callaghan, 1993).

Dance therapy has not, of course, been the only cultural means for working with those who have suffered the trauma of displacement as refugees and asylum seekers, following organised violence and torture. Drama and video have been helpful, for example, in a range of contexts from refugee camps outside the country of origin to communities affected by internal displacement. In Mozambique, for example, the use of participatory theatre was developed in areas which had been ravaged by raids during the conflicts of the 17-year civil war (during which a third of the population was internally displaced) (Scott-Danter, 1998). Participatory theatre was used as part of strategies to support individuals and communities suffering from post-Traumatic Stress – to recover ways of building trust, respect and co-operation. In a society rife with profound distrust, fear and anger rooted in prolonged conflict, Scott-Danter concluded, participatory theatre was a useful medium to bring people together. Participatory theatre has also been used in Britain, working with detainee asylum seekers, who have found the process therapeutic, as well as offering a means for engaging the wider public in dialogue about the issues and fundraising for the work of refugee support groups (Norris, 1997).

Dance therapy has particular relevance, too. As Callaghan has argued, working with survivors of torture often involves working with people from many different cultures and languages. 'Movement therapy enables verbal barriers to be transcended' (Callaghan, 1993, p. 414) (although non-verbal differences do still need to be taken into account). Torture typically involves assaults on the body – the physical and psychological site of destruction – another factor in the importance of movement therapy as a means of reaffirming people in their bodies. And movement therapy aims to treat mind and body together, enabling the survivor to 'express the unverbalizable' (Callaghan, 1993. 416), providing the space to 're-own the body and reinvest it and the world with meaning' (Callaghan, 1993, 417).

Having argued for the potential of movement therapy with refugees and asylum seekers, however, Callaghan in no way underestimated the inherent difficulties. Reflecting upon her experiences of working with a group of asylum seekers in Britain, Callaghan referred to the limbo which affected both the individuals concerned and the group process (Callaghan, 1998). The men who had all been imprisoned and tortured in their homelands were in a transient state, trying to cope with experiences of exile and loss, fears and anxieties for relatives and friends left behind, and uncertainty about their situation, applying for refugee status in Britain. These factors, together with the practical difficulties of coping with issues such as housing and benefits problems meant that their attendance at the group was erratic. These fluctuations in group membership aroused memories of separations and disappearances, Callaghan suggested, further compounding the sense of limbo in the group.

Despite these difficulties, over the course of a year, Callaghan concluded that for the group as a whole and for specific members 'the movement provided a focus and a means of expression' (Callaghan, 1998, p. 38). For some refugees, she argued 'movement is a helpful means of expressing and containing feelings' (Callaghan, 1998, p. 39) although for others, as she went on to argue, dance and movement was inappropriate – the feelings were too overwhelming to be expressed and contained in these ways.

Like dance groups for older Greek-Australians, dance movement therapy has relevance for community development in the context of concerns about community, ethnicity and identity. And as in the case of dance groups for older Greek-Australians, there are also links to concerns about individual and community health and well-being. Although there are key differences in their varying situations, being displaced for whatever reason, whether as a migrant or as a refugee or asylum seeker, poses particular challenges to people's physical, mental and sexual health, challenges arising from changes in lifestyle – diet, living and working conditions, poverty, stress, isolation and loneliness to name some of the more obvious factors. Some of these more specific issues relating to health and well-being emerge in the following chapter.

7
Cultural Strategies for Health and Well-being

Health and well-being are central to notions of development. The United Nations Human Development Report defined human development as 'a process of enlarging people's choices by empowering them to achieve their potential to lead a long healthy life' as well as 'to acquire knowledge and to have access to resources and opportunities for a decent standard of living' (UNDP, HDR: 1990). Human Development indicators such as access to safe water to drink, food, shelter, peace and security and livelihoods that enable people to raise healthy children are as key to life expectancy – itself a key indicator of Human Development – as access to health services themselves.

The promotion of health has been conceptualised both as a measure of human development and as a means for promoting economic and social development. A healthier population is potentially a more productive population, it has been suggested. As the World Health Organisation's Global Strategy for Health for All by the Year 2000 argued, the aim was for all people in all nations to attain such a level of health that 'they are capable of working productively' as well as 'participating actively in the social life of the community in which they live' (WHO, 1981, p. 15).

As the 'Global Strategy for Health for All by the Year 2000' went on to argue, these are collective issues as well as individual issues, and 'people have the right and duty to participate individually and collectively in the planning and implementation of their health care. Consequently, community involvement in shaping its own health and socio-economic future, including mass involvement of women, men and youth, is a key factor in the strategy' (WHO, 1981). What this apparently widespread view about the importance of community participation has actually meant, in practice, however, has been more

155

problematic and contested. As this chapter will argue, there have been competing approaches to the promotion of health with varying implications for cultural strategies for health and well-being.

This chapter starts with a brief summary of competing approaches to the promotion of health and well-being in the community, using community media to transmit messages about healthy living for individuals (addressing questions of diet, exercise, smoking, alcohol and drug abuse, for example) or setting these messages in their wider social context, addressing underlying issues of poverty, inequality and relative powerlessness. This sets the framework for the discussion of cultural strategies for promoting health and well-being through facilitating community participation and empowerment. Finally the chapter explores the contribution of community media to addressing issues of sexual health – issues of life and death – taking the example of a specific training programme 'Stepping Stones'. This programme was developed in Uganda, using video and drama to run workshops within communities on HIV/AIDS, communication and relationship skills, addressing issues of power and empowerment.

Competing approaches to community health promotion

The World Health Organisation's Global Strategy for Health for All by the Year 2000 built upon the declaration of the 1978 Alma-Ata Conference on Primary Care. The main thrust started from primary care, involving individuals and their families and communities. Community involvement came to be seen as 'a basic right which all people should be able to enjoy' – and as a mechanism for improving the efficiency and cost-effectiveness of limited health resources, enhancing 'the impact of investments in the health sector' (WHO, 1991, pp. 6–7). Whilst there was overall agreement about the importance of community involvement in health, however, there were differences of perspective about what this was to mean in practice.

Participation was, in fact, perceived in three different ways. Community involvement was emphasised in terms of the contributions which communities could make, whether in terms of materials and/or voluntary labour. Participation was perceived in terms of developing appropriate organisational structures. And community participation was conceptualised in relation to community empowerment 'enabling people to decide upon and take the action that they believe is essential for their development' (WHO, 1991, p. 5). While there were overlapping interests, there were also inherent tensions between these varying approaches, as will be suggested subsequently in this chapter.

The third of these perceptions of WHO policies for community participation to achieve 'Health for All by the Year 2000' was particularly relevant in relation to the development of the community health movement in Britain, as well as in the development context. As Jones and Macdonald pointed out, the principles underlying the Alma Ata Declaration, participation equity and intersectoral collaboration were all, in one form or another, preoccupations of the community health movement (Jones and Macdonald, 1993). While the community health movement which developed in the UK took up the issues raised by Health for All by the Year 2000, the movement itself pre-dated this, however, with roots in community development and self-help initiatives and campaigns from the 1960s, including roots in campaigns around women's health, black and ethnic minority action groups' initiatives and the work of health professionals themselves, organising to work with communities in new and more empowering ways (Jones, 1991).

The community health initiatives which developed from the community health movement from the late 1970s, drew upon these wider strands and related social movements. By the late eighties there were between thirty to forty community health projects in Britain, specifically committed to: a positive view of health, a collective approach to the social causes of ill health, better access to health information and resources, increased self-confidence amongst people, better relationships between clients and health professionals and greater influence over health policies and allocation of resources (CDF, 1988). Broadly the focus was upon empowering communities to challenge the underlying social causes of ill-health, poverty, inequality, inadequate housing and unsafe working conditions, as well as focusing more specifically upon redressing the unequal distribution of health care per se. The overall approach was holistic, encouraging people in disadvantaged communities to identify their own needs and to work collectively towards achieving these, through whatever combination of self-help, advocacy, inter-agency work and/or campaigning activities (CDF, 1988; Smithies, 1990). Community development health projects have worked with communities defined geographically and with communities defined in terms of common interest (including women's health projects and black and minority ethnic health action) (Sidell, 1997). And community health promotion programmes have been developed city-wide (as in the case of Healthy Sheffield 2000 for example) (Thornley, 1997).

As has already been suggested, however, community participation in health – like community development more generally – could be, and has been conceptualised in varying ways, depending upon the differing perspectives of those concerned, whether from the community health movement and/or from government and health-care agencies. Commenting on the apparent enthusiasm for user participation and community involvement, Farrant argued that:

> (T)he belated interest of the NHS in community development needs to be seen in relation to the crisis in the welfare state, and broader debates around such issues as community care, volunteerism, decentralisation and consumerism (Farrant, 1994, 14, quoted in Sidell, 1997, p. 31).

Governments, Farrant implied, may be more concerned with promoting self-help and encouraging voluntary effort to reduce the demands on resource-constrained health-care services, rather than with promoting community empowerment, to challenge the underlying inequalities of health and health care in periods of economic restructuring and welfare retrenchment. Health promotion can be addressed in terms of individual consumers' responsibilities as well as in terms of their rights – their responsibilities to give up smoking, eat healthier foods and take more exercise, for example, abstaining from drug and alcohol abuse and refraining from indulging in unsafe sex. Despite the rhetoric of community participation, this type of emphasis upon individuals as responsible consumers was characteristic of the market-dominated approaches to social policy which were predominant in the UK in the eighties and early nineties, with correspondingly less emphasis upon collective approaches to addressing the underlying causes of health inequalities which are being addressed more explicitly in the current context (Kings Fund, 1997/98).

This emphasis upon the individual consumer had resonances with the medical model of health which had predominated in the past. Jones and Macdonald defined this dominant medical model as tending:

> to ignore the complex interaction between mind and body and the social and economic realities of people's lives and environment. It

tends to medicalise and individualise social and economic problems so that the stress of the effects of poor housing, for example,
is treated as an individual depressive illness – to be treated with
psychotropic drugs. Oral rehydration therapy (ORT) is hailed as the
answer to diarrhoeal disease: a 'solution' which helps take attention away from such causes as poverty, malnutrition and lack of
clean water supplies (Jones and Macdonald, 1993, p. 201).

The impact of the medical model, Jones and Macdonald went on to
argue, has been to deepen deprived communities' perceptions of their
own powerlessness, feeling that their problems represent personal
failures.

The community development model, as they set this out in
contrast, starts from a holistic approach. The relationship between
mind and body is two-way. Material circumstances impact upon
people's health, and upon people's abilities to make healthy choices,
and so do social circumstances. It is not simply that poverty, poor
housing and unsafe working conditions are linked to ill-health –
which they are. Inequality and powerlessness are factors too – even in
relatively wealthy countries, improvements in life expectancy vary.
"(L)ife expectancy in different countries is dramatically improved
where income differences are smaller and societies are more socially
cohesive' according to Wilkinson (Wilkinson, 1996a, p. 1). People
tend to be happier or more satisfied, it has been argued, in less
unequal and more highly civic societies, and these aspects of social
development affect their health (Wilkinson, 1996b). And conversely,
feeling disempowered, lacking control over important aspects of one's
life, especially work, increases people's risks from illnesses ranging
from heart attacks, strokes and diabetes to ordinary infections
(Marmot and Wilkinson, 1999). Possible explanations include the
implications of the fact that simply being at the bottom of the heap
causes stress, particularly for men but also for women – and this stress
can, in turn, lead to a lowering of the body's immune system.

Bourdieu's concept of *habitus,* which has already been discussed in
Chapter 6, may be helpful in this context too: conceptualising
people's potential for health and well-being in terms of the continuing interactions between their economic, social and cultural
environments and their own individual genetic heritage and psychosocial development. So what might such an approach, drawing upon
Bourdieu's concept of habitus, mean in practice, for community
health promotion strategies? Rather than starting with the individual

and his/her responsibilities – to give up smoking, eat healthier foods, take more exercise and abstain from drugs and alcohol abuse and unsafe sex – this alternative approach starts from individuals in their economic social and cultural contexts. What needs to change, if the underlying causes of people's ill-health are to be addressed, and what are their own priorities for change, not only in terms of their access to appropriate health care, but also in terms of their opportunities for obtaining sufficient and sustainable incomes for themselves and their families, in safe living and working environments? And what are the economic, social, political and cultural blocks which need to be tackled before strategies for change can be effectively developed, including the blocks in people's own heads, blocks which reinforce their own sense of powerlessness and their related depression?

As the following sections will argue, from this alternative perspective, informing individuals of the benefits of healthy eating is unlikely to lead to improvements in their nutrition, if they cannot afford the ingredients in question, just as explaining the importance of safer sex to women is unlikely to reduce the incidence of HIV/AIDS, unless they feel sufficiently empowered to request their partners to use condoms (and for a number of reasons, including socially constructed constraints, in many countries, women actually do find it difficult to assert their wish for safer sex) (Doyal, 1999). Providing information, however necessary, is unlikely to be sufficient to enable people to make healthy choices. A social model of health, in contrast, sees health as a collective issue, focusing upon prevention as well as treatment and cure, reaffirming the Alma-Ata declaration's commitment to participation, equity and intersectoral collaboration. In addition, the community health movement has emphasised the importance of empowerment, as a:

> social action process that promotes participation of people, who are in positions of perceived and actual powerlessness, towards goals of increased individual and community decision-making and control, equity of resources, and improved quality of life (Wallerstein, 1993, p. 219).

Some implications for the role of community media in health promotion

As seen in previous chapters, community media have been used within health promotion strategies, in varying contexts over many decades. Popular media which have been used in health promotion have included storytelling, drama (including puppets), songs, dance and pictures (including cloth designs) (Hubley, 1993; Gordon, 1995). The key issue, for the purposes of this chapter, is not whether cultural strategies have been significant in health promotion then – they have – but how and from which perspective.

In the view of Melkote, an author who has already been quoted on competing perspectives on communication for development, the mass media have served 'largely as vehicles for top-down persuasion or as channels to convey information from experts/authorities to the people' (Melkote, 1991, p. 247). To rectify this situation, Melkote recognised that many national governments had sought to use folk media to reach people more effectively.

Melkote went on to cite the work of Kidd, commenting on the role of the Song and Dance Division (SDD) of the Ministry of Information and Broadcasting, Government of India as an example of top-down communication. The SDD, according to Kidd, started from the view that the poor are poor because they are backward and 'traditional'. The task of the SDD was to provide new information, to replace traditional ideas and bad habits with new ways of thinking and behaving. This was a one-way approach to communication, because the poor were seen as having nothing to contribute.

While the SDD provided useful information on topics such as a balanced diet, the underlying bias was to blame the receiver for his or her backwardness. 'The skits usually point out that a person is backward because he/she has too many children, or is lazy, does not eat healthy food, maintain hygienic surroundings, etc.' (Melkote, 1991, p. 249). While some of these points may have been valid, Kidd argued, the slogans failed to address the underlying political and economic conditions which made it so difficult for so many people to obtain a diet at all, let alone a balanced diet, or the lack of social security which resulted in people having large families in the hope that their families would support them in old age. In contrast, Kidd and Byram argued, on the basis of their experiences of the Laedza Batanani theatre programme in Botswana, for the use of popular theatre for developing critical consciousness. Although they also pointed out that popular theatre too could be hijacked for top-down communication 'which packages health messages in a popular and entertaining form but, in the absence of audience participation, is not so different from mass media' (Hubley, 1993, p. 143). Alternative approaches using popular theatre needed to be based upon genuine two-way dialogue, to facilitate critical thinking about social as well as individual issues; using the media in more interactive ways 'to educate and empower people for health' (WHO, 1994, p. 85).

Puppets for participation

Gordon's study of the use of puppets for health education explains the most important lessons which she drew from her experiences in the Bawku district of Ghana, lessons which have particular relevance in this context. Before working in Ghana, Gordon had used puppets in nutrition education in Northern Nigeria in 1967. Making puppets and producing plays, she had found, 'was creative work and the audience (of rural mothers attending clinics) seemed to enjoy them more than lectures' (Gordon, 1986, p. ix). But was this really helping mothers to rear their children more successfully in a harsh climate, she asked herself, after a year of this work.

The puppets had been used to convey messages about the importance of ensuring that children received a balanced diet, with sufficient protein and vitamins. 'All too often', she argued, in the past, '*we*, the workers living outside the village, decided what the farmers and parents needed to know' (Gordon, 1986, p. 1). On the basis of further experience, working in Ghana in the early seventies, living in the villages at different seasons, she came to appreciate that the main problem was not deficiencies of protein and vitamins but a deficiency of calories, particularly in the lean period before the harvest. It was not simply that mothers lacked information about nutrition for a balanced diet for their children; there were underlying issues about farming and food production, issues in which men needed to be involved as well as women.

> We should never insult people by suggesting that there are simple solutions, which even children can find, to deep-rooted problems that people have struggled with for a long time. For example, 'Give your children more groundnuts and they will grow well' is a simple message, but it is not an easy solution for most households, who sell their groundnuts to buy cheaper millet for when they are hungry (Gordon, 1986, p. 3).

Like many of the problems affecting people's health, this related to issues of resources as well as to issues of health services, issues of people's behaviour and attitudes as well as people's knowledge or lack of knowledge. 'We can only give useful information and move people to act', she concluded, 'by inviting the people themselves to take part in the puppet play, and by discussing their problems and what is important to them' (Gordon, 1986, p. 2). The experiences of the Laedza Batanani theatre in Botswana demonstrated the value of getting the extension teams and people from the community to work together to identify the problems and plan the plays, she argued.

Puppets were relevant, for this approach, as a means for presenting different views and options for thought, encouraging active community participation and self-reliance. 'Puppets can act out what people think and do. They can criticise, try out solutions and show the difficulties that face people who want to change' (Gordon, 1986, p. 3). Puppets, she argued, could build upon local culture and skills, especially in areas where storytelling and puppetry had traditionally provided local ways of exchanging information and ideas. In addition, puppets had the advantage that they cost little to make, and could be understood by everyone, whether they had been to school or not. This made puppet shows accessible to people in rural areas, whether or not they were literate. And most importantly puppet shows were enjoyable. Puppet shows attracted lots of people; the characters, jokes and songs from the puppet plays were known all over the district. This engaged people's interest more effectively than lectures on health.

Rather than simply conveying information, one-way/top-down, from health workers to local people, the use of puppets could make it easier to engage people in active dialogue, working in more participative and empowering ways. And this, in turn, made it easier to develop the processes of dialogue 'to move out from the provision of health care alone to the creation of a society and an environment where health for all becomes possible' (Gordon, 1986, p. xi). Puppetry, she pointed out, may aim to change society, not just give information. 'For centuries puppets have been used to criticise local injustice' (Gordon, 1986, p. 28). Puppet plays could continue to provide opportunities for addressing the underlying causes of ill-health.

But this last point, she pointed out, raised the following question in turn: 'If we aim to change society with puppet plays, will we stay to share the results of the struggle? Will we support those in need, or just 'stir up trouble' and go away?' (Gordon, 1986, p. 29). There are key issues here about the sustainability of health promotion initiatives, and the responsibilities of professional development workers when they stimulate the discussion of contentious social issues.

While puppetry has had the potential to contribute to participatory approaches to health promotion in rural areas in the South, puppets are not necessarily seen as so appropriate, now, especially in contexts where people are more used to contemporary media such as radio, television and film – although puppets are still being used very effectively in many contexts. The use of drama continues to have relevance, too, in participatory approaches to health promotion in both South and North. As the following section will explore in more detail, drama (including role play) has been combined with video, for example, in workshops to address the problem of HIV/AIDS in rural contexts in Africa, just as drama has been used to address issues of health and well-being in urban European contexts. Before moving on to these uses of drama, however, it may be helpful to return to the work of Augusto Boal, the Brazilian whose use of drama for community development and social action has already been outlined in Chapter 4.

Boal revisited

As Chapter 4 outlined, Boal drew upon the ideas of Freire and others, to develop the use of drama in interactive ways. The aim of Forum Theatre was conscientisation, to enable the oppressed to develop their own understanding of their situation, in order to develop collective strategies for transformation. Rather than presenting solutions, through didactic plays, Forum Theatre was pedagogic in a very different way – 'in the sense of a collective learning', actors and spectators (spect-actors) learning together as they tested out a variety of ways forward (Boal, 1995, p. 7).

Having developed the Theatre of the Oppressed in Brazil and Peru, Boal experienced exile, during which he worked in Lisbon, then in Paris and other European countries over a 15-year period. These experiences in exile provided the impetus to develop his thinking. As Boal himself explained, he worked with:

> immigrants, teachers, men and women, workers born in these countries, people who suffered oppressions with which I was well acquainted in Latin America: racism, sexism, intolerable working conditions, insufficient wages, police abuses of power, and so on (Boal, 1995, p. 7).

But he also came to develop Theatre of the Oppressed workshops with those suffering in ways which were new to him, from loneliness, the impossibility of communicating with others, the fear of emptiness.

At first he felt that:

> for someone like him 'fleeing explicit dictatorships of a cruel and brutal nature, it was natural that these themes should at first seem superficial and scarcely worthy of attention. It was as if I was always asking, mechanically: 'But where are the cops?' (Boal, 1995, p. 8).

Little by little, however, he changed his views, as he came to understand the extent of problems such as depression, drug abuse and suicide. The 'cops', he decided, had got into people's heads, although their barracks were on the outside. 'The task was to discover how these "cops" got into our heads and to invent ways of dislodging them' (Boal, 1995, p. 8).

Boal's method of theatre and therapy, set out in *The Rainbow of Desire* (Boal, 1995) explains how he and his colleagues developed the Theatre of the Oppressed, using new methods to explore both aspects of oppression, the personal and the social, the situation which is causing unwanted suffering or unhappiness. Through these methods, people could be encouraged to explore alternatives for themselves. *The Rainbow of Desire* work process involves techniques such as improvisation, including improvisation without words, freezes/human sculptures, representing images. (This use of human sculptures to enable groups to explore perceptions of issues and situations – with a view to developing strategies for change – has become a feature of a wide range of community development and adult learning initiatives, as Kane's discussion of popular education in Latin America and Scotland, for example, illustrates (Kane, 1999, p. 66).

The image might be of a word representing an issue or a relationship which is particularly important to those concerned – as it seems now perhaps, and then subsequently, as people would like it to be. For example, Boal himself has often proposed 'fear' as a workshop theme for this exercise, because, in his view, so often it is 'fear that makes us accept oppression ...'. 'For fear of losing our jobs, we submit to unacceptable conditions of work. For fear of losing a person's love or company, we accept unacceptable situations. Out of fear of death, we accept ways of life we don't like' (Boal, 1995, p. 118). Participants in the workshop would be invited to think of a fear and a concrete social situation involving this fear, and then to translate this into an image, looking at how they might *change* this situation. The workshop would then explore the different images of fear, and experiment with new ways of action for the future to tackle the fear and to work with any conflicts which might ensue, as a result of these challenges.

'Rainbow of Desire' techniques, Boal argued, could enable people to identify the 'cops' which have been internalised in their own heads. Through these methods people could explore the ambivalence of their own feelings and the complexity of their different desires. The workshops could then offer the possibility of testing out alternative ways of dealing with the particular situations which were oppressing them, or causing them unwarranted unhappiness. In the following section, there are examples of how these varying types of technique can be applied to enable people to work for change, through workshops exploring issues around relationships, communication and power, in the context of HIV/AIDS and the importance of safer sex.

The challenge of HIV/AIDS: the relevance of a community development approach

HIV/AIDS represents a major global challenge to human health and well-being, with more than 33 million people estimated to be living with HIV or full-blown AIDS in 1998 (Human Development Report, 1999). At the end of the nineties AIDS was causing 2.5 million deaths a year, more than twice as many as from malaria. This has been described as a poor people's epidemic, with 95 per cent of all HIV-infected people in developing countries, where the toll on life expectancy has been heavy. Sub-Saharan Africa has been particularly seriously affected with women being more vulnerable than men (in part at least due to biological factors). It has been estimated that for the nine countries in Africa with a prevalence of 10 per cent or more – Botswana, Kenya, Malawi, Mozambique, Namibia, Rwanda, South Africa, Zambia and Zimbabwe, life expectancy will be down to 47 years by the year 2010, back to the life expectancy of the 1960s (Human Development Report, 1999). In South Africa, for example, a country with one of the most rapidly progressing epidemic rates in the world, it has been estimated that 25 per cent of the population will be reached by the year 2010, with a fall in life expectancy from the 68.2 years previously anticipated, to an anticipated 48 years (Human Development South Africa, 1998).

This situation has devastating implications not only for the individuals and families concerned, but for development more generally, as workers and farmers in the prime of their working lives are struck down, and the burden of caring for those with HIV/AIDS is carried disproportionately by children and older women, along with the additional burdens associated with sustaining livelihoods. Here too, then, in relation to caring as well as in relation to the likelihood of infection, women are particularly vulnerable, including older women who are left to feed and care for the growing numbers of children orphaned as a result of AIDS.

There are key implications too for health and welfare services, all too often under-resourced and groaning, already, under the pressure of unmet demand. The situation has been compounded in many countries, as adjustment to the debt has led to reductions in expenditure on health care, and this in turn has led to increased risks of HIV/AIDS transmission – for example, from unsterile injections when disposable needles are unavailable (Gordon, 1995). There is a vicious circle at work, here. Lack of access to appropriate health care compounds the risks of infections associated with poverty and poor nutrition, including infections such as untreated sexually transmitted diseases, which are associated with vulnerability to HIV/AIDS – and high HIV/AIDS infection rates compound the pressures on already overstretched health-care resources.

Globally, it has been the most vulnerable groups, especially women, in the poorest countries, which have been most at risk. Over two-thirds of those living with HIV/AIDS are in sub-Saharan Africa. The spread of HIV/AIDS has been a global phenomenon, exacerbated by the risks associated with population movements, whether as a result of labour migration, civil disorder and/or international tourism including sex tourism to countries such as Thailand, which has a relatively high infection rate (Seabrook, 1996; Hall, 1997). As will be discussed subsequently in more detail, the spread of HIV/AIDS has been related to economic, political, social and cultural factors, and each of these needs to be addressed, if the spread of HIV/AIDS is to be effectively contained. The sex industry in Thailand, for example, developed for a variety of reasons, fuelled by Thailand's role as a place for 'rest and recreation' for GIs during the Vietnam War, together with economic pressures on young women and young men who lacked alternative economic opportunities for themselves and their families, or the power to resist exploitation by others. Seabrook concluded, on the basis of his study, that there were cultural factors at work too amongst the Western men who were travelling to Thailand: they were not only going to buy sex, they said. Thai women were appealing because they had been socialised to behave submissively, being less assertive than Western women (Seabrook, 1996). The risks of

HIV/AIDS infection associated with such patterns of sex tourism, are unlikely to be shifted by health promotion programmes on their own, without addressing these underlying economic, social and cultural factors, including the racism and sexism embedded in international sex tourism.

In Britain and elsewhere in the industrialised North, patterns have varied, with gay and bi-sexual men being particularly at risk. It has been estimated that between two-thirds and three-quarters of new cases in Britain, in the late nineties, involved gay and bi-sexual men (Watney, 1997). While there are important differences between their experiences of risk and the experiences of women and men in the South, there are, nevertheless key factors in common, factors which have particular relevance for the concerns of this chapter. In each context, as the subsequent section of this chapter sets out in more detail, preventing the spread of HIV/AIDS, involves much more than simply providing relevant information about safer sex. While decisions about such intimate issues as sexuality and sexual practices might appear to be pre-eminently personal ones, for individuals and their partners, these decisions actually relate to a range of wider considerations, economic, political, social and cultural factors which affect people's choices – or lack of choices. As Gordon has explained:

> The dissemination of simple 'messages' and exhortations to practice safer sex are unlikely to have a significant impact on the HIV epidemic because sexual behaviour is rooted in complex social, economic and cultural environments where choices are often seriously limited. Programmes will have to address seriously the issue of empowerment, particularly in relation to women and young people, if they are to achieve a reduction in HIV transmission and improvements in sexual health' (Gordon, 1995, p. 193).

Changing people's sexual behaviour – even when this is literally a matter of life or death – involves challenging the social and economic constraints which inhibit people from refusing dangerous sexual encounters. And this involves challenging the cultural norms which prevent people from acting upon information about safer sex, including the norms internalised inside people's heads which make it difficult for them to assert their wish for safer sex. Too often, women's biological vulnerability has been reinforced, by socially constructed constraints on their ability to protect themselves. 'Not surprisingly', as Doyal has pointed out, 'it is often the poorest women who have the fewest choices, run the most frequent risks and are most likely to become infected' (Doyal, 1999, p. 39). Sex workers are obviously particularly vulnerable, but so are wives in societies in which they are expected to have little autonomy over their own bodies. In the context of the economic and social pressures relating to structural adjustment and debt, the risks arising from women's relative power-lessness can be compounded. Migrating to urban areas in search of economic opportunities increases risks for rural women, for example, just as having sex with a teacher who pays a schoolgirl's school fees increases risks for a young woman, and having sex with a boss to keep her job increases risks for a working woman (Gordon, 1995). Empowering women in these situations to opt for safer sex involves both cultural and economic and social change.

There are relevant lessons to be drawn from experiences of promoting cultural change in gay communities in Britain and elsewhere, in the 1980s, as the seriousness of HIV/AIDS became more widely appreciated. HIV/AIDS has presented particular challenges for gay and bi-sexual men. They faced new risks to their health and well-being, due to the virus itself, and due to the associated panic which accompanied its identification in the industrialised North. AIDS has been depicted by homophobes as 'God's judgement on a society which does not live by His rules', 'the consequences of moral decadence' (quoted in Sontag, 1988, p. 61). While much of this venom has been directed at gay and bi-sexual men in Britain and the USA, elsewhere in Europe AIDS has also provided racist politicians of the extreme right, such as Le Pen in France, with opportunities for fomenting fear of immigrants as bearers of the dreaded disease. In the USA, however, the prime targets of such anti-liberal views have been homosexuals. 'More than cancer, but rather like syphilis', in Sontag's analysis of AIDS and its metaphors, 'AIDS seems to foster ominous fantasies about a disease that is a marker of both individual and social vulnerabilities' (Sontag, 1988, p. 65) fantasies which reinforce profoundly disempowering cultural prejudices and stereotypes, and discriminatory practices deeply disadvantageous to gay and bi-sexual men.

Combating the spread of HIV/AIDS has involved much more then, than 'just giving people the facts and telling them to behave differently' (Macdonald, 1998, p. 211). For gay and bi-sexual men, it has been argued, it has become widely recognised that 'self empowerment and community-based initiatives constitute the most effective interventions' (Macdonald, 1998, p. 211). Strategies have been required to address issues of oppression and inequality, the distribution of power and cultural expectations. Individual and group norms have had to be challenged, within the framework of initiatives to promote community development and empowerment.

Health education messages aimed at individuals to persuade them of the benefits of safer sex have not been so effective, it has been argued. Changing sexual practices is not like changing your hair gel or your toothpaste (Watney, 1990, p. 22). Cultural norms have needed to change, and safer sex needed to be eroticised, if it was to be acceptable over time. To achieve such changes, however, the gay community itself needed to be centrally involved; which is precisely what actually happened, it has been argued, in the eighties in Britain.

Studies have shown according to the AIDS Reference Manual:

> that a key component behind the widespread uptake of safer sex among gay men in the 1980s was the perception among gay men that safer sex was the expected norm among their friends and partners (National AIDS Manual, 1998/9).

While government and media programmes had contributed, the report argued, it was community-based campaigns for health education (that is, campaigns within and by the gay community) which had been the most effective, preventing AIDS in Britain from reaching US proportions. Watney had already come to similar conclusions about the importance of collective and community-based approaches to health promotion and community empowerment, if group norms were to be changed. He argued that:

> community development is effective AIDS education, in so far as worldwide evidence strongly suggests that gay pride has played a major factor in preventing HIV transmission by establishing safer sex not just as a set of techniques, but as a fundamental aspect of gay cultural practices (Watney, 1989, quoted in Watney, 1990, p. 23).

Collective cultural empowerment had been key 'encouraging us to think of ourselves as a community, united in response to the epidemic', building both individual and collective self-esteem (Watney, 1990, p. 24).

While recognising and valuing these achievements of the gay community itself, it is also important to avoid complacency. The AIDS Reference Manual argued that 'it is wrong to assume that gay men have it all under control' (National AIDS Manual, 1998/9, p. 63) pointing out that the fact the rate of increase amongst gay men has levelled off does not mean that all is now well. Nor should it be concluded that resources are no longer needed: health promotion resources do need to be provided, it has been argued, but health educators should take account of the strengths and weaknesses of the different approaches which have been tried both in Britain and elsewhere (Homans and Aggleton, 1988). Communities should not be expected to do it all for themselves.

> While we can each play a role in ending the epidemic by practising safer sex as a community we must also learn to fight for the funding, legal protection and attitudinal transformation necessary to ensure our future survival (Silin, 1987, quoted in Homans and Aggleton, 1988, p. 167).

Stepping Stones; a participatory training package on HIV/AIDS, communication and relationship skills

Stepping Stones is a training package, consisting of a manual and an accompanying video cassette to facilitate training workshops. The aim of each workshop is 'to enable individuals, their peers and communities to change their behaviour, individually and together, through the stepping stones which the sessions provide' (Welbourn, 1996, p. 3). Through workshop sessions communities are provided with knowledge about HIV, which sets the framework for the discussion of strategies to promote sexual health, through safer sex. Stepping Stones is not simply a training package to provide information, however. The training package sets out to explore the underlying factors which inhibit people from opting for safer choices, factors such as barriers to communication, cultural perceptions, prejudices and traditions, economic and social factors (including alcohol abuse) and issues of powerlessness and the need to develop assertiveness. Stepping Stones also offers individuals and communities support for coping with the reality of AIDS, vitally important, especially in the sub-Saharan African context.

Stepping Stones addresses both social and cultural issues (in the anthropological sense of the term, 'culture'). And Stepping Stones uses cultural tools, in the more specific sense of the term 'culture'. The video which accompanies the training manual was filmed in Uganda, showing members of a rural community who have discussed and re-enacted their own problems and developed their own solutions. Video clips are played at key points during the training programme. Each of these clips 'provides viewers with a springboard for discussion, enabling them to address their own concerns in a constructive, participatory manner' (Welbourn, 1996, p. 2). In addition, the training programme uses a range of methods from participants' drawings (especially useful where literacy skills are limited), games and exercises, songs and drama techniques, including some of those which have been discussed in the previous section, such as human sculptures.

In summary then, Stepping Stones illustrates cultural strategies for health and well-being – in both senses of the term 'culture'. The programme combines individual and community-based approaches, addressing both structural and personal barriers to empowerment and change. Stepping Stones also provides an illustration of cross-national learning: while the programme was developed on the basis of workshop experiences in Uganda, Stepping Stones draws upon approaches developed elsewhere – and such approaches have been applied in a wide variety of contexts.

The Stepping Stones workshop programme consists of a series of sessions, each with a theme, starting with group exercises to develop co-operation and trust amongst the participants, before moving on to provide information on HIV and safer sex. The programme then focuses upon helping participants to analyse why we behave as we do, recognising the factors which affect our behaviour 'such as alcohol, local traditions, the need for money, social expectations and our own personalities' (Welbourn, 1996, p. 3). And this sets the context for realistic explorations of how participants can change their behaviour to be more assertive and to take more personal, social and community responsibility for their actions.

Participants have opportunities to test out new ways of behaving, in the relative safety of their peer group, before attempting to change their behaviour with their partners. Typically this approach involves working in sub-groups of between ten and twenty participants, divided according to factors such as gender, age, educational level and socio-economic well-being. For example, if a workshop were to be divided into four sub-groups of peers these might consist of older men, older women, younger men and younger women. The use of peer group discussions is important, especially in societies in which the views of particular groups such as young women would rarely be voiced in community-wide meetings – particularly if the topic for discussion raises sensitive issues around sexuality. And this, in turn, necessitates having several facilitators, generally a minimum of four, including both men and women.

It is suggested that these facilitators are skilled professionals (such as health workers, AIDS educators) or community leaders who are already working with local groups in development settings. The whole process runs over a three to four-month period, in communities which are also being supported by an ongoing AIDS prevention and support programme. These prerequisites are important, because Stepping Stones is about much more than simply providing information; the programme aims to develop communication skills and to promote both personal and community development processes on a continuing basis.

The method is participatory, focusing upon people listening and talking to others like themselves, to enable communities to work out what they want to achieve for themselves in terms of improved care for those who are sick and improved HIV prevention for those who are not – and then pursue these goals in their communities. And this, in turn, requires support from skilled facilitators with ongoing commitment to the communities in question. Stepping Stones explicitly draws upon participatory adult education techniques. As the manual comments, reinforcing the conclusions drawn in the previous section, 'Lectures on AIDS do not work' (Welbourn, 1996, p. 20).

The following examples illustrate both the type of issues and the participatory methods used to explore them. When the participants have developed ways of communicating effectively, explored their own perceptions and prejudices and received information about HIV and safer sex (including familiarising themselves in their peer groups with how to use condoms) they move on to consider possible options for the future. One of the exercises to be used, in this context, involves working in small groups using role play and 'tableaux' (defined as 'a frozen scene representing people in a situation. No-one speaks, but their positions and expressions tell the story of what is happening to them') (Welbourn, 1996, p. 103). The second 'tableau' represents a more hopeful future. The peer group discussions of the different tableaux provide opportunities to explore options for change. Issues raised may relate to HIV/AIDS, but they may also relate to wider socio-economic issues, such as increased opportunities for income-generation, and/or more personal issues such as improved communication within the family and more equal relationships between husbands and wives. These issues are also directly relevant, when it comes to exploring the barriers to change in relation to sexual health.

The next stage is to help participants to identify the situations which involve sex and risk-taking in their own experiences, and to help them to think through other ways of handling these situations in the future. Through the use of role play in small groups, participants design a scene which is leading up to a potentially risky sexual encounter. For example, a husband might be returning home to his wife after a long journey (for example, as a migrant labourer), a young wife might be wanting a child – and this might be culturally expected of her anyway – even if she knows that her husband has been sleeping around, a 'sugar daddy' might be attempting to seduce a young girl, or a young man might fear the reactions of his wife or girl friend (who might assume that he was being unfaithful) if he suggests using a condom. Through discussion of these role plays, participants identify what was going on in each situation, what factors influenced the characters' behaviour (for example did the wife fear that she would be beaten if she did not simply agree to have sex with her returning husband, without raising questions about safer sex?) Issues raised in such discussions are likely, the manual explains, to include the following, in addition to issues around sex and the enjoyability – or otherwise – of sex itself:

- alcohol (as a significant factor in reducing inhibitions about unsafe sex)
- community beliefs and expectations regarding sex (such as men being expected to have a lot of wives and children to gain respect) and
- cultural norms and values about the sexual relations between husbands and wives, and about having children.

Having identified these factors, the next workshop sessions move on to explore these in more detail, covering a range of issues, material and resource allocation issues and social and cultural issues such as the role of traditions, and the need to change some traditions, in view of the threats posed by HIV/AIDS. For example the custom of a widow marrying her dead husband's brother traditionally offered a way of providing for the widow and her children. This is a potentially lethal tradition in communities where men are dying of AIDS.

These explorations of what needs to change sets the context for participants to work on *how* to bring such changes about. The next session starts with peer group members working in pairs to produce tableaux representing positions of power and powerlessness. This provides the basis for working on assertiveness. This session, like a number of others, is triggered off with a video clip. In this case the video clip shows relevant role plays in the Ugandan context, as a way of setting the scene for discussing alternative and more assertive ways of dealing with the situations which are portrayed by the Ugandan participants. (The first role play in the video clips for these sessions illustrates the difficulties which young women can experience when faced with unwanted sexual advances from 'sugar daddies', while the next clip goes on to explore ways in which they might be able to reject these unwanted sexual advances. The older Ugandan women's role play focuses upon a husband coming home from a journey, anxious to have sex with his wife; but having considered the risks of HIV, the wife then proposes that they use a condom). The workshop participants discuss these clips and use these discussions as the springboard for testing out alternative ways of behaving themselves, using role play to build up their confidence to take more control, more assertively – rehearsing new ways of communicating.

The resulting peer group role plays are then shown to the full group, and each role play is followed by discussion by the whole community. This process enables community members to share their ideas about what needs to change and how such changes might be made to improve their situation. The peer groups then rehearse together, in preparation for the final open community meeting, to share their requests, proposals and plans for ways forward. Having completed the process, the workshop is reviewed by participants, and follow-up workshops are planned, whether these involve peer groups on their own and/or all partipicants meeting and working together in the full community group.

Stepping Stones, in summary, illustrates a community development approach to health promotion, an approach which is participatory, from the initial planning through to the final evaluation sessions. Professionals facilitate the use of a range of community media, drawing, song, video and drama, including some of the dramatic techniques which have already been discussed, in a previous section in this chapter. And these uses of community media enable both social and cultural issues to be addressed, issues around resources and power – or the lack thereof – and issues around community traditions, norms and values. Through testing out alternative approaches, participants plan ways forward, ways of caring for those with AIDS as well as ways of preventing the spread of HIV, in their communities.

Commenting on her overall impressions of Stepping Stones, the late

Rose Mbowa, Director of the Department of Music, Dance and Drama at Makerere University, Kampala, Uganda reflected that:

> It's a powerful tool ... Basic work which inspires communities to look at their needs and really get together and discuss their problems. It's very, very empowering to the community ... transforming attitudes and so on. It's very good ... And it can work in any community, because it makes people address their own individual reality so it's not limited to any particular context (Mbowa, 1997, p. 46).

Professor Mbowa went on to comment that she had also learnt a great deal personally from being a facilitator, because this had developed her ability to listen to people. As a result her relationship with her son had improved too. 'We listen to each other a lot now' (Mbowa, 1997, p. 46).

Given the scale of the challenge of HIV/AIDS, globally, it would be unrealistic to suggest that there might be any easy solutions. Stepping Stones certainly does not suggest anything of the sort. It may be relevant to note, though, that Uganda, where the first workshop was organised and where the video was shot, was one of the worst affected areas, with over 46 000 AIDS cases reported by the end of 1994 (AIDS Reference Manual, 1998/9). Since then the spread of HIV/AIDS has been addressed. In the Human Development Report 1999 Uganda does not appear in the list of the nine countries in Africa with an HIV prevalence of 10 per cent or more. As the South African Report on HIV/AIDS and Human Development argued 'the growth of the epidemic is not irreversible'. Uganda, one of the first countries to be hard hit by HIV/AIDS has demonstrated some of the most effective ways of reversing the challenge' (UNAIDS and UNDP, 198, p. 49). Despite the challenges arising from the previous decade of crisis and civil strife (with the associated social dislocation which exacerbated the spread of the virus) rates of infection were coming down and people were avoiding high-risk behaviour. The reasons for this turnaround, the report argued, could be attributed to 'a powerful combination of clear and sustained political leadership: empowering communities: mobilising employers: addressing socio-economic issues and, above all, the full involvement of people living with AIDS' (UNAIDS and UNDP, 1998, p. 49).

This conclusion would certainly seem to endorse the value of a community development approach to the promotion of health and well-being. Facing up to the challenge of HIV/AIDS and using imaginative ways of involving communities in working in partnership with professionals to develop strategies for change, would seem potentially likely to be far more effective than more traditional approaches to health promotion, based upon telling people to do what experts think may be good for them.

Even the most imaginative and cost-effective community-based strategies cannot be put into effect, however, without ongoing resources. And that, in turn, raises questions about related policy changes. In Gordon's view:

(A) reduction in the debt burden, fair terms of trade and investment in sexual health were all urgently needed to prevent further devastating economic and social consequences of not only the HIV epidemic but also maternal and other outcomes of sexual ill-health in Africa (Gordon, 1995, p. 193).

8
Wider Strategies: 'Globalisation from Below'?

This book started from the position that issues of culture and identity *do* matter; they matter in their own right, and they also matter, more specifically, to communities and to those who work with communities. The focus upon cultures, communities and identities at the turn of the millennium, represented more than a contemporary fad, it was argued. The key questions were about how these issues were being addressed, from which perspectives, and with what differing implications for policies and practice.

This concluding chapter starts by summarising some of the key implications of the preceding chapters, arguing the case for the relevance of cultural strategies, as part of wider strategies for participation and empowerment. But this positive endorsement is not to underestimate the problems inherent in locally based strategies, more generally. In the contemporary context, local strategies need to be linked into global strategies for transformation – as the environmental slogan argues, 'think globally', as well as 'acting locally'. Such a conclusion only serves to raise a series of further questions, however, questions about what this might concretely mean and questions about how these global issues might actually be addressed, in practice. The potential scale of these discussions is vast. For the purposes of this chapter, the key issues to be addressed here are questions about 'upscaling' and questions about building alliances for change, between differing social movements and campaigns and the labour and progressive movement, on an international scale. The chapter concludes by recognising the difficulties of attempting to address these questions at all, whether in theory and/or in practice. But despite these difficulties, there *are* examples which point towards the possibility of moving forward, and these examples include the use of community media as tools for sharing experiences, building alliances and developing advocacy and campaigning at an international level.

The case so far

The opening chapters began to unpack the varying and contested meanings of culture, communities and identities, setting the scene for the discussion of policies and practice. In the remaining chapters the focus shifted to the role of community arts and media, more specifically, exploring varying examples of cultural strategies for promoting local economic development, combating political marginalisation and exclusion, and enhancing health and well-being, especially the health and well-being of oppressed groups in both First and Third World contexts. There were examples where community arts and media were being promoted within the context of market-led agendas for economic growth, whether or not the benefits were actually trickling down to the most disadvantaged groups. There were criticisms that cultural events were being used as 'carnival masks', brightening the urban scene by diverting and entertaining, a constructed fetishism 'in which every aesthetic power of illusion and image is mobilised to mask the intensifying class, racial and ethnic polarisations going on underneath' (Harvey, 1989, p. 21). And there were examples where community media were being used to convey development messages from the top downwards; telling people to give up smoking, eat healthier foods, take more exercise, abstain from drug and alcohol abuse and refrain from unsafe sexual encounters, without taking account of, let alone addressing the economic, social and cultural pressures which reinforce unhealthy lifestyles, in practice.

But there were also examples of alternative strategies, based upon more participative approaches, using community arts and media within the context of wider agendas for empowerment and social transformation. The book has been particularly concerned to explore these more interactive approaches to social transformation. The case studies in Chapter 5 included co-operative approaches to local economic development, including sustainable tourism projects, building upon local arts and crafts, for example. Chapter 6 included examples of community festivals which expressed and developed community interests, including black and ethnic minority community interests – despite powerful counterpressures, in some cases, from market forces and from state agencies. And Chapter 7 included examples of the use of drama and video as part of strategies to enable people to address the underlying issues of poverty, inequality and relative powerlessness which make healthier living so problematic for so many. In each case, cultural strategies were central rather than marginal to the processes by which communities and social movements were developing transformative alternatives.

In a study of development projects which had involved the creative arts, Gould found that a very wide variety of art forms were being used, as part of the tool kit of participatory approaches to development, ranging from circus on the Bosnian front line to puppetry teaching about landmines awareness, dance with youths in a disadvantaged area of Newcastle-upon-Tyne, UK, visual arts and creative writing in refugee camps and craft-making for income generation with homeless people in Los Angeles. There were examples of the use of drama, music, video, radio, television, film and photography (Gould, 1997). As a general observation Gould commented that the performing and visual arts were tending to be used for education and communication (including health education for example) while crafts and textiles were tending to be used for skills training and income generation. The examples quoted in the preceding chapters would broadly fit into these categories.

But, as the title to this article explained '(T)here's more than one art to creative PRA' (Gould, 1997, p. 52). The range of possibilities is actually far wider than any such simple categorisation. Projects could and did use different media in varying combinations. Gould quoted a variety of examples to illustrate this point, including examples of multi-media projects, such as 'Raw Material' based in Kings Cross, London, which used 'video, dance and street music – the language of urban youth – to get its participants to express their needs, to discuss and debate drug culture, violence, HIV and other important youth issues' (Gould, 1997, p. 54). Projects can and do also cross sector and service boundaries. Cultural strategies do not have to be confined within sector frameworks or neatly fit within the boundaries of existing service provision. The examples which have been quoted in the preceding chapters do not begin to do justice to the variety of creative arts projects which have been contributing to strategies for participation and empowerment in the both the First and Third Worlds.

In spite of this diversity of approaches, it has been argued, some incipient degree of consensus has been emerging, nevertheless, both on the need for grass-roots participation in development and on the essential role that communication plays in promoting development (Bessette, 1996). And there has been some degree of overall shift, it has been argued, away from a model of information transmission from the top downwards, 'towards practices involving the grassroots in their development' (Bessette, 1996, p. 4). This latter approach has been characterised, for example, by the use of video to reflect local issues and aspirations and to communicate these from the grass roots upwards, to outside decision-makers (Chin Saik Yoon, 1996).

In the past, the dominant approach to video, it has been argued, has been for 'educating people in the modernisation process, for disseminating messages that are formulated by experts and designed by professional producers' (Johansson and Waal, 1997, p. 59). But there have been cases where 'video has also been used in a totally different way: for giving people a voice rather than a message' (Johansson and Waal, 1997, p. 59). Johansson and Waal went on to provide contrasting examples of the impact of participatory video, drawing upon experiences of rural development in Tanzania. In one case, local messages were being communicated and connected with national and official issues – 'an interactive communication loop was established between micro and macro levels' (Johansson and Waal, 1997, p. 59). While the use of video promoted constructive dialogue in this first case, however, the reverse outcome resulted in the second case. When a community video confronted planners with local people's criticisms of development plans in another context, the planners reacted by denying the authenticity of the tape, and trying to prevent its distribution. This raises a wider set of questions about the inherent limitations of locally based strategies, the problems of communicating local needs to outside decision-makers – and being effectively heard – and the difficulties of scaling up from the local to the national level and beyond – questions which emerge too from a number of the examples which have been quoted in previous chapters.

Limitations of the local

Environmental campaigners have already been cited, in the context of the slogan, 'Think globally, act locally'. Greenpeace and Friends of the Earth, for example, have both addressed environmental issues at the global as well as the local levels, from the start. Chapter 5 concluded by similarly pointing to the need to address the wider frameworks, in this case, the frameworks of debt and international trade relations which have had such negative impact upon local economic development initiatives. Without in any way underestimating the scale of the task to be addressed globally, the chapter pointed to the challenges which had been posed through international campaigning on the debt crisis and on the need for fairer trade.

Similarly Chapter 6 explored cultural strategies for addressing the needs of migrants, refugees and asylum seekers. But here again, this raised underlying structural issues, the economic disparities which pressurise people to migrate, and the political and social conflicts which lead to forced migrations. Sadly, the escalation of such conflicts in developing countries in the latter part of the twentieth century has been identified as a continuing trend, rather than a temporary phenomenon. And this trend has been linked, in turn, to the ways in which Western nations, the USA, UK, France, Germany, Spain and the Netherlands – while expressing their anguish about conflict – 'continue to actively promote arms sales to developing countries' (Turner and Hulme, 1997, p. 227). Far from the world being a safer place since the end of the Cold War, the 'new world order' has turned out to be the 'new world disorder' (Turner and Hulme, 1997, p. 227). In this context, the problems faced by refugees and asylum seekers are being constantly reproduced into the twenty-first century.

Finally, Chapter 7 concluded with some reflections on the wider policy implications of addressing HIV/AIDS and sexual health in Africa. Even the most imaginative and cost-effective community-based strategies required ongoing resources, resources which were under increasing pressure as a result of global market forces, including the specific pressures arising from the debt and from structural adjustment. The chapter concluded by quoting the view that a 'reduction in the debt burden, fair terms of trade and investment in sexual health' were all urgently needed 'to prevent further devastating economic and social consequences of not only the HIV epidemic but also maternal and other outcomes of sexual ill-health in Africa' (Gordon, 1995, p. 193).

This brings the discussion on to the issues of 'scaling up', building communications from the bottom upwards, as well as developing communications, advocacy networks and alliances laterally, South–South as well as South–North and North–South. In recent years, there has been increasing interest in 'scaling up', drawing upon experiences of participatory approaches to development at the local level to influence – and where necessary to challenge – policymaking and practice at both national and international levels (Holland and Blackburn, 1998). As Chambers, whose work in developing participatory rural development has been so influential, has commented, '(E)mpowering poor people to conduct their own appraisal and analysis, and to present their realities is one thing. Whether their voices are heard, understood and acted upon is another' (Chambers, 1998, p. 197). While recognising the inherent difficulties, however, Chambers has also pointed to some achievements, illustrating the potential for the voices of the less powerful to have an impact on policies and practice at both national and international levels, including impacting upon the World Bank (through participatory poverty assessments, for example).

Clearly, as Chambers recognised, there are major problems involved in 'scaling up' – and getting voices from the South effectively heard. Commenting upon the limits to the potential for dialogue between North and South more generally, the late Julius Nyerere (former president of Tanzania) reflected that 'the first reaction to any question about the North–South dialogue is therefore a question: what dialogue?' (Nyerere, 1988, p. 197). In addition to underlying structural inequalities of economic power and military power, there were key imbalances of power in relation to communication and information. This, it has been argued, has had particular significance – '(C)ultural domination is one of the most insidious expressions of international power relations – it prevents the creation of a climate of dialogue in the North' (Hadjor, 1988, p. 57).

There are both opportunities and significant challenges inherent in the more specific challenge of scaling up the lessons from participatory development. Reflecting upon these challenges Gaventa has pointed to the opportunities 'for expanding the participation of the poor in development' (Gaventa, 1998, p. 153). And he has also pointed to the 'serious dangers of misuse and abuse which ultimately could discredit the concept of participation as a critical ingredient for development' (Gaventa, 1998, p. 153). Gaventa identified three interrelated dimensions of 'scaling-up' which were necessary if quality participation was to be achieved on a large scale – 'scaling-out', 'scaling-up' itself and institutional change.

'Scaling-out' involved:

the expansion of participation from one activity such as appraisal, to the involvement of people throughout the whole development process in a way that increases their empowerment (Gaventa, 1998, p. 155).

'Scaling-up' referred to:

an increase in the number of participants or places where participation, especially PRA will occur (Gaventa, 1998, p. 155).

That is, to move beyond the specifics of particular local pilot projects.
And finally 'institutional change' referred to:

> the shifts required in and among larger-scale institutions for
> scaling-out and scaling-up to occur effectively. More specifically, it
> refers to the ways in which larger-scale institutions in government
> or the civil society will interact with smaller-scale organizations or
> communities in the participatory-development process (Gaventa,
> 1998, p. 155).

While the focus here is upon participatory approaches to development
in the South, similar points apply to community participation in
urban regeneration programmes in the North – where scaling up also
raises issues about capacity-building and empowerment and the need
for institutional change.

Without effective 'scaling-out' – local capacity-building and
empowerment – Gaventa argued, policies for 'scaling-up' to the larger
regional or national level could fail, because they lacked sufficiently
strong local roots. Large-scale plans can become mandates from above
that 'participation shall occur'; an approach fraught with difficulty
because 'participation cannot be imposed from above, it will develop
differently and at differing paces, depending upon local contexts'
(Gaventa, 1998, p. 160). In addition, Gaventa argued, institutional
change was key. Large institutions, whether governments, large
NGOs, donor agencies or others also needed to change. And this, in
turn, required links, cross-sector partnerships, networks and coalitions
between local organisations and between them and larger-scale organisations. While recognising the importance of trends towards
democratisation and decentralisation in the arena of governance,
trends which were potentially favourable, Gaventa also pointed to the
simultaneous trends which were moving in the contrary direction
'towards greater inequality in the economy, greater globalization of
economic forces and an increasing concern with social exclusion'
(Gaventa, 1998, p. 165). There are connections here with a number of
themes which have been emerging in previous chapters, questions
about globalisation and increasing inequality and questions about
how to move beyond the localism of militant particularism to build
broader alliances for change. As Harvey expressed this in the context

of campaigning on environmental issues, how to 'shift from "Not in my back yard" politics to "Not-in-anyone's-backyard" principles' (Harvey, 1998, p. 349).

This once again raises issues about information and communication. While the focus has been upon contemporary preoccupations, the reality is that there has been a history of advocacy and campaigning at international levels, a history in which the exchange of information and networking has been centrally important. Reflecting upon the experiences of international campaigning, from anti-slavery campaigns and those for women's right to vote in the nineteenth century and beyond through to human rights advocacy networks, women's rights and environmental advocacy networks in the latter part of the twentieth century, Keck and Sikkink identified four key aspects (Keck and Sikkink, 1998). Since transnational advocacy groups were not generally powerful in the traditional sense, they argued, 'they must use the power of their information, ideas, and strategies to alter the information and value contexts within which states make policies' (Keck and Sikkink, 1998, p. 16). Typically this involved information politics or 'the ability to quickly and credibly generate politically usable information and move it to where it will have the most impact' (Keck and Sikkink, 1998, p. 16), as well as the use of other forms such as persuasion and pressure tactics. Links with local organisations were key, here, and local groups could benefit from these networks, in their turn, to get their information out to a wider audience. In the contemporary context, in contrast with the past, the potential for developing and maintaining such links was enhanced through new information technologies, including e-mail and fax communications. Without in any sense underestimating the scale of the task of building advocacy and campaigning networks at transnational level, then, in the current global context there needs to be some recognition of the new possibilities as well as the new challenges and constraints. Reflecting with some optimism on the developing role of NGOs in intergovernmental processes, the Secretary-General of the United Nations concluded that the global information revolution had transformed civil society (UN, 1998). He quoted the case of the International Campaign to Ban Landmines. Growing awareness among ordinary people, he argued, a grass-roots movement of conviction matched by courage, made Governments acknowledge that the cost of landmines far outweighed the need to use them.

The elimination of landmines became a truly global issue, as citizens and one thousand NGOs in sixty countries were linked together by one unbending conviction and a weapon that would ultimately prove more powerful than the landmine: E-mail (UN, 1998).

As Gaventa has argued, for NGOs 'globalization offers a series of challenges for developing new models for linking and learning on strategies for approaching common problems in both North and South' (Gaventa, 1999, p. 21). Fortunately, he went on to argue 'we are beginning to see a number of attempts by NGOs in North and South to forge such new ways of working' (Gaventa, 1999, p. 21). In the rest of this paper, Gaventa went on to illustrate this argument with concrete examples of exchanges of experiences between NGOs and community-based organisations in poor regions of the USA with their Southern counterparts.

These exchanges of experiences were potentially more meaningful to those concerned, he pointed out, within the context of increasing inequality and uneven development within the North. Levels of income inequality, in the particular case of the USA, were higher than in many countries in the South – the 'development of the "South within the North"'. Global processes of restructuring were leading to some convergence of conditions between the poorer, low-wage areas of the North and the more successful areas of the South. To illustrate this point he quoted the example of a South Korean plant which had relocated to South Wales, UK, 'lured by the low-wage levels and favourable business incentives' (Gaventa, 1999, p. 23). These exchanges of experiences between Northern and Southern NGOs and community-based organisations were rendered potentially more meaningful, then, as a result of the increasing connections between poor regions of the North and South, 'economic connections brought on by multinationals or capital mobility, or by cultural connections encouraged by global media and information technologies' together with 'social and intellectual connections involving shared development strategies and concepts – including in the voluntary sector' (Gaventa, 1999, p. 23). As the following examples illustrate, community media including video played a valuable role in building these global links.

Globalisation from below: examples of the use of video and the internet for sharing experiences and building networks and alliances, transnationally

Chapter 4 included an example where video was used – in Vietnam – both to explore local issues, needs and solutions and to represent these local perspectives to other communities and to decision-makers and potential donors, both nationally and beyond (Braden, 1998). Examples from Tanzania have already been quoted in this chapter, both the case where the participative use of video succeeded in communicating local messages upwards, developing an interactive communication loop between the micro and macro levels, and the case where the reverse outcome occurred – where critical messages were ignored and their validity denied (Johansson and Waal, 1997).

Gaventa's examples, to illustrate his arguments about building links and learning between NGOs and community-based organisations in North and South, also included a case study where video played a significant role. This was an example involving common issues in occupational and environmental health in Appalachia, USA and in India. In Appalachia there were problems arising from the movement of wastes and toxic materials. As a relatively poor area, characterised by low wages and weak enforcement of environmental protection laws, it became a preferred location for the development of more dangerous industries. With increasing global competition, as well as increasing costs and stronger environmental and occupational regulation in the North, during the seventies and eighties, these same dangerous industries began to expand also into countries of the South.

In 1984 two staff members (John Gaventa and Juliet Merrifield) from the Highlander Research and Education Center – an NGO with a history of carrying out education and training for grass-roots communities in Appalachia and the rural south of the USA – were invited to share their experiences with the Society for Participatory Research (PRIA) in India. They took with them videos made with American workers and community groups who had organised around occupational and environmental health issues. As Gaventa's account explains:

'(A) key workshop was held in Bombay with NGOs and workers for whom this was a relatively new field. A few months after this workshop, the Bhopal disaster occurred, in which a gas leak from the

United Carbide's chemical factory killed an estimated 10,000 and maimed thousands more' (Gaventa, 1999, p. 30).

The Bhopal plant, as it turned out, was modelled on a similar Union Carbide plant in a relatively poor Appalachian community.

Because of the links which had been made between Highlander and PRIA, they were able to respond rapidly, developing joint research and learning on Union Carbide's record in the US, India and elsewhere. This collaboration included the production of a video tape in the US, sharing the results of similar (although far smaller) industrial accidents; the video was for use in India. A delegation of health and worker activists also visited the US to share their experiences and to learn more about dealing with occupational and environmental health. And in 1984 a joint report was produced, exposing the record of Union Carbide worldwide. This report, entitled 'No Place to Run: Local Realities and Global Issues of the Bhopal Disaster (Agarwal, Merrifield and Tandon, 1985) drew upon information from Belgium, Canada, Chile, India, Japan, New Zealand, Puerto Rico, the UK and USA. Through this international collaborative research, information was provided to activist workers, community groups, organisers and popular educators.

As a result of these links and joint work, it was possible to counteract attempts to shift the blame for the disaster onto the Indian management, demonstrating that similar problems had also occurred in the USA. And when the company flew an Indian doctor out from its West Virginia plant to Bhopal to assure residents there that there would be no major health problems, US groups were able to demonstrate that the very same doctor had declared the opposite to be the case in the US context.

In addition to the immediate impact of collaborative work, there were long-term effects in both places. In poor communities in the US Appalachians there was greater awareness of the vulnerabilities which they shared in common with communities in other parts of the world. And in India the exchanges triggered off a set of activities focusing upon worker awareness and occupational health. Fifteen years later, the impact of the exchange was still being felt.

Clearly the use of video was but one part of the development of this collaborative work and campaigning. But video did have a relevant contribution to make in facilitating these people-to-people exchanges and lateral learning. Reporting upon a trip to Zanzibar participating in setting up a digital video unit in 1998, Kamal Singh from the

Participation Group at the Institute of Development Studies, University of Sussex, UK, reflected on the potential uses of video. In particular he was impressed by the ways in which video could capture and transmit local people's voices and perspectives without interpretation. He was also struck by how easily people took control of the editing process (Singh, 1998).

Commenting on the villager-to-villager networking that took place when five Tanzanian villagers came from the mainland during his visit, he wrote 'What a brilliant experience' (Singh, 1988, p. 3). The videos which they showed from mainland Tanzania sparked off discussions on local issues. Local people also made their own video about a controversial seaweed farming project. Tanzanian donors were promoting this, but local women in Zanzibar explained the difficulties and disadvantages of seaweed farming, setting out the reasons why they would have preferred to return to their previous activity of fishing. As Singh explained '(T)here was a strong desire to take back the film being made on Seaweed farming to fisher-women in Tanzania who were being urged by donors to leave fishing' (Singh, 1998, p. 4) so that they could share the experiences of the women in Zanzibar. Singh reflected on the power of video to convey local people's voices, to promote these sharing processes and to facilitate people-to-people networking.

Two of the mainland villages had been part of an exchange visit to India, and this had also been filmed. Here again, the use of video enabled the experience to be shared more widely. One showing of the video had apparently been attended by 2000 people. A villager explained that the video 'made the distance between Tanzania and India very short' (Singh, 1998, p. 4). Singh concluded, overall, that the visit had left him convinced that the use of video in PRA work should be pursued with more energy, and that there should be no substitute for people's own voices being heard. This conclusion has relevant implications both for the issue of scaling up and for the related issue of people-to-people exchanges and networking, both locally and transnationally.

Of course video has its inherent limitations. Video cameras are still relatively expensive and to be an effective tool, local groups also need access to editing equipment – although newer digital technologies are potentially more user-friendly for local people, once they do have the necessary equipment. On the positive side, however, participatory video has some advantages over other media, such as drama. Video scenes can, for example, be played again and again, for clarification and further discussion. Even in rural areas with relatively high illiteracy rates, such as Nepal, for example, video tapes can be produced by people themselves to represent their own issues as they see these themselves (Tuladhar, 1999).

Despite these limitations then, video has considerable potential, as a tool for creating dialogue between local people in different contexts and between local people and decision-makers. Video has also come to be used, as the Bhopal example illustrated, in campaigning and advocacy at transnational level. ActionAid's International Education Unit has been developing a participatory video pilot project as a tool for involving marginalised people in ActionAid's global Education Rights Campaign. The pilot project aims to enable people who do not have access to education conferences or political meetings – people who may not be able to read or write a report – to contribute their own experiences and testimonies. The videos which are produced through these participatory processes will then be used in connection with the 'Elimu' – Education Rights – Campaign both at local level as an empowerment and communication tool, and at international level as an information and advocacy tool (Hille, ActionAid, 1999). As the report on the project explains '(P)articipatory video is special because these productions are made from the perspectives of the poor and with their direct involvement and authorship.' ... 'Their stories are not told *for* them; they are telling their own stories, in their own language and using their own oral traditions' (Hille, ActionAid, 1999, p. 2). Through this project ActionAid aims to involve local people in the Education Rights Campaign on a global scale, developing models for the use of participatory video as a tool for empowerment and advocacy more widely, in the future.

The use of video has also been linked to the use of the internet for people-to-people exchanges of experiences and for advocacy and campaigning purposes at global level. Christian Aid, for instance, has an online news service which includes information about videos along with other forms of news and campaigning information. For example, through the internet, people have been enabled to send virtual postcards to key decision-makers such as the President of the United States and British Chancellor of the Exchequer, reminding them about the Jubilee 2000 campaign on debt. As Christian Aid's web page on campaigning explains '(C)ampaigning is an essential part of Christian Aid's work with the poor. We believe that it is only by changing the unfair structures that create and perpetuate poverty that we can hope to make a real difference to people's lives' (Christian Aid,

1999). Those who visited the web site were invited to join the campaigns (on poor country debt and on ethical consumerism) through joining the e-mail network of urgent action campaigners.

The debt campaign and the campaign on ethical consumerism have already emerged, in Chapter 5, as examples of local actions, linked together to tackle global issues – and to make an impact. A number of the Jubilee 2000 coalition members both developed their own web sites and linked these to one another and to the central Jubilee 2000 site. This represented an innovative approach to ensuring that local campaigning made the maximum impact globally. The e-mail campaign was an experiment which proved to be particularly successful. Overall, the campaign was effective in raising the issue of the debt at the G8 Summit and at meetings of the World Bank and the IMF in 1999, it has been suggested, because these innovative tactics built upon local people's actions – acting in concert with each other 65 million people around the world were prepared to take action to press for change.

So the Jubilee 2000 campaign used a range of strategies to mobilise, locally as well as globally. These strategies have included the use of drama performed at community festivals and other events, information packs, magazines by and for young people (such as the CAFOD magazine *Between the Lines* making links between sports issues and development issues – CAFOD, 1999) and a free video 'Fair Deal for the Poor'. And there were high-profile media events such as the meeting in September 1999 between popular musicians – including Bob Geldof and David Bowie – and the Pope, to discuss the debt issue.

It is, of course, important to remember that the Jubilee 2000 campaign built upon a range of local campaigns in the South in the preceding years. In Latin America in the 1980s, for example, there were riots, political demonstrations and strikes in what has been described as a 'singular and unprecedented wave of social unrest' (Walton, 1989, p. 299). There is not the space here to explore these mobilisations in detail. The point is simply to recognise the significance of these earlier roots in the South when celebrating the achievements of subsequent campaigning.

Oxfam have also been involved, along with other partners, in using the internet to facilitate people-to-people exchanges as well as advocacy and campaigning work on other issues too. The Meridian Line initiative, for example, was devised by Oxfam and others to mark the millennium by linking people in the eight countries through which the Greenwich meridian line passes – UK, France, Spain, Algeria, Mali,

Burkina Faso, Togo and Ghana. The intention was to build partnerships, promote exchanges and cultural events such as a making music project – with a particular focus upon working with children through schools (Oxfam, 1999).

If video has limitations, particularly limitations of access, so too does the internet, of course. Clearly there are technology-poor communities and regions, just as there are technology-rich ones. The preceding points about the potential uses of the internet have to be set within the context of this extremely unequal reality. There is absolutely no way in which these structural inequalities can be resolved through any quick technological fix.

While recognising these limitations, however, it is also noteworthy that there have been some moves to begin to address at least some aspects of these technological inequalities. In the UK for example, in 1999, the BBC Webwise Campaign provided information on the website to help communities to get online (http://www.bbc.co.uk/webwise). This included advice on how to create community web sites, discussion sites and other services for community benefit. One particular feature was a Neighbourhood Online game, a game to help people to work through ways of using new media technologies to tackle local issues. While recognising the importance of such attempts to address these technological inequalities, though, the significance of the gaps which still remain can hardly be underestimated.

Back to the theoretical starting points

This key point about the limitations of new technologies brings the discussion back to underlying arguments about the structural features of inequality both within countries and regions and globally. Inequalities of access to community media reflect wider patterns of inequality, in terms of both power and of access to economic, political, social and cultural resources. These structural inequalities are not going to be resolved by technological quick fixes. Nor are global patterns of economic, political and social inequality going to be resolved by cultural strategies alone.

This chapter opened by arguing that issues of culture and identity do matter; they matter in their own right. And cultural strategies matter to communities and to those who work with communities to promote participation and empowerment. But cultural strategies are not going to be effective as substitutes for economic, political and social strategies. The choice for communities and for those who work with them is not an *either/or* choice. They have a variety of potential choices about *whether* and *how* cultural strategies could contribute to strategies for empowerment, building labour and progressive movement alliances to work towards transformation, both locally and beyond.

Culture, defined as 'the arts and media' in society, is not, and should not be considered only or even primarily in these terms – reduced to the role of a weapon for winning people's consciousness. The arts and media do have the potential for enhancing people's consciousness, but they are about far more than that. The point, as Chapter 1 argued, is not to negate aesthetic pleasure, unless this serves to provide specific propaganda for particular political causes.

But culture, as Chapter 1 summarised, has also been defined in the wider sense – culture as 'a whole way of life', 'a design for living'. In this sense of the term, culture is centrally important for agendas of empowerment and social transformation. From this wider definition, it follows too that cultural strategies are not usefully separated from economic strategies, political strategies or social strategies, let alone substituted for them. Culture as a way of life was defined as including both values and norms and the material goods produced, a society's patterns of work as well as its customs, its social relations as well as its leisure pursuits. Strategies for empowerment need to address each aspect, and the ways in which they interact, both locally and beyond.

References

Introduction

S. Aronowitz and H. Giroux (1986) *Education under Siege* (London: Routledge).

D. Atkinson (1994) *The Common Sense of Community* (London: Demos).

D. Atkinson, ed. (1995) *Cities of Pride* (London: Cassell).

A. Boal (1979) *Theatre of the Oppressed* (London: Pluto).

P. Caplan ed. (1987) 'Introduction' to *The Cultural Construction of Sexuality* (London: Tavistock) 1–30.

M. Castells (1983) *The City and the Grass Roots* (London: Edward Arnold).

R. Chelliah (1999) *Arts and Regeneration* (London: Local Government Information Unit).

G. Crow and G. Allan (1994) *Community Life* (Harvester Wheatsheaf: Hemel Hempstead).

K. Epskamp (1989) *Theatre in Search of Social Change: the relative significance of different theatrical approaches* (The Hague: Center for the Study of Education in Developing Countries).

A. Etzioni (1993) *The Spirit of Community* (New York: Crown Inc.).

P. Freire (1970) *Cultural Action for Freedom* (Harmondsworth: Penguin).

P. Freire (1972) *Pedagogy of the Oppressed* (Harmondsworth: Penguin).

F. Fukuyama (1992) *The End of History: the Last Man* (London: Pergamom).

P. Gilroy (1987) *There Ain't no Black in the Union Jack* (London: Hutchinson).

P. Gilroy (1993) *Small Acts* (London: Serpent's Tail).

A. Gortz (1982) *Farewell to the Working Class* (London: Pluto).

D. Harvey (1990) *The Condition of Postmodernity* (Oxford: Blackwell).

D. Harvey (1993) 'Class Relations and Social Justice' in M. Keith and S. Pile, eds (1993) *Place and the Politics of Identity* (London: Routledge) 41–66.

K. Hughes (1995) 'Really Useful Knowledge: Adult Education and the Ruskin Learning Project' in M. Mayo and J. Thompson, eds (1995) *Adult Learning, Critical Intelligence and Social Change* (Leicester: National Institute of Adult Continuing Education), 97–110.

M. Jacobs (1996) *The Real World Coalition: the Politics of the Real World* (London: Earthscan).

H. Kean (1995) 'Radical Adult Education: the Reader and the Self' in M. Mayo and J. Thompson, eds (1995) *Adult Learning, Critical Intelligence and Social Change* (Leicester: National Institute of Adult Continuing Education), 58–68.

M. Keith and S. Pile, eds (1993) *Place and the Politics of Identity* (London: Routledge).

W. Kymlicka (1990) *Contemporary Political Philosophy* (Oxford: Clarendon).

C. Landry, L. Greene, F. Matarosso and F. Bianchini (1996) *The Art of Regeneration* (Stroud: Comedia).

M. Loney (1983) *Community against Government* (London: Heinemann).

A. Manghezi (1976) *Class, Elite and Community* (Uppsala: The Scandinavian Institute of African Studies).

S. Melkote (1991) *Communication for Development in the Third World* (London: Sage).

L. Morris (1994) *Dangerous Classes: the Underclass and Social Citizenship* (London: Routledge).

K. Popple (1995) *Analysing Community Work* (Buckingham: Open University Press).

M. Rustin (1999) 'Editorial: a Third Way with Teeth' in *Soundings*, Issue 11, Spring 1999, 7–21.

B. Smart (1992) *Modern Conditions, Postmodern Controversies* (London: Routledge).

A. Touraine (1974) *The Post Industrial Society* (London: Wildwood House).

J. Weeks (1987) 'Questions of Identity' in P. Caplan, ed. (1987) *The Cultural Construction of Sexuality* (London: Tavistock) 31–51.

P. Worsley (1984) *The Three Worlds: Culture and World Development* (London: Weidenfeld and Nicolson).

1 Culture and Cultural Strategies in the Context of 'Global' Restructuring

L. Althusser (1984) *Essays on Ideology* (London: Verso).

P. Anderson (1979) *Considerations on Western Marxism* (London: Verso).

S. Aronowitz and H. Giroux (1986) *Education under Siege* (London: Routledge).

D. Bell (1961) *The End of Ideology* (New York, Free Press; London: Collier-Macmillan).

P. Bourdieu (1984) *Distinction* (London: Routledge).

P. Bourdieu (1988) *Homo Academicus* (Cambridge: Polity Press).

A. Cheater (1989) *Social Anthropology* (London: Unwin Hyman).

J. Clarke *et al.*, eds (1979) *Working Class Culture* (London: Hutchinson).

I. Davies (1995) *Cultural Studies and Beyond* (London: Routledge).

M. Ferguson and P. Golding (1997) 'Cultural Studies and Changing Times: an Introduction' in M. Ferguson and P. Golding, eds (1997) *Cultural Studies in Question* (London: Sage) xiii–xxvii.

M. Foucault (1979) *Discipline and Punish* (Harmondsworth: Penguin).

P. Freire (1972) *Pedagogy of the Oppressed* (Harmondsworth: Penguin).

P. Freire (1995) *Paulo Freire at the Institute* (London: Institute of Education).

F. Fukuyama (1992) *The End of History: the Last Man* (London: Pergamom).

N. Garnham (1997) 'Political Economy and the Practice of Cultural Studies' in M. Ferguson and P. Golding, eds (1997) *Cultural Studies in Question* (London:

Sage) 56–73.

A. Giddens (1989) *Sociology* (Cambridge: Polity Press).

H. Giroux and S. Aronowitz (1991) *Postmodern Education* (Minneapolis, USA: University of Minneapolis University Press).

T. Gitlin (1997) 'The Anti-political Populism of Cultural Studies' in M. Ferguson and P. Golding, eds (1997) *Cultural Studies in Question* (London: Sage) 25–38.

S. Hall (1991) 'Introductory Essay: Reading Gramsci' in R. Simon (1991) *Gramsci's Political Thought* (London: Lawrence and Wishart) 7–10.

M. Haralambos and M. Holborn (1991) *Sociology: Themes and Perspectives* (London: Collins).

D. Harvey (1990) *The Condition of Postmodernity* (Oxford: Blackwell).

F. Jameson (1984) 'Postmodernism, or the Cultural Logic of Late Capitalism' in *New Left Review*, 146, 53–92.

C. Jenks (1993) *Culture* (London: Routledge).

A. King (1991) 'Introduction' in A. King, ed. (1991) *Culture, Globalization and the World System* (London: Macmillan) 1–18.

A. Johnson (1995) *The Blackwell Dictionary of Sociology* (Oxford: Blackwell).

R. Johnson (1979) 'Culture and the Histories' in J. Clarke *et al.*, eds (1979) *Working Class Culture* (London: Hutchinson) 40–71.

R. Johnson (1979) 'Three Problematics: elements of a theory of working class culture' in J Clarke *et al.* (1979) *Working Class Culture* (London: Hutchinson) 201–37.

S. Lash (1993) 'Pierre Bourdieu' in C. Calhoun *et al.*, eds (1993) *Bourdieu: Cultural Perspectives* (Cambridge: Polity Press) 193–211.

M. Ledwith (1997) *Participating in Transformation* (Birmingham: Venture Press).

J. McGuigan (1997) 'Cultural Populism Revisited' in M. Ferguson and P. Golding, eds (1997) *Cultural Studies in Question* (London: Sage) 138–54.

M. Mayo (1997) *Imagining Tomorrow* (Leicester: National Institute of Adult Continuing Education).

P. Mayo (1999) *Gramsci, Freire and Adult Education* (London: Zed).

K. Marx (1968) 'The Eighteenth Brumaire of Louis Bonaparte', in K. Marx and F. Engels, *Selected Works* (London: Lawrence and Wishart).

K. Marx (1970) *The German Ideology* (London: Lawrence and Wishart).

I. Meszaros (1991) 'Lukacs' in T. Bottomore *et al.*, eds (1991) *A Dictionary of Marxist Thought'* (Oxford: Blackwell) 325–7.

Novosti Press Agency (1983) *Fundamentals of Political Knowledge* (Moscow: Novosti Press Agency Publishing House).

K. Popple (1995) *Analysing Community Work* (Buckingham: Open University Press).

M. Postone, E. LiPuma and C. Calhoun (1993) 'Introduction: Bourdieu and Social Theory' in C. Calhoun, E. LiPuma and M. Postone, eds (1993) *Bourdieu: Critical Perspectives* (Cambridge: Polity Press).

E. Said (1994) *Culture and Imperialism* (London: Vintage).

J. Scott (1990) *Domination and the Arts of Resistance: hidden transcripts* (Yale, USA: Yale University Press).

D. Sholle (1992) 'Authority on the Left: Critical Pedagogy, Postmodernism and Vital Strategies' in *Cultural Studies*, Vol. 6, No. 2, 271–88.

B. Smart (1992) *Modern Condition, Postmodern Controversies* (London: Routledge).

T. Steele (1995) 'Cultural Struggle or Identity Politics: Can There Still be a 'Popular Education?' in M. Mayo and J. Thompson, eds (1995) *Adult Learning, Critical Intelligence and Social Change* (Leicester: National Institute for Adult Continuing Education) 47–57.

R. Taylor (1979) *Film Propaganda: Soviet Russia and Nazi Germany* (London: Croom Helm).

I. Wallerstein (1990) 'Culture as the Ideological Battleground of the Modern World-System' in *Theory, Culture and Society*, Vol. 7, Nos 2–3, June 1990, 31–55.

S. Watson and K. Gibson, eds (1995) *Postmodern Cities and Spaces* (Oxford: Blackwell).

R. Williams (1976) *Keywords* (London: Fontana).

P. Willis (1977) *Learning to Labour* (London: Saxon House).

J. Wolff (1991) 'The Global and the Specific: Reconciling Conflicting Theories of Culture' in A. King, ed. (1991) *Culture, Globalization and the World System* (London: Macmillan) 161–73.

2 Communities, Identities and Social Movements

P. Abberley (1987) 'The Concept of Oppression and the Development of a Social Theory of Disability' in Disability, Handicap and Society, Vol. 2, No. 1, 5–20.

B. Anderson (1983) *Imagined Communities* (London: Verso).

S. Aronowitz (1992) *The Politics of Identity* (London: Routledge).

D. Atkinson (1994) *The Common Sense of Community* (London: Demos).

D. Atkinson (1995) *Cities of Pride* (London: Cassell).

C. Barnes and G. Mercer (1995) 'Disability: Emancipation, Community Participation and Disabled People' in G. Craig and M. Mayo, eds (1995) *Community Empowerment* (London: Zed) 33–45.

H. Becker (1963) *Outsiders* (New York: Free Press).

M. Bulmer (1986) *Neighbours: the Work of Philip Abram* (Cambridge: Cambridge University Press).

C. Calhoun, ed. (1994) *Social Theory and the Politics of Identity* (Oxford: Blackwell).

P. Califia (1997) 'San Francisco: Revisiting "The City of Desire"' in G. Brent Ingram, A.-M. Bouthillette and Y. Retter, eds (1997) *Queers in Space* (Washington and Seattle, USA: Bay Press) 177–98.

M. Castells (1983) *The City and the Grassroots* (London: Edward Arnold).

M. Castells (1997) *The Power of Identity* (Oxford: Blackwell).

J. Cowley (1979) *Housing for People or for Profit?* (London: Stage One).

G. Crow (1997) 'What do we Know about the Neighbours? Sociological perspectives on neighbouring and community' in P. Hoggett, ed. (1997) *Contested Communities* (Bristol: Policy Press).

G. Crow and G. Allan (1994) *Community Life* (Hemel Hempstead: Harvester Wheatsheaf).

M. Davis (1999) *Sylvia Pankhurst: a Life in Radical Politics* (London: Pluto).

D. Della Porta and M. Diani (1999) *Social Movements: an Introduction* (Oxford: Blackwell).

A. Escobar and S. Alvarez (1992) 'Introduction: Theory and Protest in Latin America Today' in A. Escobar and S. Alvarez, eds (1992) *The Making of Social Movements in Latin America* (Boulder, CO and Oxford: Westview Press) 1–10.

A. Etzioni (1993) *The Spirit of Community* (New York: Crown).

S. Fainstein and C. Hirst (1995) 'Urban Social Movements' in eds D. Judge, G. Stoker and H. Wolman (1995) *Theories of Urban Politics* (London: Sage).

V. Finkelstein (1993) 'The Commonality of Disability' in J. Swain, V. Finkelstein, S. French and M. Oliver, eds (1993) *Disabling Barriers – Enabling Environment* (London: Sage, in association with Open University).

J. Foweraker (1995) *Theorizing Social Movement* (London: Pluto).

F. Fox Piven and R. Cloward (1982) *The New Class War* (New York: Pantheon).

P. Freire (1972) *Pedagogy of the Oppressed* (Harmondsworth: Penguin).

E. Gellner (1987) *Culture, Identity and Politics* (Cambridge: Cambridge University Press).

A. Giddens (1991) *Modernity and Self-Identity* (Cambridge: Polity Press).

A. Giddens (1994) *Beyond Left and Right* (Cambridge: Polity Press).

A. Giddens (1994) 'Living in a Post-Traditional Society' in U. Beck, A. Giddens and S. Lash (1994) *Reflexive Modernization* (Cambridge: Polity Press) 56–109.

T. Gitlin (1994) 'Fragmentation of the Idea of the Left' in C. Calhoun, ed. (1994) *Social Theory and the Politics of Identity* (Oxford: Blackwell) 150–74.

K. Gould, A. Schnaiberg and A. Weinberg (1996) *Local Environmental Struggles* (Cambridge: Cambridge University Press).

D. Harvey (1989) *The Urban Experience* (Oxford: Blackwell).

D. Harvey (1990) *The Condition of Postmodernity* (Oxford: Blackwell).

D. Harvey (1993) 'Class Relations and Social Justice' in M. Keith and S. Pile, eds (1993) *Place and the Politics of Identity* (London: Routledge) 41–66.

D. Harvey (1998) 'What's Green and Makes the Environment Go Round?' in F. Jameson and M. Miyoshi, eds (1998) *The Cultures of Globalization* (Durham and London: Duke University Press) 327–55.

P. Heelas (1996) 'Introduction: Detraditionalization and its Rivals' in P. Heelas, S. Lash and P. Morris, eds (1996) *Detraditionalization* (Oxford: Blackwell) 1–20.

P. Hoggett, ed. (1997) *Contested Communities* (Bristol: Policy Press).

b. hooks (1993) *Sisters of the Yam: Black Women and Self-Recovery* (Boston: South End Press).

M. Jacobs (1996) *The Real World Coalition* (London: Earthscan).

S. Lash (1994) 'Reflexivity and its Doubles: Structure, Aesthetics, Community' in U. Beck, A. Giddens and S. Lash (1994) *Reflexive Modernization* (Cambridge: Polity Press) 110–73.

S. Lash (1996) 'Tradition and the Limits of Difference' in P. Heelas, S. Lash and P. Morris, eds (1996) *Detraditionalization* (Oxford: Blackwell) 254–74.

E. Lemert (1972) *Human Deviance, Social Problems and Social Control* (NJ: Englewood Cliffs).

K. Loach (1996) *Modern Times: the Flickering Flame*, Videocassette.

S. Lowe (1986) *Urban Social Movements* (London: Macmillan).

I. Martin (1999) 'Introductory Essay: Popular Education and Social Movements in Scotland Today' in J. Crowther, I. Martin and M. Shaw, eds (1999) *Popular Education and Social Movements in Scotland Today* (Leicester: National Institute of Adult Continuing Education) 1–25.

D. Massey (1994) 'Double Articulation: a Place in the World' in A. Bammer, ed.

(1994) *Displacements* (USA: Indiana University Press) 110–21.

M. Mayo (1994) *Communities and Caring: the Mixed Economy of Welfare* (London: Macmillan).

M. Mayo and G. Craig (1995) 'Community Participation and Empowerment: the Human Face of Structural Adjustment or Tools for Democratic Transformation' in G. Craig and M. Mayo, eds (1995) *Community Empowerment* (London: Zed) 1–11.

G. Mead (1934) *Mind, Self and Society* (Chicago: University of Chicago Press).

A. Melucci (1988) *Nomads of the Present*, (London: Hutchinson).

B. Morris (1994) *Anthropology of the Self* (London: Pluto).

B. Morris (1996) *Ecology and Anarchism* (Malvern: Images Publishing).

J. Morris (1991) *Pride against Prejudice* (London: The Women's Press).

C. Mouffe (1998) 'The Radical Centre: a Politics without Adversary', *Soundings*, No. 9, 1998, 11–23.

N. Nelson and S. Wright (1995) *Power and Participatory Development* (London: Intermediate Technology).

L. Paterson (1999) 'Social Movements and the Politics of Educational Change' in J. Crowther, I. Martin and M. Shaw, eds (1999) *Popular Education and Social Movements in Scotland Today* (Leicester: National Institute of Adult Continuing Education) 41–54.

S. Pile and N. Thrift, eds (1995) *Mapping the Subject* (London: Routledge).

K. Popple (1995) *Analysing Community Work* (Buckingham: Open University Press).

Red-Green Study Group (1995) *What on Earth is To Be Done?* (Manchester: Red-Green Study Group).

R. Samuel, B. Bloomfield and G. Boanas, eds (1986) *The Enemy Within: Pit villages and the miners' strike of 1984–5* (London: Routledge and Kegan Paul).

A. Scott (1990) *Ideology and the New Social Movements* (London: Allen and Unwin).

V. Seddon, ed. (1986) *The Cutting Edge: Women and the Pit Strike* (London: Lawrence and Wishart).

L. Sklair (1998) 'Social Movements and Capitalism' in F. Jameson and M. Miyoshi, eds (1998) *The Cultures of Globalization* (London: Duke University Press) 291–311.

M. Stacey (1969) 'The Myth of Community Studies' in *British Journal of Sociology*, Vol. 20, No. 2, 134–47.

M. Taylor, 'Dangerous Liaisons: Policy Influence through Partnership'. Paper presented at the Centre for Voluntary Organisation symposium, 'Third Sector Organisation in a Changing Policy Context', 17–18 September 1998.

V. Taylor (1995) 'Social Reconstruction and Community Development in the Transition to Democracy in South Africa' in G. Craig and M. Mayo, eds (1995) *Community Empowerment* (London: Zed) 168–80.

A. Touraine (1974) *The Post Industrial Society* (London: Wildwood House).

I. Whitt and J. Slack (1994) 'Communities, Environments and Cultural Studies' in *Cultural Studies*, Vol. 8, No. 1, 5–31.

F. Williams (1989) *Social Policy* (Cambridge: Polity Press).

E. Zaretsky (1994) 'Identity Theory, Identity Politics: Psychoanalysis, Marxism, Post-Structuralism' in C. Calhoun, ed. (1994) *Social Theory and the Politics of Identity* (Oxford: Blackwell) 198–215.

3 'Race', Racism, Anti-Racism and Identities

ACR (1999) ARC in Secondary Schools: 'Up Front and Personal in Ooh Ah Showab Khan', http://www.acrctheatre.com.

L. Back (1996) *New Ethnicities and Urban Cultures* (London: UCL Press).

L. Back, T. Crabbe and J. Solomos (1998) 'Lions, Black Skins and Reggae Gyals': *Race, Nation and Identity in Football, Critical Urban Studies: Occasional Paper* (New Cross, London: Centre for Urban and Community Research, Goldsmiths).

H. Bhabha (1990) 'The Third Space: Interview with Homi Bhabha' in J. Rutherford, ed. (1990) *Identity, Community, Culture, Difference* (London: Lawrence and Wishart) 207–21.

M. Castells (1997) *The Power of Identity* (Oxford: Blackwell).

J. Clifford (1997) *Routes* (Cambridge, MA: Harvard University Press).

P. Gilroy (1987) *There Ain't no Black in the Union Jack* (London: Hutchinson).

P. Gilroy (1993) Small Acts (London: Serpent's Tail).

C. Guillaumin (1995) *Racism, Sexism, Power and Ideology* (London: Routledge).

S. Hall (1990) 'Cultural Identity and Diaspora' in J. Rutherford, ed. (1990) *Changing Identities* (London: Lawrence and Wishart) 222–37.

S. Hall (1991) 'Old and New Identities, Old and New Ethnicities' in A. King, ed. (1991) *Culture, Globalization and the World-System* (London: Macmillan) 41–68.

S. Hall (1996) 'Response to Saba Mahmood' in *Cultural Studies* 10 (1), 12–15.

D. Harvey (1997) 'Contested Cities: Social Process and Spatial Form' in N. Jewson and S. Macgregor, eds (1997) *Transforming Cities* (London: Routledge) 19–27.

R. Herrnstein and C. Murray (1994) *The Bell Curve* (New York: The Free Press).

A. Johnson (1995) *The Blackwell Dictionary of Sociology* (Oxford: Blackwell).

M. Kohn (1996) *The Race Gallery: the Return of Racial Science* (London: Vintage).

K. Malik (1996) *The Meaning of Race* (London: Macmillan).

M. Mayo (1999) 'Organising Young People': New Unionism's Challenges for Youth and Community Workers' in *Youth and Policy*, No. 64, Summer 1999, 28–40.

H. Meekosha (1993) 'The Bodies Politic: Equality, Difference and Community Practice' in H. Butcher *et al.*, eds (1993) *Community and Public Policy* (London: Pluto) 171–93.

K. Mercer (1990) 'Welcome to the Jungle: Identity and Diversity in Postmodern Politics' in J. Rutherford, ed. (1990) *Identity, Community, Culture, Difference* (London: Lawrence and Wishart) 43–69.

R. Miles (1982) *Racism and Migrant Labour* (London: Routledge and Kegan Paul).

T. Modood (1997) '"Difference", Cultural Racism and Anti-Racism' in P. Werbner and T. Modood, eds (1997) *Debating Cultural Hybridity* (London: Zed) 154–72.

P. Parmar (1990) 'Black Feminism: the Politics of Articulation' in J. Rutherford, ed. (1990) *Identity, Community, Culture, Difference* (London: Lawrence and Wishart) 101–14.

E. Rose *et al.* (1969) *Colour and Citizenship: a Report on British Race Relations* (Oxford: Oxford University Press).

N. Rose (1989) *Governing the Soul: the shaping of the private self* (London: Routledge).

S. Rose (1997) *Lifelines* (Allen Lane: Penguin Press).

B. Schwarz (1994) 'Memories of Empire' in A. Baumer, ed. (1994) *Displacements* (USA: Indiana University Press) 156–71.

A. Scott (1990) *Ideology and the New Social Movements* (London: Allen and Unwin).

L. Segal (1987) *Is the Future Female?* (London: Virago).

K. Shukra (1997) 'The Death of a Black Political Movement' in *Community Development Journal*, Vol. 32, No. 3, July 1997, 233–43.

K. Shukra (1998) *The Changing Pattern of Black Politics in Britain* (London: Pluto).

A. Smith (1994) *New Right Discourse on Race and Sexuality* (Cambridge: Cambridge University Press).

R. Sondhi (1997) 'The Politics of Equality or the Politics of Difference? Locating Black Communities in Western Society' in *Community Development Journal*, Vol. 32, No. 3, July 1997, 223–32.

A. Stoller (1995) *Race and the Education of Desire* (USA: Duke University Press).

Trades Union Congress (1996) *Testament of Youth* (London: TUC).

4 Community, Culture and Cultural Strategies: Alternative Approaches in Community Development

B. Ashcroft and K. Jackson (1974) 'Adult Education and Social Action' in D. Jones and M. Mayo, eds (1974) *Community Work One* (London: Routledge and Kegan Paul) 44–65.

P. Beresford and M. Turner (1997) *It's Our Welfare* (London: National Institute of Social Work).

A. Boal (1979) *Theatre of the Oppressed* (London: Pluto).

A. Boal (1992) *Games for Actors and Non-Actors* (London: Routledge).

A. Boal (1995) *The Rainbow of Desire* (London: Routledge).

A. Boeren (1992) 'Getting Involved: Communication for Participatory Development' in A. Boeren and K. Epskamp, eds (1992) *The Empowerment of Culture: development communication and popular media* (The Hague: CESO) 47–59.

S. Braden (1978) *Artists and People* (London: Routledge and Kegan Paul).

S. Braden (1998) *Video for Development* (Oxford: Oxfam).

A. Briggs and A. Macartney (1984) *Toynbee Hall* (London: Routledge and Kegan Paul).

D. Brokensha and P. Hodge (1969) *Community Development: an interpretation* (San Francisco: Chandler).

M. Bulmer (1987) *The Social Bases of Community Care* (London: Allen and Unwin).

CDP (1977) *Gilding the Ghetto* (Newcastle upon Tyne: CDP Publications).

R. Chambers (1983) *Rural Development* (London: Longman).

R. Chambers (1997) *Whose Reality Counts?* (London: Intermediate Technology Publications).

S. Collins, P. Curno, J. Harris and J. Turner (1974) 'Community Arts' in D. Jones and M. Mayo, eds (1974) *Community Work One* (London: Routledge and Kegan Paul) 171–85.

G. Craig and M. Mayo, eds (1995) *Community Empowerment* (London: Zed Books).

G. Crow and G. Allen (1994) *Community Life* (Hemel Hempstead: Harvester Wheatsheaf).

L. Dominelli (1990) *Women and Community Action* (Birmingham: Venture Press).

A. Dunham (1970) 'Community Development – Whither Bound?' in *Community Development Journal*, Vol. 15, No. 2, April 1970, 85–93.

A. Escobar (1995) *Encountering Development: the making and unmaking of the Third World* (Princeton, NJ and Chichester, UK: Princeton University Press).

M. Etherton (1982) *The Development of African Drama* (London: Hutchinson).

F. Field (1995) 'Political and Moral' in D. Atkinson (1995) *Cities of Pride* (London: Cassell) 24–8.

A. Frank (1969) *Capitalism and Underdevelopment in Latin America* (New York: Monthly Review Press.

J. Harris (1999) *Personal Communication*.

J. Holland, ed. (1998) *Whose Voice?* (London: Intermediate Technology Publications).

R. Johnson (1988) 'Really Useful Knowledge: 1790–1850' in T. Lovett, ed. (1988) *Radical Approaches to Adult Education* (London: Routledge) 3–34.

T. Kelly (1970) *A History of Adult Education in Great Britain* (Liverpool: University Press).

D. Lerner (1958) *The Passing of Traditional Society* (New York: Free Press).

O. Lewis (1968) *La Vida* (London: Panther).

M. Loney (1983) *Community against Government* (London: Heinemann).

T. Lovett (1975) *Adult Education, Community Development and the Working Class* (University of Nottingham: Department of Adult Education).

D. McClelland (1967) *The Achieving Society* (New York: Free Press).

V. McGivney and F. Murray (1991) *Adult Education in Development* (Leicester: NIACE).

M. Mayo (1975) 'Community Development: a Radical Alternative?' in R. Bailey and M. Brake eds (1975) *Radical Social Work* (London: Edward Arnold) 129–43.

M. Mayo, ed. (1977) *Women in the Community* (London: Routledge and Kegan Paul).

M. Mayo (1994) *Communities and Caring* (London: Macmillan).

M. Mayo (1997) *Imagining Tomorrow* (Leicester: National Institute of Adult Continuing Education).

S. Melkote (1991) *Communication for Development in the Third World* (London: Sage).

J. Midgely, with H. Hall, M. Hardiman and D. Narine (1986) *Community Participation, Social Development and the State* (London: Methuen).

L. Miniclier (1969) 'Community Development as a Vehicle of US Foreign Aid' in *Community Development Journal*, Vol. 4, No. 1, 8–12.

P. Mlama (1991) *Culture and Development* (Uppsala, Sweden: Scandinavian Institute of Africa Studies).

B. Morris (1996) *Ecology and Anarchism* (London: Pluto).

D. Mosse (1995) 'People's Knowledge' in *Project Planning: the Limits and Social Conditions of Participation in Planning Agricultural Development*, Overseas

Development Institute, Network paper 58 (London: ODI).

C. Murray (1990) *The Emerging British Underclass* (London: IEA Health and Welfare).

B. Orton (1996) 'Community Arts: Reconnecting with the Radical Tradition' in I. Cooke and M. Shaw, eds (1996) *Radical Community Work* (Edinburgh: Moray House).

K. Popple (1995) *Analysing Community Work* (Buckingham: Open University Press).

W. Rostow (1960) *The Stages of Economic Growth* (Cambridge: Cambridge University Press).

United Nations (1971) *Popular Participation in Development: Emerging Trends in Community Development* (New York: United Nations).

A. Weaver (1970) 'An Experience of Educational Theatre in Community Development in Nicaragua' in *Community Development Journal*, Vol. 5, No. 1, January 1970, 44–6.

M. Weber (1958) *The Protestant Ethic and the Spirit of Capitalism* (New York: Charles Schiber).

M. Wolfe (1993) *Adult Basic Education in Nineteenth Century Britain* (Study Unit) (London: YMCA).

P. Worsley (1984) *The Three Worlds: Culture and World Development* (London: Weidenfeld and Nicolson).

M. Zakes (1993) *When People Play People* (London: Zed Books).

5 Cultural Strategies and Community Economic Development

Arts Council of Great Britain (1993) *A Creative Future – the way forward for the arts, crafts and media in England* (London: HMSO).

Barraclough, J. (1992) 'Development Tourism – Personal Views of Oxfam's Volunteer Tours Overseas' in *Community Development Journal*, Vol. 27, No. 4, 396–401.

M. Beazley, P. Loftman and B. Nevin (1997) 'Downtown Redevelopment and Community Resistance: an International Perspective', in N. Jewson and S. MacGregor, eds (1997) *Transforming Cities* (London: Routledge) 181–92.

F. Bianchini (1993) 'Remaking European Cities: the role of cultural policies' in F. Bianchini and M. Parkinson, eds (1993) *Cultural Policy and Urban Regeneration: the West European Experience* (Manchester: Manchester University Press).

P. Booth and R. Boyle (1993) 'See Glasgow, See Culture' in F. Bianchini and M. Parkinson, eds (1993) *Cultural Policy and Urban Regeneration: the role of cultural policies* (Manchester: Manchester University Press) 21–47.

E. Cater (1994) 'Product or Principle? Sustainable Ecotourism in the Third World: problems and prospects' in *The Rural Extension Bulletin*, No. 5, August 1994 (University of Reading) 3–10.

E. De Kadt (1992) 'Making the Alternative Sustainable: Lessons from Development for Tourism' in V. Smith and W. Eadington, eds (1992) *Tourism Alternatives* (Philadelphia: University of Pennsylvania Press) 47–75.

W. Eadington and V. Smith (1992) 'Introduction: the Emergence of Alternative Forms of Tourism' in V. Smith and W. Eadington, eds (1992) *Tourism*

Alternatives (Philadelphia: University of Pennsylvania Press) 1–12.

D. Fennell (1999) *Ecotourism* (London: Routledge).

B. Goff (1993) 'Reviving Crafts and Affirming Culture: from Grassroots Development to National Policy' in C. Kleymeyer, ed. (1993) *Cultural Expression and Grassroots Development* (Boulder and London: Lynne Rienner Publishers) 121–34.

J. Gough (1986) 'Industrial Policy and Socialist Strategy: Restructuring and the unity of the working class' in *Capital and Class*, Vol. 29.

The Greater London Council (1985) *The London Industrial Strategy* (London: Greater London Council).

D. Harvey (1989) 'Down Towns' in *Marxism Today*, January 1989, 21.

K. Healey and E. Zorn (1993) 'Taquile's Homespun Tourism' in C. Kleymeyer, ed. (1993) *Cultural Expression and Grassroots Development* (Boulder and London: Lynne Rienner Publishers) 135–47.

R. Hewison (1995) *Culture and Consensus: England, art and politics since 1940* (London: Methuen).

C. Landry, L. Greene, F. Matarosso and F. Bianchini (1996) *The Art of Regeneration: Urban renewal through cultural activity* (Stroud: Comedia).

H. Lovel and M.-T. Fuerstein (1992) 'After the Carnival: Tourism and community development' in *Community Development Journal*, Vol. 27, No. 4, 335–52.

C. Marien and A. Pizan (1997) 'Citizen Participation in the Planning Process' in S. Wahab and J. Pigram, eds (1997) *Tourism, Development and Growth* (London: Routledge).

F. Matarosso (1998) *Vital Signs – Mapping Community Arts in Belfast* (Stroud: Comedia).

G. Mooney and M. Danson (1997) 'Beyond' Culture City: Glasgow as a 'Dual City' in N. Jewson and S. MacGregor, eds (1997) *Transforming Cities* (London: Routledge) 73–86.

G. Mulgan (1986) *Saturday Night or Sunday Morning? From Arts to Industry – New Forms of Cultural Policy* (London (now Stroud): Comedia).

M. Mowforth and I. Munt (1998) *Tourism and Sustainability* (London: Routledge).

I. Munt and E. Higinio (1997) 'Belize: Ecotourism Gone Awry' in L. France, ed. (1997) *Earthscan Reader in Sustainable Tourism* (London: Earthscan) 98–101.

J. Myerscough (1988a) *The Economic Importance of the Arts in Britain* (London: PSI).

J. Myerscough (1988b) *The Economic Importance of the Arts in Glasgow* (London: PSI).

R. O'Grady (1990) *Third World Stopover* (Geneva: Rish Books, World Council of Churches).

N. Oatley (1996) 'Sheffield's Cultural Industries Quarter' in *Local Economy*, August 1996, 172–9.

J. Perez de Cuellar (1995) Our Creative Diversity, UNESCO, Report of the World Council on Culture and Development.

T. Robson (2000) *The State and Community Action* (London: Pluto).

University of Ulster Video (undated) 'Between Street and State: Derry and the Co-operative Movement', University of Ulster, Community Development Studies Unit, Magee College, Derry, N. Ireland.

P. Wilkinson (1992) 'Tourism – the Curse of the Nineties?' in *Community Development Journal*, Vol. 27, No. 4, 386–93.

6 Nationality, Ethnicity, Identity and Displacement: Cultural Strategies to Find Ways of Feeling 'at Home'

A. Alonso (1990) 'Men in "Rags" and the Devil on the Throne: a study of Protest and Inversion in the Carnival of Post-Emancipation Trinidad', in *Plantation Society in the Americas*, Carnival in Perspective Special Issue 1990, 73–120.

R. Arshad (1999) 'Making Racism Visible: an Agenda for an Anti-racist Scotland' in J. Crowther, I. Martin and M. Shaw, eds (1999) *Popular Education and Social Movements in Scotland Today* (Leicester: National Institute of Adult Continuing Education) 279–89.

A. Barnett (1989) 'After Nationalism', in R. Samuel, ed. (1989) *Patriotism: the Making and Unmaking of British National Identity* (London: Routledge) 140–55.

L. Bertal (1997) 'Dancing into Freedom' in *ADMT UK Quarterly*, Vol. IX, No. 3, 10–12.

M. Berman (1983) *All That is Solid Melts into Air* (London: Verso).

J. Besson (1989) *Caribbean Reflections: the Life and Times of a Trinidad Scholar (1901–1986), An Oral History Narrated by William W. Besson*, Edited and Introduced by Jean Besson (London: Karia Press).

G. Bottomley (1992) *From Another Place* (Cambridge: Cambridge University Press).

K. Callaghan (1993) 'Movement Psychotherapy with Adult Survivors of Political Torture and Organized Violence' in *The Arts in Psychotherapy*, Vol. 20, 1993, 411–21.

K. Callaghan (1998) 'In Limbo: Movement Psychotherapy with Refugees and Asylum Seekers' in D. Doktor, ed. (1998) *Arts Therapists, Refugees and Migrants* (London: Jessica Kingsley) 25–40.

E. Carter, J. Donald and J. Squires, eds (1993) *Space and Place: Theories of Identity and Location, Introduction* (London: Lawrence and Wishart) vii–xv.

M. Cernea (1996) 'Bridging the Research Divide: Studying Refugees and Development Oustees' in T. Allen, ed. (1996) *In Search of Cool Ground: War, Flight and Homecoming in Northeast Africa* (London: UNRISD and James Currey) 293–317.

S. Chant and S. Radcliffe (1992) 'Migration and Development: the Importance of Gender' in S. Chant, ed. (1992) *Gender and Migration in Developing Countries* (London: Belhaven Press) 1–29.

M. Chussudovsky (1998) *The Globalisation of Poverty* (London: Zed).

A. Cohen (1980) 'Drama and Politics in the Development of a London Carnival' in *MAN*, Vol. 15, 1980, 65–87.

A. Cohen (1982) 'A Polyethnic London Carnival as a Contested Cultural Performance' in *Ethnic and Racial Studies*, Vol. 5, 1982, 23–41.

A. Cohen (1993) *Masquerade Politics* (Oxford: Berg).

V. Dodd (1999) 'Police Cameras Ring Notting Hill' in the *Guardian*, Monday, 30 August 1999, 9.

E. Erikson (1968) *Identity, Youth and Crisis* (London: Faber and Faber).

A. Giddens (1990) *The Consequences of Modernity* (Cambridge: Polity Press).

D. Gilmore (1998) *Carnival and Culture: Sex, Symbol and Status in Spain* (New Haven and London: Yale University Press).

S. Hall (1987) 'Minimal Selves' in *Identity: the Real Me, ICA Documents No. 6*

(London: ICA) 44–6.

J. Hampton, ed. (1998) *Internally Displaced People* (London: Earthscan).

C. Hill (1989) 'History and Patriotism' in R. Samuel, ed. (1998) *Patriotism: the Making and Unmaking of British National Identity*, Vol. 1, History and Politics (London: Routledge) 3–8.

S. Howe (1989) 'Labour Patriotism, 1939–83' in R. Samuel, ed. (1989) *Patriotism: the Making and Unmaking of British National Identity*, Vol. 1, *History and Politics* (London: Routledge) 126–39.

A. Johnson (1995) *The Blackwell Dictionary of Sociology* (Oxford: Blackwell).

V. Landon (1999) 'Sydney's Carnival Queens', *Observer*, London, 25 April 1999, Escape Section, 8.

J. Macdonald (1997) *Transnational Aspects of Iu-Mien Refugee Identity* (London: Garland Publishing).

T. Malyon (1998) 'Tossed in the Fire and They Never Got Burned: the Exodus Collective' in G. McKay, ed. (1998) *DiY Culture* (London: Verson) 187–207.

D. Morley and K. Robins (1993) 'No Place Like Heimat: Images of Home (land) in European Culture' in E. Carter, J. Donald and J. Squires, eds (1993) *Space and Place: Theories of Identity and Location* (London: Lawrence and Wishart) 3–29.

C. Morris (1999) 'Pride or Profit?' in *Time Out*, London, April 21–28, 1999, 108.

T. Nairn (1981) *The Break-up of Britain* (London: Verso).

A. Norris (1997) 'Asylum' – Theatre for Development in Oxford, *PLA Notes*, 29, June 1997, 50–1.

B. O'Connor (1997) 'Safe Sets: Women, Dance and "Communitas"' in H. Thomas, ed. (1997) *Dance in the City* (London: Macmillan) 149–72.

J. O'Malley (1977) *The Politics of Community Action* (Nottingham: Spokesman).

B. Orton (1996) 'Community Arts: Reconnecting with the Radical Tradition' in I. Cooke and M. Shaw, eds (1996) *Radical Community Work* (Edinburgh: Moray House Publications) 171–85.

J. Pieterse and B. Parekh (1997) 'Shifting Imaginaries: decolonization, internal decolonization, postcoloniality' in J. Pieterse and B. Parekh, eds (1997) *The Decolonization of the Imagination* (Delhi: Oxford University Press) 1–19.

E. Pryce (1990) 'Culture from Below: Politics, Resistance and Leadership in the Notting Hill Gate Carnival: 1976–1978' in H. Goulbourne, ed. (1990) *Black Politics in Britain* (Aldershot: Avebury) 130–48.

A. Radcliffe-Brown (1964) *The Andaman Islanders*, Free Press of Glencoe (New York and London: Macmillan).

F. Rust (1969) *Dance in Society* (London: Routledge and Kegan Paul).

R. Samuel (1989) 'Introduction: Exciting to be English' in R. Samuel, ed. (1989) *Patriotism: the Making and Unmaking of British National Identity* (London: Routledge) xviii–lxvii.

J. Scott (1985) *Weapons of the Weak* (New Haven, NJ: Yale University Press).

H. Scott-Danter (1998) 'Between Theatre and Therapy: Experiences of a Dramtherapist in Mozambique' in D. Doktor, ed. (1998) *Arts Therapists, Refugees and Migrants* (London: Jessica Kingsley) 94–109.

V. Seidler (1989) *Rediscovering Masculinity: Reason, Language and Sexuality* (London: Routledge).

A. Smith (1995) *Nations and Nationalism in a Global Era* (Cambridge: Polity Press).

A. Subramanyam (1998) 'Dance Movement Therapy with South Asian Women in Britain' in D. Doktor, ed. (1998) *Arts Therapists, Refugees and Migrants* (London: Jessica Kingsley) 175–90.
United Nations (1997) *Report on the World Social Situation* (Geneva: United Nations).
P. Van Koningsbruggen (1997) *Trinidad Carnival* (London: Macmillan).
A. Ward (1997) 'Dancing around Meaning (and Meaning around Dance)' in H. Thomas, ed. (1997) *Dance in the City* (London: Macmillan) 3–20.
N. Yuval-Davis (1996) *Gender and Nation* (London: Sage).

7 Cultural Strategies for Health and Well-Being

A. Boal (1995) *The Rainbow of Desire* (London: Routledge).
Community Development Foundation (1988) Action for Health (London: Community Development Foundation/Health Education Authority).
L. Doyal (1999) 'Sex, Gender and Health: a New Approach' in S. Watson and L. Doyal, eds (1999) *Engendering Social Policy* (Buckingham: Open University Press) 30–51.
G. Gordon (1986) *Puppets for Better Health* (London: Macmillan).
G. Gordon (1995) 'Participation, Empowerment and Sexual Health in Africa' in G. Craig and M. Mayo, eds (1995) *Community Empowerment* (London: Zed) 181–93.
C. Hall (1997) 'Sex Tourism in South-East Asia' in L. France, ed. (1997) *Earthscan Reader in Sustainable Tourism* (London: Earthscan) 113–21.
H. Homans and P. Aggleton (1988) 'Health Education HIV Infection and AIDS, in P. Aggleton and H. Homans, eds (1988) *Social Aspects of Aids* (London: Falmer Press) 154–76.
J. Hubley (1993) *Community Health* (London: Macmillan).
J. Jones (1991) 'Community Development and Health Education: Concepts and Philosophy' in *Roots and Branches*, Papers from the Open University/Health Education Authority Winter School on Community Development and Health, Open University.
J. Jones and J. Macdonald (1993) 'Who Controls Health Care?' in *Community Development Journal:* Special Issue on Control of Health Care, Vol. 28, No. 3, 199–205.
L. Kane (1999) 'Learning from Popular Education in Latin America' in J. Crowther, I. Martin and M. Shaw, eds (1999) *Popular Education and Social Movements in Scotland Today* (Leicester: National Institute of Adult Continuing Education) 54–69.
Kings Fund (1997/98) Health Care UK (London: Kings Fund).
T. Macdonald (1998) 'Perspectives on Sexual Health Promotion' in M. Morrissey, ed. (1998) *Sexuality and Healthcare; a Human Dilemma* (Wiltshire: Quay Books, Mark Allen) 209–23.
M. Marmot and R. Wilkinson (1999) *The Social Determinants of Health* (London: Routledge).
R. Mbowa (1997) 'Rehearsing for Reality: Using Role-play to Transform Attitudes and Behaviour' in *PLA Notes*, 29, June 1997, 43–7.
S. Melkote (1991) *Communication for Development in the Third World* (London: Sage).

National AIDS Manual Publications (1998/9) *AIDS References Manual*, National AIDS Manual Publications.

J. Seabrook (1996) *Travels in the Skin Trade: Tourism and the Sex Industry* (London: Pluto).

M. Sidell (1997) 'Community Action for Health' in L. Jones and M. Sidell, eds (1997) *The Challenge of Promoting Health* (PLACE: Macmillan) 20–36.

J. Smithies *et al.* (1990) *Community Participation in Health Promotion* (London: Health Education Authority).

S. Sontag (1988) *AIDS and Its Metaphors* (London: Penguin Books).

P. Thornley (1997) 'Working at the Local Level' in L. Jones and M. Sidell, eds (1997) *The Challenge of Promoting Health* (PLACE: Macmillan) 55–72.

United Nations (1990) *UNDP Human Development Report* (New York: United Nations).

United Nations (1999) *Human Development Report* (New York: United Nations).

UNAIDS and UNDP (1998) *HIV/AIDS and Human Development South Africa* (New York: United Nations).

N. Wallerstein (1993) 'Empowerment and Health: the Theory and Practice of Community Change' in *Community Development Journal*, Vol. 28, No. 3, July 1993, 218–27.

S. Watney (1990) 'Safer Sex as Community Practice' in P. Aggleton *et al.*, eds (1990) *AIDS: Individual, Cultural and Policy Dimensions* (Basingstoke: Falmer) 19–44.

A. Welbourn (1996) *Stepping Stones* (London: ActionAid).

R. Wilkinson (1996a) *Unhealthy Societies*, Routledge, London.

R. Wilkinson (1996b) 'How Can Secular Improvements in Life Expectancy be Explained?' in D. Blone, E. Brunner and R. Wilkinson, eds (1996) *Health and Social Organisation* (London: Routledge)109–22.

World Health Organisation (1981) *Global Strategy for Health for All by the Year 2000* (Geneva: WHO).

World Health Organisation (1991) *Community Involvement in Health Development* (Geneva: WHO).

World Health Organisation (1994) *Health Promotion and Community Action for Health in Developing Countries* (Geneva: WHO).

8 Wider Strategies: 'Globalisation from Below'?

A. Agarwal, J. Merrifield and R. Tandon (1985) *No Place to Run: Local Realities and Global Issues of the Bhopal Disaster* (Tennessee, USA: Highlander Center).

G. Bessette (1996) 'Development Communication in West and Central Africa: Toward a Research and Intervention Agenda', http://www.idrc.ca/books/focus/802/bessette.html.

J. Blackburn and J. Holland, eds (1998) *Who Changes? Institutionalizing Participation in Development* (London: Intermediate Technology Publications).

S. Braden (1998) *Video for Development* (Oxford: Oxfam).

CAFOD (1999) *Between the Lines: a magazine by and for young people*, Issue 8, Summer 1999 (London: CAFOD).

R. Chambers (1998) 'Afterword' in J. Holland and J. Blackburn, eds (1998) *Whose Voice? Participatory Research and Policy Change* (London: Intermediate Technology Publications) 197–200.

Chin Saik Yoon (1996) *Participatory Communication for Development*, http://www.idrc.ca/books/focus/802/chin.html.

Christian Aid News (1999) http://www.christian-aid.org.uk/news/index.htm.

J. Gaventa (1998) 'The Scaling-up and Institutionalization of PRA: Lessons and Challenges' in J. Blackburn and J. Holland, eds (1998) *Who Changes? Institutionalizing Participation in Development* (London: Intermediate Technology Publications) 153–66.

J. Gaventa (1999) 'Crossing the Great Divide: Building Links and Learning between NGOs and Community-based Organizations in North and South' in D. Lewis, ed. (1999) *International Perspectives on Voluntary Action: Reshaping the Third Sector* (London: Earthscan) 21–38.

G. Gordon (1995) 'Participation, Empowerment and Sexual Health in Africa' in G. Craig and M. Mayo, eds (1995) *Community Empowerment* (London: Zed) 181–93.

H. Gould (1997) 'There's More Than One Art to Creative PRA' in *PLA Notes*, 29, June 1997 (Sussex: Institute of Development Studies, University of Sussex) 52–4.

K. Hadjor (1988) 'Issues in North–South Dialogue', in K. Hadjor, ed. (1988) *New Perspectives in North–South Dialogue* (Third World Communications) 46–60.

D. Harvey (1989) 'Down Towns' in *Marxism Today*, January 1989, 21.

D. Harvey (1998) 'What's Green and Makes the Environment Go Round?' in F. Jameson and M. Miyosho, eds (1998) *The Cultures of Globalization* (Duke, USA and London: Duke University Press) 327–55.

M. Hille, ActionAid (1999) *Elimu Pilot Project: Participatory Video for Influencing and Empowerment* (London: ActionAid).

J. Holland and J. Blackburn, eds (1998) *Whose Voice?: Participatory Research and Policy Change* (London: Intermediate Technology Publications).

L. Johansson and D. Waal (1997) 'Giving People a Voice Rather Than a Message' in *PLA Notes*, 29, June 1997 (Sussex: Institute of Development Studies, University of Sussex) 59–62.

M. Keck and K. Sikkink (1998) *Activists beyond Borders* (New York and London: Cornell University Press, Ithaca).

J. Nyerere (1988) 'At the Receiving End of the North–South Dialogue' in Kofi Hadjor, ed. (1988) *New Perspectives in North–South Dialogue* (London: Third World Communications) 197–213.

Oxfam (1999) On the Line Explained, http://www.ontheline.org.uk/otlexplain/otlindex.htm.

K. Singh (1998) *Travel Report*, http://www.zanzibar.org/maneno/pvideo/kamal.html.

S. Tuladhar (1999) *Participatory Community Video: Post Literacy*, http://www.panasia.org.sg/nepalnet/education/video.htm.

M. Turner and D. Hulme (1997) *Governance, Administration and Development* (London: Macmillan).

J. Walton (1989) 'Debt, Protest, and the State in Latin America' in S. Eckstein, ed. (1989) *Power and Popular Protest: Latin American Social Movements* (Berkeley and Los Angeles, CA and London: University of California Press) 299–328.

United Nations (1998) Statement of the Secretary-General to Parlatino, Sao Paulo, 14 July 1998, 'The UN and Civil Society', UN Website, http://www.un.org.

Index

ActionAid 190
adult education 16–17, 25:
  learning programmes 9
  origins of 87–8
  politics and 17
Africa 103, 106, 108, 135, 166, 171, 182
AIDS 164, 166–77, 182
Albany Settlement, Deptford, London 99–100
alcohol 171, 172, 174, 179
Alma Ata Declaration 156, 157, 160
Althusser, Louis 24, 27, 28, 34
Anderson (1979) 19; (1983) 39
anthropologists 44, 77, 143
anti-racists 69
Appalachia 187–8
Aristotle 103
arms sales 182
Aronowitz and Giroux 4, 29
arts: audit of 119
Arts Council 111, 114
Arts and Regeneration 9
Asian people 79
see also India
asylum seekers 133, 135, 153, 154, 182
Australia, Greek dance in 141, 150–1, 154

Back (1996) 83–4
Balkans 135
Barnes and Mercer 58–9
Barnett, Canon 88
Beazley, Loftman and Nevin 120
Belfast 130–1
Belize 123–4
Bell, Daniel 20
Between the Lines 191
'Between Street and the State: Derry

and the Co-operative
  Movement' 127
Bhopal 187–8, 190
bi-sexual men 169
Bianchini (1993) 111, 114, 120
Birmingham 120, 132
black people:
  arts and 81
  biology and 72
  class and 70–1, 81
  community politics 82
  definitions 70
  feminism 82
  identity 70–72
  petite bourgeoisie 74–5
  politics 80, 81
  race relations industry and 80
  self-identification 70
  self-organisation 70
  writers 72
Boal, Augusto 103–6, 164–6
Boeren (1992) 105–6
Booth and Boyle 121
Botswana 106, 161
Bottomley (1992) 141, 150, 151
Bourdieu (1988) 33–5, 159
bourgeois culture 23
Bowie, David 191
Braden (1998) 107–8, 109
Brazil 164
Brecht, Bertold 103, 104
Brougham, Lord 87

CAFOD 191
Callaghan (1993) 153, 154
Canada 106–7
capitalism:
  control mechanisms 50
  global 3, 20
  individuality and 46

variousness 31
Castells (1997) 40, 44, 52, 55, 56–7, 70
Centre for Contemporary Cultural Studies 27, 80
Césaire, Aimée 71
'Challenge for Change' 106–7
Chambers (1983) 107; (1998) 182–3
Chiang Mai 122
Christian Aid 132, 190–1
Chussudovsky (1998) 137
Citizens' Commission on the Future of the Welfare State 97
City Challenge 98
class politics 53–4
Clifford (1997) 73–4
Cohen (1982) 144, 145, 146, 147
Colhoun (1994) 46, 47
Colombia 126
colonialism 91, 92
'Colour and Citizenship' 64–5
communication skills 131
communities:
    culture and 5, 10
    empowering 7, 8
    identity and 2, 3, 5, 10, 45, 57
    of interest 39, 41–6
    of locality 39–41
    professionals working with 6–7
community:
    concepts of 36–41
    definition 2, 36, 37, 39, 66
    exclusivity 66
    politics 4, 54–61
    see also preceding and following entries
community arts:
    community development and 7, 98–102, 111–32, 141
    market and 102
    problems 100
community development:
    community arts and 7, 98–102, 111–32, 141
    contradictions 92
    critics 5–6
    critiques 94–6
    culture and 89–90, 95, 96, 97–102, 111–32

education and 90–1
film and 106, 107
market economy and 131
modernisation and 91, 92
origins of 87–8
urban areas 92
video and 106, 107–9
Community Development Journal 122, 123
Community Development Projects 95, 96, 101
community media 7, 93, 105, 160–2
community politics: social movements and 54–61
community video 107–9
community work: origins 88–9
condoms 174, 175
Costs of Industrial Change 96
craft industries 112, 113–14, 126, 127–9, 132
Craigmillar Festival Society 100–1, 141–2
Cranhill Arts Project 101
cultural capital 34, 35
cultural industries 115, 116–17
cultural politics: development of 16, 33
cultural strategies:
    debates on 15, 16–18, 19
    globalisation and 178–93
    market and 117–22, 131
    politics and 17
Cultural Studies:
    criticisms of 32
    emergence of 1, 16
    Gramsci and 26–7
    politics and 17
culture:
    anthropological sense 5, 19
    arts 14, 99, 193
    change 35, 72
    community development and 89–90, 95, 96, 97–102, 111–32
    debates on 17, 32
    definition 2, 13–15
    differing perspectives on 18–24
    evolutionists and 18–19
    global factors and 15, 19
    as mask 118

political economy and   4, 33
racism and   66–7
significance of   5, 6
structuralists and   18, 19
variousness of   72
way of life   14, 19, 99, 193
see also preceding entries

dance   85, 141, 148–54
debts, developing world   167, 169,
    181, 182, 190, 191
Della Porta and Diani   48–9
Derry   127
diet   179
Disabled Peoples' Movements   57–9
Disabled Peoples' International (DPI)
    58
diversity and difference:
    celebration of   4
    nationalism and   139–40
    social transformation and   47
    subordination and   77–8
    transversal politics and   139–40
    women and   47
Doyal (1999)   168–9
drama:
    community development and
        92–4, 102
    people's theatre   103, 104
    racism and   85
    theatre of the oppressed   103,
        104, 165
    as therapy   153
drugs   179
Du Sautoy, Peter   92
Dunham (1970)   96
Dunstable   148

e-mail   191
Eastern Europe   3, 95
economic development:
    communication and   90
    paradigms   90
'Economic Importance of the Arts in
    Britain'   119, 120
Edinburgh   101, 141, 142
education:
    colonialism and   90, 91
    community   102–3

community development and
    90–1
employment   115, 116, 121, 130
Englishness   138–49
Enlightenment   76–7
environmental movements:
    campaigns   59–60, 61
    characterisation of   52
    global   181
    identity politics and   51
    local and global connections   59–61
    video and   187–8
Erikson (1968)   151
Escobar and Alvarez   48
Etherton, Michael   94, 108
ethnic group   64
ethnicity:
    globalisation and   133–41
    nation-states and   137
    race and   64
Etzioni (1993)   37
eugenics   68
exile   134
Exodus Collective   148

Fainstein and Hirst   51–2
fair trading   112, 114, 132, 182
false consciousness   24–6
Farrant (1994)   158
feminism:
    black   82
    identity and   47, 49
Fennell (1999)   123–4
festivals   141–8
film   106, 107
Forum Theatre   164
Foucault, Michel   25, 34, 45
France: student unrest, 1968   34,
    50
Frankfurt School   20
Freire, Paulo   6, 8, 23, 25, 26, 42, 99,
    102, 107, 164
Freud, Sigmund   42
Friends of the Earth   181
Fukuyama, Francis   3, 20

G8   191
Garnham (1997)   33
Gaventa, John   183, 186, 187–8

Gay and Lesbian Mardi Gras carnival
     142
gay people:
   AIDS   168, 169, 170–
   1
   community   2, 56
   genes and   68
   organising   56
   rights   47
Geldof, Bob   191
Gellner (1987)   39
Germany: holocaust   64
Ghana (Gold Coast)   92–3, 162
Giddens (1989)   13, 43, 44
Gilding the Ghetto   96
Gilmore (1998)   143
Gilroy (1987)   72, 79–80; (1993) 65,
     75; (1995) 67
Gitlin (1997)   32; (1994) 46
Glasgow   101, 119, 121
Goff (1993)   126
Gold Coast   92–3
Goldman, Emma   148
Gordon (1986)   162; (1995) 168, 177
Gortz and Touraine   3, 49
Gould (1997)   180
Gould, Schnaiberg and Weinberg
     60, 61
Gramsci, Antonio:
   adult culture and   23–4
   Cultural Studies and   26–7
   hegemony and   23–4, 26, 27, 102
   ideology   6, 23
   influence   22–3
Greater London Council (GLC)   114,
     115–16
Greenpeace   181
Guillaumin (1995)   77

habitus   141, 151, 159
Hall, Stuart   22–3, 24, 63, 73, 79, 136
Harvey (1989)   118; (1990) 28, 30–2,
     39, 40, 54; (1993) 46–7; (1998) 185
health:
   circumstances affecting   159
   community promotion of   156–60
   community media and   160–2
   cultural strategies for   155–77
   medical model of   158

Healy and Zorn   124, 125
Heelas (1996)   44
hegemony   23–4, 25, 26, 27, 102
Henson, Matthew   74
heritage   112, 113
Herrnstein and Murray   67–8
Hewison (1995)   120
Hill (1989)   139
history, end of   3
HIV/AIDS   164, 166–77, 182
Hoggart, Richard   24
Homans and Aggleton   171
homosexuals *see* gay people; lesbians
hooks, bell   47
Howe (1989)   139
Hungary: Soviet suppression of   20

identity:
   communities and   5, 10, 57
   complexity of   45, 62
   concept of   41–2, 45
   definition   2
   differences over   41–2
   displacement and   134–41
   exclusion and   63
   multiple   134, 135
   oppression and   47–8
   political economy and   62
   politics   4, 33, 45, 46–8, 78, 79
   racism and   66–7
ideology   23, 24, 27, 28
ILO   58
IMF   191
immigration controls   66
India:
   Community Development
          programme   95
   dance   151–2, 161
   video   187–88, 189
individuality:
   differing degrees of   42
   multi-dimensionality of   42, 44
   neo-liberalism and   62
   psychological theories about   42
   society and   42, 43
   tradition and   44
information technology   185, 191
International Campaign to Ban
     Landmines   185

internet   190–2
investment   117, 119, 120
Ireland, Northern   127–31
Irish Set Dance   149–50
Iu-Mien refugees   140

Jenks (1993)   18, 19
Jews, murder of   64
Johansson and Waal (1997)   181
Jones and Macdonald (1993)   157,
     158–9
Jordan, Jane   82–3
Jubilee 2000 Campaign   132, 190,
     191

Kane (1999)   165
Kean (1995)   9
Keck and Sikkink   185
Kenya   8
Kings Cross, London   180

La Rose brothers   147
Laedza Batanani theatre   161, 163
landmines   185–6
Laos   140
Lash (1993)   33, 44; (1994) 46
Latin America   52, 104, 191
Lawrence, Stephen   147
lesbians   47, 142
Lévi-Strauss, Claude   34
Lima   105
Liverpool   96
Local Government Information Unit
     Report *Arts and Regeneration*   9
London:
     demonstrations   132
     Free School   144
     Gay Pride march   142
     Industrial Strategy   116
     Kings Cross   180
     Notting Hill Carnival   143–8
Los Angeles   180
Lukacs,   20, 22
Luce, Richard   119

Macdonald (1997)   140
Malik (1996)   67, 76–7, 78
Marxism:
     culture and   21

economic sphere   4, 21, 29
     exhaustion of   20
     material factors and   18, 21
     as meta-theory   31
     mode of production and   27
     New Left and   22
     postmodernism and   29–30
     working class as agent   50
Massey (1994)   41
Matarosso (1998)   111
Mayan temples   123
Mbowa, Rose   176
Mead (1934)   42
Mechanics' Institutes   87
Melkote (1991)   90, 94, 161
Melucci (1988)   56
Mercer (1990)   80
Meridian Line Initiative   191–2
Merrifield, Juliet   187
'meta' narratives   29, 30, 31
migrants   133, 134, 135, 136, 182
Miles (1982)   64
Miniclier (1969)   91
Mlama (1991)   102–3
Modood (1997)   71
Moe family   73–4
Montreal   118
Morley and Robins   134
Morris (1994)   41–2; (1996) 59
Mosse (1995)   110
Mouffe (1998)   38
Mowforth and Munt   123
Mozambique   153
multinational corporations   59, 186
Munt and Higinio   124
museums   112
music   10, 73
Mussolini   23
Myerscough (1988a)   119

Nairn (1981)   138
nation-states, nations and   137, 138
nationalism:
     ethnic   134
     exclusion and   66
     globalisation and   133–41
     nation-states and   138
nationality, globalisation and
     133–41

nations
  definition of   137–8
  nation-states and   137
  see also preceding entries
Neighbourhood Online Game   192
Nepal   190
New Left   17, 19, 20, 21, 22:
  false consciousness and   26
  Gramsci and   23, 24
  Marx and   22
  Stalin and   27
New Social Movements:
  coalescing of   53
  communities of identity and   3
  critics of   51
  cultural action and   115
  definition   48–9
  divisions within   53
  identity and   48–9
  politics and   4, 115
  social transformation and   50,
    51–2, 53, 80, 81
  theorists' concerns   49–50
Newcastle-upon-Tyne   180
Ngugi   8
Nicaragua   93
Nigeria   162
non-governmental organisations
  (NGOs)   37, 185, 186, 187
North West Musicians Co-operative
  128, 129
Northern Ireland   127–31
Northern Ireland Co-operative
  Development Agency   129
Notting Hill Carnival   143–8
Nyerere, Julius   183

O'Connor (1997)   148–50
Olympics   118
oppressed people:
  identity and   47–8
  oppressors' views internalised   42
Orton (1992)   98, 100, 101
Oxfam   107, 108, 132, 191

Parmar (1990)   83
Paterson (1999)   54
Peary, Robert   74
Peru   104, 105, 124–6, 164

Pieterse and Parekh   134
Pile and Thrift   43
Piltdown Video Project   101
PLA/PAR methods   107, 108, 110
Plato   148
police:
  Notting Hill Carnival and   147–8
  racism   145, 146, 147
Popple (1995)   39
'Popular Participation in
  Development'   106
postmodernism:
  capitalism and   31
  challenges   28–35
  communications and   30
  culture and   1, 29, 30
  geography and   31
  history and   3
  identity and   1
  Marxism and   29–30
  outlines   28–9
  universalism and   76
poverty:
  alleviating   101
  causes   95, 96
  culture of   69, 92, 97
Powell, Enoch   65
Pryce (1990)   147
public sector, marketisation of   32
puppets   162–4

race
  community of locality and   40–1
  concept problematical   63–9, 70,
    71
  identity and   63, 70–5
  purity, the myth of   65
  travel and   73–4
  universalism vs particularism
    75–8
  see also ethnicity
racism
  alternative strategies   78–86
  biological   67, 68, 69, 72
  combating   83–4
  culture and   64, 65, 66–7, 68
  drama and   85
  football and   10, 84, 85
  intelligence and   67–8

jokes   84
Notting Hill Carnival and   145
police   145
trade unionism and   85, 86
Radcliffe-Brown (1964)   149
Raquira   126
'Raw Material'   180
Reagan, Ronald   54
refugees   133, 134, 153, 154, 182
Regional Arts Associations/Arts
   Boards   114
religious fundamentalism   44, 49,
   134
Rose (1989)   62, 63; (1997) 69
Rushdie, Salman   73
Ruskin College, Oxford   9
Rust (1969)   149

Said (1994)   14
Samuel (1989)   139
San Francisco   2, 56
scaling-up   181–6
Scotland, devolution of   138
Scott (1990)   25, 70
Scottish National Party   138
Seabrook (1996)   167
Segal (1987)   70
self   43, 44, 62–3
Senghor, Leopold   71
Settlement Houses   88, 89
sex, safer   166, 168, 169, 170, 171,
   179
sex tourism   167
sex workers   169
Sheffield   117, 118, 158
Shell UK Prize for Open Learning
   127
Shukra (1997)   80–2
Singh, Kamal   188–9
Single Regeneration Budget
   programme   98
Sklair (1998)   61
Smith (1995)   133–4, 138
smoking   179
social classes   34
Social Exclusion Unit Policy Action
   Team Report   108
social movements:
   community politics and   54–61

social transformation and   50,
   51–2, 53, 57
social self, development of   42
social transformation   7, 8
   culture and   15
   education for   26
   social movements and   50, 51–2,
      53, 57
socialist states   3
society, existence of   2
sociology, interactionist approaches
   42, 43
Sondhi (1997)   71
South Africa   166
   Apartheid   55, 77
   Civic Organisations   55
Spain: Citizen's Movements   55
Stacey (1969)   36
Stalin, Josef   20, 21–2, 27
Steele (1995)   16–18
Stepping Stones   171–7
Subramanyam (1998)   152
Sussex University, Institute of
   Development Studies   189
Sydney   142, 151

Tanzania   181, 183, 187, 189
Taquile   124–6, 131
Tebbit, Norman   65–6
Templemore Crafts Co-operative
   127, 128, 129
Thailand   91, 122, 167
Thatcher, Margaret   114, 117
theatre *see* drama
'Third Way'   38
Third World:
   communication in   94
   craft industries   132
   development in   94
   heritage   121
   tourism   121
Thompson, E. P.   17
Titicaca, Lake   124–6
torture   152–3, 154
tourism:
   alternative approaches   123, 132
   culture and   8, 113, 117–18, 119,
      121–2
   environmental concerns and   123

heritage and   113
sex   167
support for   112
trade unions   51, 81, 85, 86
traditionalism   44
tragedy   103–4
training   115, 130, 131
transnational companies   61
transversal politics   139–40
Trinidad carnival   143–4, 146

Uganda   171–6
Ulster, University of – Magee College
   127, 128
underclass   5, 69, 97
UNDP   113
unemployment   119, 127
UNESCO   58, 111, 113, 114, 122,
   124
Union of Soviet Socialist Republics
   3, 21–2, 95
Union Carbide   188
United Nations   37, 58, 95, 106,
   135, 185
United Nations High Commission for
   Refugees   135
United Nations Human Development
   Report   155
United States of America:
   Appalachia   187–8
   community development and   91
   environmental racism   59
   Iu-Mien refugees in   140
   new social movements   48
   NGOs   186
   poverty in   95, 97
   red-lining neighbourhoods   40
   urban regeneration   120–1
   War on Poverty   95
urban regeneration:
   arts and   8, 9
   culture and   8, 9, 111, 113–17
   market-led   112, 117–22

Van Koningsbruggen (1997)   144
video   106, 107–9, 181, 188–90

Vietnam   91, 107–9, 187
Vietnam War   167
'Vital Signs'   130

Wales 186
Wallerstein (1991)   16
Watney (1990)   170
Weaver (1970)   93
web sites   190
Weber, Max   90
Welbourne (1996)   171, 172
welfare dependency   69, 97
Wilkinson (1995)   159
Williams (1989)   40
Williams, Raymond   13, 17, 19, 37
Willis (1977)   27
Wolff (1991)   14
Women's Liberation Movement:
   difference and diversity and   47
   fragmentation   54
   gender roles and   6
   personal/political   50
   social transformation and   51
women's suffrage   51
Workers' Movement   27
working-class communities   40
working-class culture, valuing   19
working-class people
   black people and   79
   education and   16–17
   empowering   16
   politics   53
World Bank   37, 113, 183, 191
World Congress of Rehabilitation
   International   58
World Health Organisation (WHO)
   155, 156, 157
Worsley (1984)   5, 95

xenophobia   134

youth work   88, 89
Yugoslavia   136–7
Yuval-Davis (1996)   137, 139–40

Zanzibar   188, 189